# TAKE ME AS I AM

# Take Me As I Am

*The true story of evangelist
Geordie Aitken*

PAUL WATSON

The Pentland Press
Edinburgh – Cambridge – Durham – USA

First published in 1995 by
The Pentland Press Ltd
1 Hutton Close,
South Church
Bishop Auckland
Durham

ISBN 1-85821-344-4

Typeset by Carnegie Publishing, 18 Maynard St, Preston
Printed and bound by Antony Rowe Ltd, Chippenham

*Dedicated*

*To Gwen, St Martha's, Sunderland*

*To my mam, Pat, Jordan,
Pauline and Indi*

*To Margaret and George Aitken*

# Contents

# Illustrations

# Foreword

'Whatever you have done Jesus loves you. Come to him just as you are'. This message resounds through all of the mission of Geordie Aitken. It is a message that tells how the Christian revelation can literally turn a human being around and alter his or her life from top to bottom irrevocably.

In more simple terms Geordie reveals the story of his conversion from a life of selfishness, hatred, misery and failure into one of vibrant love and conviction. Every word redolent of that love.

His story relates how he was guided to take his message of faith into the highways and byways. Claiming nothing for himself he reaches out to the prostitute, the down-and-out and the prisoner replacing the anguish and degradation of being 'rubbished' with the vigour of the caring love of God. His is a message that transfigures lives.

The latter half of the twentieth century, despite all of its huge scientific and social advances has left many people victim to the twin enemies of stress and loneliness. For all of its claims to be a caring society modern life with all of its speed and rush leaves vast numbers of people in its wake suffering from new disorders such as crippling depressions or the age-old problems of falling through the net of either welfare or charity. For most people faith is a quality that is out of date and which has been inadequately replaced by the medical pundit or social worker however competent or sincere they may be. There is also the plain fact that there are alarmingly many whom these facilites fail to reach.

The liberality and technological advances of the welfare state, excellent in themselves, do not provide the whole answer and there are those, and not so few, who are beyond even that. It is inadequate to reach those who are troubled if you have either no or only a partial message and many are not reached at all. The message that consumes

Geordie Aitken in his mission is one of universal love. He talks of literally 'hugging' people into the Kingdom. He speaks of bringing a prostitute to Jesus telling her in all of her degradation 'I love you' and tells her of his own degraded loveless life now transformed with divine light of joy.

Geordie Aitken is not only able to reach those in the gutter of spiritual depths, what he has to communicate is powerful and he is a great communicator. Taking nothing for himself he gives all of the credit to God. Nonetheless, so positive is what he has to give that aching voids are filled.

This bringing of people in darkness to joy is so much needed in this day and age for so many 'haves' and 'have-nots' alike are without inner purpose or spiritual satisfaction. The pace of life is so fast that those with problems cannot find anyone to talk out what is on their mind. Everyone is too busy. Many aching wounds go ignored. Hence the huge need for telephone Samaritans, the massive growth in the number of paid counsellors, the appalling rise in alcoholism and indeed suicides. There are so many who if they could only take a break or had someone to listen would be able to work out their problems and lead successful lives. Often the victims are from the most worthwhile professions and those who care most. It is the doctors the nurses and the lawyers who end up on skid row – the ultimate of modern stresses and modern social carelessness. So many too of the most worthwhile of people fall through the net of the health service and social security while the rest of us assume they are taken care of because we pay taxes. It is a universal malaise and the end results a scandal. The dimensions of the problem of homelessness have increased and are continuing to increase at an alarming rate. Those who believe that those on the streets or sleeping rough do it from choice simply do not realize that in Scotland, for example, 71% of them are suffering or have suffered from mental illness and have been excluded from psychiatric hospitals before they can cope. Of those, 27% are actually senile. The sick are victimized all over again. There is a hidden half-world but it is becoming less and less hidden.

It is to such as these, with their self respect taken from them by the rest of us either too busy or too self-preoccupied to show that we care that the evangelism of Geordie Aitken and a few like him is so particularly meaningful. It is a message that nobody would be the worse for so full of warmth and purpose that it is. He reaches the neglected and his answer is filling. The 'unco guid' would do well to listen too for their need is great also. It is not good for a man to pass by on the other side like the Levi or the Pharisee in the parable.

Thank God for samaritans like Geordie and above all thank God for their message which transforms lives.

Hugh M Douglas Hamilton
Begbie Farmhouse
Haddington
1994

If a book is written to the glory of God then it is going to touch lives and people are going to be changed.

They are going to come to the Lord and be saved.

It will make a difference to hundreds of thousands and maybe indirectly millions of people across the world.

This book is a very important undertaking.

Pastor Benny Lee
St Charles, Missouri.

# Preface

Apart from the physical change in Geordie Aitken many people are amazed at the depth of inner feeling and ability to put his thoughts on paper, coming from a man who had a torrid childhood and missed much of his regular schooling.

Over the years Geordie Aitken has written some beautiful poems which he now uses as part of his powerful testimony and which reveal his inner feelings and deep love of the Lord.

My name is Geordie Aitken and I've a tale to tell
there is a man called Jesus who saved my soul from Hell
In the past he walked in Galilee
but now he walks with a guy like me

I am a sinner saved by grace
I looked upon the Saviour's face
I asked him once to save my soul
in an instant flash he made me whole

No more shakes or tears with booze
my born-again heart cannot lose
I am as helpless as a babe in arms
without my Saviour's loving charms

In the past my life was dead
with evil thoughts inside my head
Lust and hate dwelled in my heart
my filthy sin tore me apart

Jesus, it's great to be born again
and work with you in saving men
What an assurance you died for me
when you hung on a filthy Roman tree.

My Saviour.

Following his conversion My Saviour was one of the first poems written by Geordie Aitken to the glory of God. Over the years he has written numerous poems and often includes them in the countless number of comforting letters he writes to people on a weekly basis.

# Introduction

In a one-room Glasgow tenement block a screaming ten pound Geordie Aitken came into the world.

Fifty-eight years on he still lives in Glasgow and still screams.

But he screams a different tune to that of his early violent days when the only things on his mind were fighting Catholics, finding money for drink and ripping off anyone who had enough money to count.

Those exploits were carried out in filthy back lanes, heaving bar rooms and rat-infested tenement blocks.

His evangelical exploits have been performed in such similar places, but also in church halls, prisons, hospitals and in schools across the world.

Many of the people in his life today are from the same mould as they were in 1950s Glasgow. Killers, terrorists, gangsters, alcoholics, conmen, down-and-outs, Catholics and Protestants. But for more than the last decade Geordie Aitken has talked and preached with them, taken comfort into their lives and led them to God.

A far cry from the days when he would run with hardline Orange Lodges, smash skulls for the price of a drink and savagely attack his fellow man in the name of religion.

A wild Geordie Aitken himself admits he was only ever allowed to march with the devout Orangemen because he was a 'nutter'. Many terrorists still serving massive sentences in Irish jails for their bloody sectarian beliefs are now telling a different tale. They and Geordie Aitken, once had their own way of helping people meet their maker. Usually with a knife, cut throat razor, pistol or bomb. Now many of them have given their lives to Christ and thank Geordie Aitken for leading them along a Christian path. Their only fighting done with the tongue and a pen.

These and countless others who have seen the light will testify to the remarkable life story of the man who made a screaming entry into the world and is determined to go out in a similar fashion.

God's Unique Servant – Geordie Aitken.

Bridgeton is where I ran around
The punters there loved the sound
Dolly's Braes and No Surrender
Those songs to me brought inner splendour

There is The Sash, our number one
Its words would make my blue blood run
Give me also Sweet Derry's Walls
With No Surrender my battle call

The hurry up wagon would sound eeeee awwww
I had better run here comes the law
When caught and battered I would fight like hell
As I knew police tactics Oh so well

The judge would say sixty days
just for singing Dolly's Braes
I would think about another bottle
and the many Catholics I would like to throttle

This life of mine sure is tough
I think my friend I've had enough
But who do I turn to to find an answer
For Geordie Aitken the Bridgeton cancer

I will try this Jesus, He may hear my plea
His power might set this captive free
Jesus, help this sinner such as I
My stinking life is one big lie

I'll try my best to follow you
as all I've followed is the colour blue
Use me, Jesus, to preach your word
as the life I led was so absurd

My brother Orangemen I say today
I will pray for you all come what may
Give your hearts to the Lord
Let's sing His anthem in one accord

Let's march through heaven's open gate
with flute and drum in sober state
Beat the drum for the heavenly call
come to Christ yes one and all.

The Bridgeton Lad

# CHAPTER I

# Born a Rebel

Rebellion and hatred were welling up in Geordie Aitken at a very early age. In later years such emotions were to prove his downfall yet, ironically, also his salvation. Still to reach the age of 7 he was already a seasoned streetwise kid, into violence and cons. Life on the mean Glasgow streets was hard and fast but he loved every minute of it. Born in a rat-infested slum tenement block, the small but stocky bundle of hatred learned about life the hard way. Raking through sodden middens for empty beer bottles which he washed in street puddles and sold for a penny each outside local pubs was his way of getting pocket money, asking for any brought a different response, a hefty lashing with a belt, administered by either parent.

Already a street scavenger, Geordie Aitken was picking up the wrong kind of wisdom. On the streets he could cope, but back indoors he was becoming a timebomb waiting to explode. Because of his misguided emotions he admits he would have gladly taken an axe to his parents for what he believed to be a lack of love towards him. Though in reality his frantic parents were being strict and seemingly callous towards him simply to keep him in check, he decided their actions were born out of hatred. He reckoned he should have been the most important thing in the world to them and wasn't bothered that war had just broken out. They lived in a filthy block of flats, money was tight, and his proud parents had to share their house not only with three squawling children but bugs, mice and beetles. Elsewhere in the damp, leaking flat his parents shared a wooden bed in the kitchen; in another room their children slept three to a tiny bed. But as far as rebellious Geordie Aitken was concerned those were minor worries compared to his welfare. Often his frantic mother had to deal with everything, with her husband usually working away as a lorry driver. She saw more of the rats and mice than of her wayward son, the streets were his real home. On them he did what he wanted and loved every minute of it.

At home he had to do what he was told and hated every minute of it. In lashing her wild son his desperate mother often cursed him before God. Those curses were to leave more of a mark on the youngster than the marks of any leather belt could. His only respite from the mean streets of Glasgow was during the summer, when he would be shipped out to his grandmother's cottage in Cambus, Stirling, for his six-week school holidays. He always called her his 'Wee Ma'.

It was there that he had his first experiences of the supernatural. As a young boy he would lie curled up at the bottom of his grandmother's bed and listen as she spoke to 'Unseen People'.

Despite the darkness, the eerie silence and weird experience he was never scared. There were invisible guests in the house and she spoke to them on a regular basis. 'At night time I would lie awake hoping these spirits would speak to me'. He would also sit on her knee and watch as she read tea leaves. He later began copying her and from that very early age he was introduced to spiritualism. In later days it was to lead him into the psychic world, and the world of the occult. He was to spend sixteen years in the frightening realms of the satanic world.

It was another radical part of his life, along with the militant Orange Lodge beliefs, alcoholism and hatred of God that was to be replaced by his deep Christian beliefs when he gave his life to God nearly forty years later. But long before that was to happen he had plenty of dark days and bitter experiences ahead of him.

Away from his grandmother's and back on the rough streets of Glasgow, education and schooling took a back seat. For forty years Geordie Aitken really believed that God had cursed him, and hatred and disregard of God dogged his every step.

At the age of 7, and weighing about the same, he developed bronchitis and doctors diagnosed him as being riddled with threadworms. They came courtesy of the filthy, starving dogs with which he shared the back streets of Glasgow's East End. In a bid to cure his condition doctors sent him to a special day school on the outskirts of Glasgow. It offered him little respite from the filthy back streets he had learned to love. Under the guise of offering the bronchial cases fresh air the school heads ordered the sick children out into the fields to pick vegetables. A young wheezing Geordie Aitken was to later learn that a teacher had established a lucrative business selling off the produce to Glaswegian shops. Had he known at the time he would have happily stabbed him.

Worse for the little bundle of fiery frustration was the manner in which the sick children were taken to school in the infamous 'grey van'. The surface emotions of hatred and resentment began to take root in the very heart and soul of his young frame. Other Glasgow children would shout and laugh at the bus as it headed in and out of the city because it also transported the area's mentally ill children and numerous polio sufferers. Many a laughing youngster was to suffer at the hands of a young Geordie Aitken for ridiculing the occupants of the bus. Not because he felt sorry for the polio sufferers and mentally ill children sitting on the wooden benches as the bus trundled through Glasgow, but because they had the cheek to compare him to his fellow travellers. The travelling was bad enough but once there things were not much better for the hardened schoolboy. Memories of the school medical remain with him today.

Classes would be lined up in a freezing green-painted corridor where strapping nurses would publicly declare who had problems. The boys, in short vests and underpants, stood facing the girls, lined up along the facing wall in their short vests and black knee-length knickers. Those with head lice had a steel comb run through their hair. Those with scabies had their hair cut military style and a blue disinfectant rubbed into their skulls. Many a blue head was seen running around the yard of the special school. Geordie Aitken escaped the shame thanks to his mother conducting a weekly inspection in the cold of their tenement block. Many children were sent home with the dreaded letter. Those deemed to be filthy were given a note from the school nurse demanding that their parents cleaned them up before returning them to school. If that failed sanitary inspectors were sent round and if that, too, failed the children were taken from their parents who would be charged with neglect. 'The dirty kids lives were made hell by the other children and I was as guilty as anyone in adding to their hurt and shame. But that was life in the East End of Glasgow.'

School dinners left a lot to be admired and many a time the contents of the stew bowl were left stuck to the undersides of the dinner benches for cleaners to prise off.

Fighting was an everyday occurence and many a sore face peered out from behind desks after another playtime bell sounded. Most kids hated what was happening at the school for obvious reasons. Geordie Aitken only hated the school because it kept him from his beloved streets. 'I could never wait until school finished so that I could get back to the streets. Little did I know that in years to come I would be chosen by Christ to become an evangelist and go back to the streets with a different message.'

The fresh air cleared his congested lungs but implanted something far more serious in a little Geordie Aitken. Four years of travelling in the detested grey van had sown the seeds of a vicious violent hatred. Admittedly he became: 'A very rebellious and nasty kid because of my lousy time at the special school'.

Back in mainstream education his secondary school life was doomed to failure. Firmly rooted at the bottom of the class because of a terrible truancy record at the special school an active mind was the last thing Geordie Aitken was concerned about boasting of. Active hands and feet were all he wanted to be proud of, many battered pupils knew it was no idle boast.

Homework consisted of running with an apprentice Protestant gang of teenage thugs. The 'Young Derry' gang was a feeder for the violent elders of the Bridgeton Senior Derry group. Lessons there were easy. 'It was easy for me to hate so I had no trouble in using the tools of the young gang trade. Open razors, studded belts and cycle chains were our weapons of war.' But anything that could be used to hurt the hated Catholics was wielded with relish. That was to be proved in graphic yet childish detail.

One of his secondary school's history teachers kept a proud collection of ancient weapons. Following a burglary at the school those were used to stock up the Young Derry Brigade's already frightening arsenal.

Now a hardened street fighter, at the age of 11, Geordie Aitken found himself armed to the teeth and wielding a weapon that was bigger than him. 'I gladly used our normal tools of war but I felt terribly awkward trying to hit an opposing gang member with a Highland Claymore.'

The Protestant families stuck together in the tenements and displayed a remarkable community spirit despite the conditions many of them endured. But such a community spirit was to distance the rebellious and confused schoolboy even further from his family. He mistakenly believed that his mother showed more kindness to the neighbours than to her own children. Many families shared a communal pot of home-made Scottish broth with a massive ham bone lodged at the bottom. Geordie Aitken remembers his mother taking great pleasure in making the broth for the other families. 'It blew my mind thinking about the love and kindness my mother showed to our neighbours and those people outside our family.'

It was outside the family circle that Geordie Aitken began to run riot. Aikie, as he was known to his young friends, was only happy with a weapon in his hand and a Catholic to fight with. Many of his young gang members either finished up murdered or charged with murder later in life. The vicious inbred streak in all of them never went away. Whatever the reason, nearly all of the youngsters died early deaths.

School was passing him by but he did not care. But care or not he was to have no say about his next educational establishment. That was provided by way of the local magistrates. Because of violent, wanton behaviour and in a bid to sort out his troubled mind a 13-year-old Aikie was on his way to a residential school. He headed down that path on St Patrick's Day 1949. The local Catholic schoolchildren, on a day's holiday, paid their Protestant enemies a school visit but made the mistake of throwing a green-painted brick through the window where Aikie was sitting at his desk. After school he rounded up his gang and set out to seek revenge.

Every window in the Sacred Heart Church chapel was duly smashed before the gang embarked on a similar wrecking spree at the nearby Sacred Heart School.

That satisfied their lust for revenge and in their tiny minds evened the score for the earlier attack on their own school.

But even then, coupled with the violent streak was an old streetwise head on the shoulders of the bitter boy. Having attacked the church for reasons of revenge the school had been targeted for other less sectarian reasons. Aikie knew that his friend's uncle was the resident glazier and would be thankful for the extra hours of overtime. Not that the magistrates knew, not that the teenage rebel cared, and off to Colintraive in Argyll he went for two years. The fact that there was no escape from Scotland's Devil Island did not bother him. He hated his home life so much that even if he could have fled from the school he would have rather stayed with his new-found criminal cronies. The only thing he missed was the street fights and the young gang members he mixed with but now he was in a place full of such vicious youngsters. They were the type of people the 13-year-old hardman could appreciate. They were 'my brand new family'.

Even visits by his family were rushed and he was pleased when the allotted two hours were up and he was back with his friends. He still mistakenly thought that his mother hated him and that visiting days were simply 'going through the motions'. Life at the residential school brought conflicting emotions for the loveless youngster and his inbred distrust and hatred of the Catholic teachings deepened thanks to the hypocritical and cruel teaching of the school staff.

After morning prayers the boys were regimentedly taken out into the fields to pick enough produce to line the pockets of the establishment. The only privileges the boys got were being allowed to go walking, under strict supervision, and receiving parcels from home without certain people taking their pick of the contents. But even what little they were allowed was to come to an abrupt end when a vindictive Geordie Aitken blew the exhaust off a local farmer's tractor by ramming a potato down it. The reason for the rebellious action was that the farmer, whose crops they had been sent to pick, had tried to cut short their lunch break.

Violent and rebellious actions came easy for young Aikie but he was left confused when it came to affection. His first experience of affection came in the shape of the motherly Mrs Davidson. In his misguided and confused state he would often wish that she was his mother. Not only did she look after him at the school but took him to visit her home where he saw real, loving and happy family life at close quarters. He began to respond to this strange feeling of love but also knew that he responded a lot quicker to feelings of hatred.

On leaving the residential school he made a solemn promise to Mrs Davidson to keep out of trouble and left the school with a tear in his eye. Weeks later he was back with the street gangs and taking his first drink of the cheap wine that was to later nearly ruin his life and put him in an early grave.

Only a few months out of the residential school and he was ready to leave Bernard Street Secondary School. He had never bothered much with school before being sent away and since his release bothered even less. He had missed two years of mainstream education and was not about to try to catch up in the last couple of months left after his return.

The alcohol, the hatred and the lost schooling saw Geordie Aitken leave education with a chip on his shoulder the size of Ben Nevis.

His first experience of work was a farce, the 15-year-old rebel took a job his mother wanted him to take and managed to last one week. Ironically, it had been making waterproof coats for policemen and prison warders. The people he was to have his fair share of trouble with in later life.

His second attempt at legal money making did not last much longer after he battered a fellow apprentice at the upholstery firm in the East End of Glasgow. The two warriors met in the yard during the dinner break and were cheered on by just about the entire workforce. Ten vicious minutes later and Geordie Aitken was the new hero of the warehouse. But his new found fame saw him overstep the mark and when he was found brazenly stealing from the warehouse it was back on the dole and the mean streets of Glasgow.

Girlfriends came and went because of his violent escapades with the warring street gangs. Fighting was his first love and other romantic interludes had to fit in with his lifestyle. One had 'hair like coconut fibre and a face that only a mother could love', while another of the young Aitken conquests was 'so ugly that as a baby she would have needed shutters on her pram'. He dearly wished he could find a decent respectable girl but knew it was a choice between that or running with his heroic Protestant gangs. He chose the gangs, in what was not really a contest, and 'gave up looking for birds that looked like film stars'. Girls could not stop his violent descent into alcoholism and trouble but his fighting days in the East End of Glasgow were brought to an abrupt, albeit temporary, end when the Aitken clan moved to the outskirts of the city to an area known as the Glasgow overspill.

Geordie Aitken was now 16 and this was the first time he had lived in a house with an inside toilet and bath. His days of bathing in a metal tub or a kitchen sink or patiently sitting cutting up newspaper to use as toilet roll in the communal tenement block were over.

But it was with great regret and rebellion that the teenager left his wild fighting friends behind to roam the East End streets without him. But fears that he was moving from his beloved concrete jungle into the peaceful wilds of the countryside were dispelled when he reached the overspill of Barlanark. It was to become just another battlefield for the hardened East End street warrior and much to the dismay of his family his wild fighting days were anything but over.

Their housing estate happened to be the home of a particularly vicious street gang. And Geordie Aitken had the right credentials for membership. Not only did he walk straight into that but he discovered, to his delight, that a district branch of his beloved Orange Lodge was also in existence on the estate. Despite the change of address he was right back into his old fighting ways. But the chance of salvation was close at hand for his frantic family.

A glimmer of hope came when their rebellious boy set off for Newmarket, in England, to make his name as a jockey.

He left home as a raw 16-year-old without a fuss or fond farewells. 'My family had no hesitation in letting me go because the last time they got an element of peace was when I was sent to the approved school.' But any thoughts of becoming a champion jockey went at the first fence after yet another violent outburst. One of many that were to blot his early years.

Six months after crossing the English border he was on his way home with violence the root of his problems. His days had never been particularly happy at the stables and one day his frustration at everything not being what he had hoped spilled into near-bloodshed. While working as a tack boy he took a pitchfork to a trainer who had whipped one of his young Scottish workmates. Geordie Aitken did not particularly like the young Edinburgh lad, he just disliked the trainer. When his employers duly attended Sunday service he broke into the stable office, tore up his contract, grabbed his insurance cards and hitched-hiked back to Glasgow. 'I left feeling nothing but deep rooted hatred for them.'

Two days later the grey swirling smoke billowing from Glasgow chimneys was a welcoming sight for the failed jockey. He had sampled life in the South, decided it was not for him and was now back where he belonged.

In later years he was to have another attempt at working in England but that was to end in similar acrimonious circumstances. Despite the welcoming sight of his home city the ensuing family reunion was far from happy.

Disinterested parents met him with the words: 'Here comes the worlds greatest jockey. I wonder how many races he won?' Any hopes of a professional racing career firmly ground into the Newmarket turf, the muddy building sites of Glasgow soon beckoned.

The construction game was heaven on earth for the 16-year-old who now saw himself as one of the men he had always adored. 'They worked hard, drank hard and fought hard.' He could manage one of those, the fighting, and he soon learned the other two.

Drink was now becoming an integral part of his life and, as in later years, went hand in hand with violence. His favourite pastime of fighting was now beginning to be fuelled by drink. Being back in Glasgow also gave him plenty of time to pursue his Orange Lodge beliefs which he set about doing with a great fervour. Even a barbaric initiation ceremony into the senior ranks did not quell his fighting ardour. On joining he had to accept orders under oath and prove his fighting spirit. Blindfolded, with trouser legs rolled up and shirt torn open he had to run a gauntlet of fanatical lodge members during which he was punched, kicked and even stabbed.

But the Protestant cause formed the nucleus of Geordie Aitken's young life and the physical pain he had to endure was nothing compared to that which he was to eagerly dish out. 'I passed with flying colours because I had been used to physical pain since I came out of my mother's womb.' Along with the scars came the rebellious tattoos, and his membership of various bands attached to the Orange Order. To show his dedication the name of 'King Billy' soon adorned his muscular, powerful arms. That first tattoo sickened his parents and earned him yet another beating. The beating did not bother him and to thank them for it he promptly went out for more rebellious and hardline Protestant tattoos. Soon he was sporting over thirty tattoos on his arms publicly declaring his militant Protestant beliefs. Ironically, those rebellious tattoos were to play a major role in the one time Orange Lodge member's later evangelical work.

Most of the flute bands he was involved with were made up of drunken revellers looking for trouble and fuelled, not always by religious beliefs, but by booze and hatred. 'I had no problem as I was at the front of the queue when it came to drinking and hating.' He was never far from the front either when it came to fighting.

His first taste of prison came courtesy of the yearly 12th of July celebrations. Every summer the Orangemen proudly marched to commemorate the battle of the River Boyne at which King William III, Prince of Orange, defeated King James II and his hated Catholic army in Co. Meath. 'When we walked with the lodge bands it was the modern day version of the Battle of Boyne.' His blood was spilt as was the blood of countless Catholics. To add reverence to the marches a Bible was carried by a bearer at the head of the lodge but to most of the men it would have been better used as toilet paper. Yet lodge members had to attend church before being allowed to march, and a bored Geordie Aitken sat through many a service so that he would be allowed on the streets. He decided that watching a minister speak from a church pulpit was a small price to pay to be let loose on the hated Catholics with his custom-made lead-filled baton. Already believing he was cursed by God he left many a service convinced that God actually hated the Geordie Aitkens of the world. It stemmed from snide remarks of 'stiff necked phony Christians'. They were the ones who would ask: 'who let the scum in?'

The question was normally posed after a quick look around the congregation at the young Orangemen's bruised, battered faces complete with black eyes and stitches. Far from feeling full of salvation, fuelled with hatred the lodge members would take to the Glasgow streets. Thoughts that God hated them for drinking and fighting and only loved the church-going middle classes fuelled the fires of hatred already deeply rooted in Geordie Aitken. Excitement grew to fever pitch as: 'I walked along in my uniform and the crowds waved to me from the pavements of the Protestant areas of Glasgow.'

Geordie Aitken did not need a reason to fight but if he ever needed an excuse the fanatical rivalry between Catholics and Protestants on the tough streets of Glasgow provided one.

His hatred of Catholicism was inbred and he had also decided that God hated him as well. What a brilliant time he was having.

Such were his family's fanatical Protestant beliefs that they repeatedly told him that if ever a nun walked past him and her habit brushed him he had to run straight home and change his clothes. 'They needn't have worried because I would never have let a nun get that close in the first place.' To tell him then that in later years he would be willingly helping out two sisters in a soup kitchen would have met with violence, the kind he loved. Any Catholics that did get within striking distance were duly dispatched in a wicked manner. He liked hurting his enemies.

His job in the flute bands was to march as a marshal ensuring the onlookers never broke ranks. He wore his uniform with pride but never managed to master a flute or an accordion. Instead, he carried his own instrument, the favoured lead-filled baton. 'When I hit someone with it they definitely stayed down. I only ever aimed for their heads. The outside of the baton was covered in a nice orange and purple silk ribbon but to me it was a weapon of war against the opposing forces called Catholics.' His early days in the Orange Lodge as a wild teenager, were paved with booze, bigotry, violence, which by this time were well planted in his frame.

Away from the sectarian violence life continued in a similar fashion as he continued along the road to ruin in the company of his building site heroes.

He was now loving life and revelled in the pain and sorrow he caused. Not only to his family but to anyone who crossed his path. After all, he thought, he was cursed and hated by God so what did he have to lose. Weekdays he was a drunken thief. Weekends a drunken thug.

Stealing became an obsession for the wild 19-year-old with the proceeds of his criminal capers needed to fuel his rapid descent into the depths of alcoholism. But it was that very thieving which was inadvertently to lead him to the doorstep of the nearest army recruiting office and also, temporarily, away from the streets of Glasgow and the violence of the Orange Lodge.

Despite his wild and wicked ways he never lost his steetwise way of thinking, it was now inbred to keep one step ahead. Following a police investigation into the theft of tons of copper cable from a construction company he decided to join up rather than face a prosecution. He joined the army on the same day that he fled from the building site. His partners in crime didn't get away. They were sent to Barlinnie prison. And as for Geordie Aitken?

'I got sentenced to nine years in the Highland Light Infantry.'

The world is sure a sinful place
the way folks act is a sure disgrace
What we need to set men straight
is a man to lead them through the narrow gate

That man is Jesus our heavenly King
love and joy he will bring
First he must own your heart
from sin my friend you will depart

Ask right now to be set free
call on the Lord on bended knee
Jesus died for your sinful cure
he rose again that's for sure

What a gift to know the Lord
and praise his name in one accord
So come along and have no fear
your cry for help the Lord will hear

He will come and dine with you
and eat the manna with heavenly stew
Set the table here I come
Lord Jesus, you are my number one

In heaven you have prepared my place
saved by your love and heavenly grace
Thank you, Jesus, for saving me
I'm so happy I jump with glee

The World.

# CHAPTER 2

# Wild Army Days

Age 19, a proud Geordie Aitken stood outside the army recruiting office in the middle of the Argyle Street area of Glasgow. With excitement in his heart and full of wild spirit he deliberately dithered outside of the main door in the busy shopping precinct, hoping everyone would notice that Geordie Aitken was joining up. Such was his ego.

In the window of the recruiting office was a huge poster of a handsome strapping soldier standing in his Highland Light Infantry uniform kilt of McKenzie tartan, green doublet, glengarry bonnet with its beautiful red feathered plume, hair sporran, dice hose, spats, brogue shoes and banana-shaped smile nearly the size of his impressionable target's ego. That's me, he thought as he lapsed into a Walter Mitty-style trance. It never crossed his mind that this man had not been created by the Highland Light Infantry but by an army artist. He was as real as Geordie Atiken's chances of winning the Victoria Cross.

Having decided that everyone now knew he was joining up for active service he proudly strode into the front office to be confronted by three stoney-faced recruiting sergeants. Amazed at their interest in him, his massive ego was further inflated. He later discovered that his khaki clad admirers had actively vied for his signature because they received ten shillings for each new recruit to their particular regiment. Despite the financial carrot one recruiting officer did not bother with the five feet two Geordie Aitken. The Scots Guards. 'Can you imagine a five feet two me in a busby hat standing amongst a load of six footers? The Highland Light Infantry was the regiment I joined. I did not realize what I was letting myself in for, and as time would tell, neither did the HLI.' It was to be the worst ten bob the army had ever spent. He soon realized that the only thing he did right on that fateful day was to take out the three year option on his nine years service. After three days he was ready to get out never mind three years.

His pending battle with the medical officers was to be one of the hardest fought of his army career. 'To me the doctors looked as if they themselves needed a medical.' He came through it thinking the one who tested his reflexes must have been a battered child himself thanks to the way he swung a hammer at the 19-year-old's kneecaps. 'He seemed hell bent on letting others know what it felt like to be battered.'

The big moment came in the shape of the X-ray machine. This would show whether his earlier broncial problems or years of fighting had left their inner mark. A midget of a doctor stretched his neck so it would fit into the machine's grooves, pulled a few levers and up he went a further two inches. With his feet almost off the ground, his trousers still dangling around his ankles, a bemused Geordie Aitken was passed fit to join the army.

The physical pain out of the way, the hard part was still to come. Education had never played a major part in his life and here he was due to sit an exam. Memories of earlier school exams flooded back. He had once been asked what eight miles and seven miles added up to. An answer of nineteen was the reply which had his teacher branding him stupid. But a defiant schoolboy had an answer, and this time it was right. 'Stupid I might be but I'm the nearest in the class.'

Banishing such thoughts from his head he sat smiling at his army inquisitor. 'What is twelve and twelve?' 'Twenty-four, sir' came the reply. 'Well done, Mr Aitken.' 'What is the capital of Scotland?' 'Edinburgh, sir.' 'Well done again.' 'When was the battle of Bannockburn?' 'Errr, don't know, sir.' 'Don't worry, Mr Aitken,' came the reply, 'you've passed with flying colours.' Feeling fit, educated and important, it was back to the Aitken residence in Barlanark to inform the family. After skirting round why he had left the building site in the first place.

Age 19 he was on his travels for the third time, following his forced trip to the boarding school, and his ill-fated attempt to become a Newmarket jockey. Two days later the usual farewells in the bag, he jumped on a tramcar for the Maryhill Barracks for his initial eight weeks training period. On arrival he had thought he had taken the wrong tram and mistakenly gone to the infamous Barlinnie prison. On the other side of the massive iron gate stood his drill sergeant who welcomed him to the camp in a far from complimentary manner.

'Hey, stupid, where did you get that suit from — the circus?' Following more snide remarks, directed at his Marlon Brando-style haircut Geordie Aitken was already wondering how to get out of the army. Further sarcastic encouragement followed from the hefty sergeant who told him that he had only been joking about his hair. 'It's all coming off anyway, son. What is under your army bonnet is yours but what's outside of it is the army's.'

It was bad enough getting it cut but he plummeted to new depths of panic when the barber turned out to be the duty bugler. 'You could see he was a bugler. He had sagging jaws like a pedigree bloodhound and even smelled like a canine friend. He was about as interested in cutting my hair as I was in joining the army.' No salon treatment for the little Glasgow hardman. An army bonnet was planted firmly, albeit unevenly, on his head and a pair of electric shears ran around the rim. A terrible fear welled up inside the Glasgow nutcase, but trouble, and possibly the bugler's life, was spared when the bugler revealed there wasn't a mirror in the room. Feeling like an alien, and unknown to him, looking like one, he was marched to the quartermaster's stores to be kitted out.

Before he went in he had already decided he should never have joined up. By the time he came out he was near suicidal and laying plans to desert.

The shock of all shocks was in store for the five feet two would-be soldier when he went in for his uniform. 'What size head have you got, son?' was the first question. Having never actually measured his cranium and having only ever used his head to bend a few noses and black a few eyes the teenage recruit was stumped. Out came a 'flying saucer' of a bonnet. 'A wee bit too big, sir,' came a sarcastic response as the hat covered his eyes and hung down over his ears. 'Never mind, son, you'll grow into it', was the equally sarcastic reply from the disinterested, seen-it-all-before bored quartermaster.

The rest of the prized HLI uniform came in similar sizes and with the same advice from the army. 'Bloody hell they must be going to stretch me on a rack next to get this stuff to fit.' That night Geordie Aitken lay on his hard army bed wishing he was back in civvy street. He had been a soldier for less than twenty-four hours. The recruiting poster would have been the first thing to bear the brunt of his anger as he compared himself to the tall, handsome and smiling soldier beaming down at him from the window. How he had let himself be taken in thinking that creation in the window was actually him. 'The kilt that I so wanted to wear looked like a tartan table lamp when I put it on, my spats looked like two plaster of Paris moulds around my slim legs and my shoes resembled two paddle steamers.'

He never slept much that night and come the following morning the grey misty dawn matched his mood. A far from happy raw recruit was ready to take on the world. But only after he had taken on his own regimental leaders. Mostly that was done in a drunken stupor as his heavy boozing not only continued throughout his army life but got worse. Basic training was a joke. If he thought his uniform was bad it was nothing compared to the small soldier's rifle. 'It was that heavy it felt like a gun from a Centurian tank.' And throughout his three years his rifle was to cause him plenty of trouble. Usually because he kept losing it or throwing it away.

He got through the initial training period and was sent to 'B' company as a rifleman and posted to Germany. 'They insisted on calling me a rifleman but this was another crazy part of my army life. Out on the shooting range it was a joke. If I had been shooting for food I would have died of starvation.' His spirits rose when he learned the German base of Luneberg was nothing more than an alcoholic's paradise. Maybe army life isn't all bad he thought. But before he even got there he was in trouble with his superiors, because of his cursed rifle.

Having made the trip from Harwich, in England, across to Holland the raw recruits headed for Germany by train. By the end of the four hour trip he and a bunch of squaddies were blind drunk and shouting filthy remarks to their sergeants and officers. On arrival at the barracks the drunken Geordie Aitken and his friends were charged with being drunk in charge of a rifle. Any thoughts of sightseeing were put on hold, when, having not even been in Germany for twenty-four hours the guilty men were confined to barracks for fourteen days.

Three months on and the Highland Light Infantry were branded the worst regiment to be based in Germany for many years. Many local bars were soon out of bounds to the wild fighting men of the Highland Light Infantry. And they were proud of the fact.

Compared to the English regiments stationed there the Scottish soldiers were undisciplined, drunken yobs. But Geordie Aitken also loved the cleanliness of the European country compared to the squalor of the Glasgow tenements.

'I used to watch the German frauleins hanging clean bed linen out of their windows and think back to my Glasgow. The only things that hung out of bedroom windows in the East End of Glasgow were people trying to get away from the police.' Night life for the soldiers consisted of drinking in the aptly named 'Bucket of Blood' pub. It got its name due to the amount of blood spilled during fights between the HLI and its English enemies.

Women came and went as in Geordie Aitken's early days he put drink first and invariably ended up with the less tasty frauliens. 'The only girlfriends we could get were the left overs from the First World War.' But romance was to play a part in his early days. 'I dug up a local girl who came second in a beauty contest. She lost out to a gorilla. Her name was Imguard but she would have been better christened mudguard. She was filthy and the dirt seemed to be etched into her wrinkled skin.' That relationship didn't last too long when the proud Scotsman discovered he had become the laughing stock of the whole British Army posted to the Rhine. Dejected yet again, he longed for the tenements of Glasgow and the welcoming grey smoke which he knew meant he was home.

He often thought of deserting and admits the only stumbling block was the thought of having to hitch-hike from Germany. He decided to make the best of a bad job. But such thoughts quickly disappeared back at barracks and the daily doses of army training. He was soon to spend most of his time in an army jail or confined to base. Cross country runs and endurance tests were the order of the day for the hapless squaddies. Those who kept the company of Geordie Aitken invariably struggled. 'The last time I ran anywhere was to get away from the police.' They were expected to complete a ten mile course, but for the Geordie Aitkens of the regiment their feats were normally measured in yards. 'About forty of us hung-over runners started to run the ten miles but usually after about a quarter of a mile collapsed absolutely knackered.'

Bedecked in their army PT shorts, the thirsty Geordie Aitken and his friend decided to call it a day with the running and popped into

the local guest house for a drink. Having been reported missing by
their company they were duly rounded up by two military policemen,
handcuffed half drunk to a jeep and driven back to the barracks and
into the guardhouse.

Bars were to be the mainstay of his army days and by the time he
left he had spent most of his time in them or behind them. 'There
were courts martial just about every day. Men were literally carried
into the cells because of the drink or because they refused to march
in.' Whenever Geordie Aitken served a sentence he celebrated by
hitting the town, getting drunk and invariably locked up again. 'I was
not in the cells all of the time just every other week.' Mostly after
being found in an out-of-bounds drinking hole, where he would drink
himself half senseless on twenty-five pence bottles of cheap wine.

But despite his intoxicated states the streetwise squaddie usually had
a trick up his sleeve when cornered. On one occasion when he had it
didn't save him from the guardhouse. Having borrowed a fellow
squaddie's civilian clothes to visit yet another off-limits bar, he found
himself in a vicious fight. He managed to get out of the bar just as the
Special Investigation Branch piled in to quell the near riot and find the
culprits. He was half-way to freedom when the SIB jeep pulled him
over. In brazenly trying to con his way out of the trouble he had
forgotten that the clothes he had borrowed belonged to a five feet
eight inch friend. On his five feet two inch frame they were a dead
giveaway. But still the defiant conniving soldier tried his hand. All the
way back to the barracks he insisted, in pigeon German, that he was
a local. Unfortunately for him, the only phrases he had bothered to
learn were how to order a drink. With coat sleeves down past his hands
and trousers trailing the ground a sozzled Geordie Aitken was herded
back to the guardhouse still uttering German phrases.

If he could not get out of the barracks then the next best thing was
to bring the booze and the birds in. But whatever he tried seemed to
land him behind bars.

One night nearly a dozen local girls were smuggled into one of the
camp huts. Things were going well until squeals of drunken laughter
reached the ears of an alert guard commander. Many a naked fraulein
was unceremoniously squeezed into a metal army locker before the
room was searched. As was his way with women Geordie Aitken had

once again picked the wrong one. His girlfriend-for-the-night was too fat to fit in his locker. Undeterred, he squeezed her under his bed and covered her in a thick grey wool blanket seconds before the hut doors burst open and the men were ordered to stand to attention at their beds. Knowing that they were in there, it didn't take the guards too long to find the naked women crammed in the lockers.

A smug Geordie Aitken for once thought he had escaped capture. Until his girlfriend decided to pass wind. Up with the bed blanket, and out she was dragged to be added to the line of naked women standing far from proudly to attention. The women were marched to the detention centre to await the arrival of German police who had to escort them back to town. They were later charged with trespassing and the soldiers once again confined to barracks.

But a change of scenery was looming for the troublesome soldier. In a bid to curb his ways Geordie Aitken was transferred to General HQ, and posted to the sergeants' mess as a waiter. His new uniform was to rival his army one in the ill-fitting stakes. The only difference this time was that he was issued with a pair of tartan trousers, crisp shirt and dicky bow. But his job as waiter was not as it first appeared. Indeed he was more of a general caretaker and dogsbody. Everything had to be cleaned by him from the toilet bowls down to the soup bowls. And usually the rebellious squaddie used the same cloth. 'I hated everyone of the sergeants I had been assigned to wait on. The resentment in me was thicker than the porridge I used to serve them'.

Geordie Aitken in 'borrowed' sergeant's uniform.

The only way he could take revenge on the three-striped men, who were usually behind his spells in the guardhouse, was on the quiet. He knew that any outright physical violence would earn him at least 112 days behind bars. He decided the best way to exact revenge was to bring them all down with food poisoning and dreamed up various choice ways of doing just that. One of his favourites was to wipe the toilet bowls and urinals with the cloth he used to wipe the tops of sauce bottles and polish the cutlery. Another was to pick his nose and to deposit the contents into the sauce bottles. A mouthful of saliva also mysteriously found its way into bowls of steaming soup on more than one occasion. 'This was the only way I could get back at these people who I absolutely hated. All of them had at one time or another, been responsible for me being locked up.' But a vindictive Geordie Aitken was not content at having the last laugh in secret. Often he wanted to publicly ridicule them.

One in particular was the fat sergeant nicknamed 'The Pig'. 'He looked like a pig, ate like a pig, and even grunted like a pig'. During a quiet moment Geordie Aitken took a screwdriver to the Pig's chair, loosened the screws and waited gleefully to serve him his meal. He just happened to be handing him his soup when he sat down, and revenge was certainly sweet. Not only did the scalding soup splash all over the obese NCO but on the way down he took half of the table with him after grabbing hold of the tablecloth in a vain bid to stop his descent. He regained his feet with soup dripping from his nose and his face a deep scarlet. A Geordie Aitken stood there a deep purple from trying to keep his laugh in.

Despite being away from his squaddie mates his thoughts never strayed far from B Company. One Christmas Eve he duly stole three dozen chickens from the sergeants' mess and set off for a midnight feast with his comrades in arms. But there was a price to pay for the soldiers. Mounds of chicken bones were found on the floor of B Company's billets and every squaddie spent Christmas Day in the guardhouse. But Geordie Aitken was a happy man. His comrades had not said where the chickens had come from. But more importantly, in the sergeants' mess his hated superiors were having boiled ham for their Christmas dinners.

His waiting on days were soon to be over after an eventful bingo evening in the mess. By now his craving for alcohol was taking its toll and he had stooped to drinking left-over beer and whisky which had stood all night and which he was supposed to clear away. Instead of pouring the flat beer down the sink he threw it down his throat before setting the breakfast table. Often he was drunk before it came to dinner time. Usually he could get away with it but one night at an officers formal social evening he overstepped the mark. As the bingo numbers were being called Geordie Aitken passed around drinks from a massive tray and lost his footing. Up went the tray and down went the wine glasses on top of the Regimental Sergeant Major, his wife and their charming daughter, None of them was too pleased. The RSM standing there soaking and the two most important women in his life sobbing hysterically. But a sozzled Geordie was too drunk to care, until the next morning when he was formally charged with being drunk while on duty. That meant another seven days' detention and transfer back

Geordie Aitken as mess orderly.

to B company. But his taste of freedom only served to send him back aiming to make up for lost time amongst his boozing mates and the local frauleins.

Back where he belonged on the bottom rung, his drinking and fighting continued. But for once his army fighting days were within legal limits when he took up boxing. A friend and he duly represented their unit in the Army on the Rhine boxing championships. Geordie Aitken fared well and knocked out his opponent in the first round. But trouble was in store when his over-enthusiastic fellow Glaswegian entered the ring for his bout. Never a natural boxer, but an accomplished street-fighter, he reverted back to what he knew best when things started to go against him. 'He actually came out for one round and started headbutting and kicking his opponent. It ended up with a bloodbath and he nearly killed him.' Referees had to wade in and stop the fight before dragging the now half-crazed Glaswegian from his battered foe, a private from the Army Pay Corps.

That pugilist, far from being declared the winner, was charged with serious assault and consigned to the guardhouse. 'We never actually found out what the official result of that bout was.' Geordie Aitken gave up his boxing career after that one bout when it came to receiving his prize – a brass button polisher. To make sure he was never invited back to boxing training he tore up the Pig's dress hat during one training session in the camp gym. 'He should have known better than to go to the toilet and leave it lying around where I was. Anyway I didn't fancy having my head punched in for a brass button polisher and needed an excuse to get out of boxing.'

He got out of boxing but went straight back to the guardroom. When out of there he was back in the town. Which usually meant back to the guardroom. Another night of drunken depravity finished up with the expected outcome. This time after he battered a prostitute who he accused of stealing his money as they flirted in the off-limits beer house.

He blamed it on the fact that the landlord had been selling them nothing but dyed methylated spirits. His commanding officer was not convinced so it was back behind bars. Even while in the guardhouse Geordie Aitken got into trouble and was given yet another sentence. In stacking his wooden bed up against the wall to peer out of the bars it duly collapsed and left the tiny soldier dangling from the bars. All the while his regulation boots were digging into the plaster. Thinking the rebellious squaddie had purposefully defiled his cell he was charged with wilful damage and given an extended sentence.

Back in training the hapless Geordie Aitken could do nothing right. And again it was his cursed rifle that was to land him in trouble. During army manoeuvres the fed up squaddie and three friends soon tired of 'playing soldiers', and decided to have a rest behind a bush. Their fits of laughter at one of Geordies Aitken's not too reverential jokes gave the game away, and their position. A furious company commander discovered his four AWOLs behind a bush and screamed at them to come out double quick.

They duly did, but in four different directions and fled across the rolling fields into the distance. To aid his escape Geordie Aitken slung his rifle away and ran off across the fields. He had never run so fast since joining up. He later discovered that had he discarded his 'best friend' in the heat of a real battle he would have been in serious trouble. As it was only while on exercise he was dispatched yet again to the guardhouse. He was charged with carelessness and given seven days. It took nearly as long to find his rifle. Under military police escort he was taken back to the field to find his weapon but to his dismay, and that of the MPs every bush in the massive field had taken on a similar appearance in the close light of day. Furious at having been given the sentence in the first place the rebellious soldier smashed up his cell and tore up his uniform. It was not the last time he was to rip up his coveted but oversized uniform.

By the time he was discharged all of his army credit money was taken up to cover the cost of damaged uniforms. He did not realize at the time but he was eventually to leave the army penniless because of his actions against his uniforms.

While he was behind bars another recruit had joined the regiment who was to prove a blessing in disguise to Geordie Aitken. Captain Williams was a Church of Scotland minister who had joined the British Army Chaplains Corp because of a lifelong ambition to be part of a regiment that wore a kilt. Both Geordie Aitken and his company commander realized that regular army life was not for the skiving squaddie. Miraculously, Captain Williams proved the answer to their problems. The chaplain needed a batman. But in solving B Company's problems he was only adding to his own. By the time his new batman was finished with him he was heading for a nervous breakdown. Not that Geordie Aitken cared.

The transfer to batman duties, responsible for the officer's kit meant he was taken off regular duties including guard duty. Which to Geordie Aitken meant more free time to enjoy a drink. 'This poor chaplain didn't know what he was letting himself in for.'

With a hatred of religion, and a hatred of the army and a general hatred of authority, things were doomed from the start. One of his main functions was to dress the captain but ironing both the dress uniform and ceremonial uniform were a chore for the newly appointed batman. Usually because he was so hungover from the night before he could hardly concentrate.

'My job was primarily to keep this holy man tidy but after hitting the booze again the poor guy became the dirtiest officer in the regiment if not the entire army. His dress belt and sword were so dull because of the lack of attention you would have thought they were turning rusty. Often I would burn a hole in the leg of his dress trousers because the iron was too hot and the backside of his trousers were that glossy they looked like a mirror. You could have walked behind him and combed your hair in them.'

Realizing he needed divine intervention to cure the hapless batman Captain Williams ordered him to attend a course in the village of Verden, in the Black Forest. It was scheduled to last three weeks but Geordie Aitken lasted two days. On his day of enrolment he arrived half drunk from the night before despite a solemn promise to Captain Williams, that he would not do anything to embarrass the chaplain. 'He sent me off on the course hoping it would do something about my thirst for alcohol. He was right as it made me drink even more.'

During the course the classes were not allowed out of the barracks and were expected to take part in nightly Bible discussion groups. Geordie Aitken had other plans and on the first night set off to find a pub in a nearby town. To fuel his addiction for alcohol he took with him a hussar's dress helmet which he planned to sell off for beer money. Off he went over the eight foot perimeter wall in search of a drink clutching the feathered helmet and wearing his kilt. 'I went over the wall like a tartan parachute.' He duly sold the hat, got drunk and set off back to the barracks. Getting back over the wall was a bigger problem thanks to the local brew and he was, not surprisingly, caught rolling around singing and telling everyone what he thought of the church course. 'Sod your barmy church course you are all a shower of Bible-thumping perverts.'

Duly charged with theft, absconding, and being drunk he was facing yet another stint in the guardhouse. Fortunately, the camp did not have one and the next morning he was put on a train and returned to Luneburg. Thankfully for everyone, his three years were nearing an end. The unit was shipped back to Scotland and Geordie Aitken only had months to go. But still he could not earn himself a little respect, as his unsuspecting family were to discover. Having decided to urinate on the sacred drill square Geordie Aitken was once again in the guardhouse when his proud relatives decided to pay him a surprise visit.

Relatives from Canada had arrived in Edinburgh for the annual military tattoo and decided to pop in and pay their own hero a visit.

Geordie Aitken with other members of HLI in Germany.

They didn't have to wait until the military tattoo to see a proud Scottish rifleman in his kilt when they had their own to look at. Unfortunately, when they arrived at Redford Barracks in Edinburgh, Geordie Aitken was once again behind bars. In a show of sympathy, and knowing that his hapless soldier only had days left anyway, the company commander allowed the troublesome squaddie out of the jail to greet his relatives. That was how Geordie Aitken finished his army days. The day he joined he ended up in the guardhouse and on the day he was leaving he had just left it yet again.

Three years after joining up he was on his way home. To the delight of himself and the Highland Light Infantry he was returned to the streets of Glasgow at the age of 22 with a word of warning from his company commander. 'If you feel like joining the British Army again make sure you join a bloody English regiment.'

The disco sound is their delight
mention Jesus the kids take flight
What is the cause they turn their back?
and paint our Jesus a deep jet black

Drugs and sex is their thing
with booze and violence for a fling
When will their filthy sinning end
as their way of life is round the bend?

But churches fall so very short
in dealing with kids who like to snort
Their doors are closed to gutter folk
to teenage addicts they will not yoke

Jesus loves the kids so much
he will take them out of Satan's clutch
But churchy people you must change
and keep traditions out of range

The kids need help, not your rules
to stop them using Satan's tools
Jesus lives and is here to stay
get rid of religion and change your ways.

The Teenage Scene.

# CHAPTER 3

# Drunken Violence

In October 1959 a 22-year-old Geordie Aitken walked out of Redford Barracks straight back into a life of drunken violence. He couldn't even leave his army tormentors at the gates without branding them all a 'shower of puffs'.

There he stood on the Scottish streets in denims and a pair of scruffy trainers without any laces. Near penniless, his army discharge money had been witheld to cover the cost of the numerous uniforms he had ripped up during his spells in the guardhouse. But before letting the world know he was back in circulation he decided to have a drink. Rather than wait until he got back to his native Glasgow he headed for an Edinburgh pub. Instead of spending what little he had on smartening himself up he went off to spend it on getting tanked up.

Only hours after his army discharge he was in a bar room brawl. As he sat savouring his freedom in Edinburgh's Black Bull pub a nasty argument broke out between a man and a woman standing at the bar but unknown to Geordie Aitken the woman was a prostitute and the man a potential punter. He launched himself straight in and headbutted the unsuspecting sailor leaving him in a pool of blood. That argument quickly settled he turned to find another stranger at his shoulder. This one was more friendly and turned out to be the woman's grateful pimp who duly offered to buy him drinks for the rest of the day, and throw in the choice of twelve girls he had on his books.

A heavy night's drinking out of the way Geordie Aitken returned to Glasgow nursing his customary hangover to let his friends know he was back on the streets.

All he left behind was his new-found pimp friend. A few years later he didn't even have that. He learned that the pimp had been stabbed to death in a street fight.

Back in his native Glasgow the building sites, scrapyards, thieving, fighting, drinking and Orange Lodge fanatacism beckoned. The only improvements were made to his dress. Out of uniform it was back to his dapper suits and milk and margarine hair styles. Dressed to kill, he was also prepared to, as his customary role in the flute and accordion bands continued. 'I still never bothered to learn an instrument. The bands only wanted me because I was mental.'

Not a lot had changed since he left the back streets to join up. Only now he was a tougher fighter thanks to his army training. Despite the initial happiness at leaving the army it didn't take long for him to slip back into a life of drunken depravity. 'I thought I was taking a drink but the drink was actually taking me.'

Now working in a scrapyard, a chance of salvation came along in the shape of his girlfriend Mae. He had liked her since his school days and here she was still single and accepting his advances. But he blew it. In no uncertain terms. Here was his chance to settle down and curb his wicked ways and marry the girl of his dreams. But two days before the couple were due at the altar the wedding was called off after Mae's drunken excuse for a boyfriend savagely attacked her mother's boy-friend. She was also to discover that her lying fiancé had blown all of their savings, sold their wedding presents to buy booze and had been letting his drunken mates sleep off their hangovers in the little rented flat that was meant to be their marital home.

During the run up to the wedding things were looking bleak but Mae persevered in the hope that things would change after the big day. They were not to get that far.

Throughout their courtship Mae could not curb his drinking. Often a night at the cinema would end in violence and Mae return home in tears.

The Royal Cinema was the scene of many acrimonious partings. By virtue of what it was, it was perhaps not the best place to take his beloved girlfriend, but as was often the case Geordie Aitken viewed things through drink affected eyes. He was even smuggling drink into the cinema in a lemonade bottle, not to evade cinema staff but to try to kid his girlfriend that he was off the booze. 'I must have been the only person in Glasgow who could get drunk on a bottle of lemonade. Before the movie was finished I would be up singing my rebellious Protestant songs.' As the drunken singing started another night's courting ended. But Geordie Aitken wasn't bothered. Memories of his childhood days at the Royal returned. Usherettes never lasted more than a week thanks to the customers groping them, grabbing their takings and lifting whatever refreshments they wanted. Geordie Aitken usually took his own, a large bag of whelks. Not that he particularly liked the taste but because the empty shells made excellent missiles to pelt at the heads of viewers.

Another favourite pastime was firing metal staples from an elastic band at the cloth cinema screens ripping them to shreds. Or even urinating in the ice-cream cartons and hurling them at cinema staff. Whatever they did it usually ended up with a police presence in the ramshackle cinema. No comfy seats in that place just rows of wooden benches. Not least because the cinema was regularly flooded after thieving customers ripped out the lead and copper pipes from the toilet. 'It was a miracle if we ever got through a movie without the lights going up or the police being called.' After a night at the pictures it was back to the scrapyard and the now frantic Mae. She was still prepared to give him yet another last chance. But his chances were running out.

At one wedding rehearsal the scruffy shipyard worker turned up at

Geordie filthy after work in the scrapyard.

the church straight from work, covered in oil and reeking of cheap wine. The minister, not surprisingly, mistook him for a tramp, and asked the embarrassed Mae where her intended was. When the disillusioned groom-to-be jumped up and snarled at the minister that he was the lucky man an almighty row ensued. It ended in blows, the young couple thrown out of the church and a hysterical minister warning a tearful Mae: 'don't marry that man he's a nutter.' As it happened the wedding never did take place but not because of the minister's warning. As the wedding presents started to roll in so did an alcoholic Geordie Aitken, by now on his hundreth last chance; he started to pawn them to buy cheap wine. When that money ran out he sold the pawn tickets to buy more drink.

He was also lying to Mae about the flat they had and which had been left in his hands ready to furnish for married life. The money intended for that was also firmly in the hands of the owner of the nearest wine shop. All along he had been promising his fiancée that their flat was 'coming along great'. Indeed, the door was left propped open with a library book so that his street friends could use it as a drinking den and then sleep off their hangovers on the floor. Far from knowing what was going on Mae readily accepted her husband-to-be's excuses of 'wait until we are married' whenever she asked to see their intended new home. 'It's bad luck to see it before then.' It would have been for him had she known what was really going on. As it happened the state of the flat paled into insignificance.

Following his drunken fight with Mae's mother's boyfriend it was finally ended. Mae's intended maid of honour had a different duty to perform from the one she expected and was dispatched to the Aitken home to tell him the news. The words took a while to sink in. Not because he was emotional but because he was still hungover from the night before and trying to remember how badly he hurt his planned mother-in-law's boyfriend, and what to say about the wedding presents.

All that was left of them was a frying pan and that was being used by his family. It was duly washed out and handed back to the maid of honour to return to Mae. The expected trouble never materialized when Mae got word to him saying she was just so pleased to have got away from him with her sanity that she couldn't care less about the flat, the presents, or him.

Back to being a batchelor boy the ill-fated wedding saga was still not fininshed. After hearing that Mae had married his mate a drunken and jilted Geordie Aitken set out for revenge. 'I knew everything had been my fault and was actually quite relieved not to be getting married but I still thought the world of Mae. With a drink inside of me I could not handle the thought of her with this friend of mine.' After following the two of them to her mother's home Geordie Aitken set about the new groom. Far from hurting him he very nearly half-killed him. He did that with a wooden fence post with a six-inch long nail still sticking out from where he had ripped it from a garden fence.

The innocent one-time best friend of his drunken attacker, was left lying with the post stuck to his face and the nail embedded in his jaw having penetrated his lower jaw and gums. The only concern Geordie showed was the next morning when he bought a copy of the *Daily Record* newspaper to read about the attack and to see how badly injured his victim had been left. That was to set a pattern of newspaper buying. Many a time he would buy a morning paper just to see what he had been up to the night before. 'I was terrified to buy a newspaper after a night's drinking in case someone had been murdered.'

Two years out of the army and life was rapidly heading downhill. Not that Geordie Aitken cared. Every time things looked bleak he took a drink, and drinking was what he liked doing best. To feed his habit his life centred around crime and thieving. Now back on the building sites he was ideally placed to do both.

One of his hobbies, stealing non-ferrous metals, earned him the nickname of David Copperfield. Another hobby, stealing cables, nearly earned him an early grave. 'If it was not screwed down, or quickly missed, then I would steal it. Before too long every building site in Glasgow was being warned not to take David Copperfield on.' While working as a cement mixer in the early days of the Strathclyde University project the boozed up builder started to break the habit of a lifetime by going into work an hour early. Not to court favour with his bosses but to steal enough cable before they arrived, more money to spend on the drink. But one such ploy left him with a bad head that for once had nothing to do with the booze.

One misty morning he thought that all of his Christmases had come at once. A veritable goldmine in the shape of an exposed telephone cable. Twelve feet of that, he thought, and I'll be able to get drunk for a week. He could barely get through the day thinking about the prized cable and hardly slept waiting for the next morning to come. This time he and his thieving sidekick even went in two hours early to make sure they had time to take what they wanted. They knew that this was no ordinary telephone cable and was indeed heavy duty cable but what they did not know was that it had been re-connected during the night and was now powering the street lights and the nearby Rotten Row maternity hospital. With the promises of riches in their minds the two dawn thieves took a pick to the cable. Taking turns they managed to hack their way through the outer casing to unearth the prized copper. It was Geordie Aitkens turn with the pick. Down went the pick head and up went the hungover thief. Out went the street light and emergency operations at the Rotten Row hospital had to be conducted courtesy of a standby power generator. The pick head shrivelled from two and a half feet down to eight inches, the handle turned black. and Geordie Aitken's partner in crime duly fled the scene. Thanks to his rubber boots he had been saved, but only just. 'I was fired about thirty feet up into the air and landed bursting open my head. I was lying there in the middle of a complete blackout thinking I was having a heart attack and all I could hear was my mate scarpering off up the road.' He swore from then on he would never steal copper again.

A few bottles of cheap wine later, his head firmly bandaged and he soon broke yet another promise. It lasted about as long as the solemn promise he had made to Mrs Davidson on leaving the residential school.

Getting money for drink was all that mattered and a few broken promises were nothing to him. Having recovered enough to return to work, and having escaped police prosecution, his thieving ways were finally to catch up with him. His thieving was costing construction companies fortunes. Dozens of building sites later, he was finally barred from the construction game. 'I would lie to everyone saying I had stopped the drink but before I barely got started on a new job I would be stealing again.' Other jobs came and went but the drinking and stealing didn't, the streets and the pubs were his life.

None more so than the infamous Cactus Colorado, at least that was one of its names. It was so bad its name was changed nearly every

other week just to win back customers. 'I was getting barred every
night of the week.' Once for nearly burning the place down after a
misguided cigarette end landed on a padded chair and started a blaze
which was only put out with the help of the local fire brigade.

Geordie Aitken's intended target had been the strapping well-dressed
commissionaire who was employed to give the pub an air of respect-
ability. Anywhere else in the city he would have been called a bouncer.

On his jacket hung various war medals to let people know he was
a war veteran, but they meant nothing to the vicious street gangs he
was now doing battle with. 'They never counted to us. We just kicked
right into him  and booted him to the ground. We used to rip his cap
up and throw it into the street before throwing him out after it. We
went through commissionaires like we went through pints.' Because
of his antics he was barred from just about every pub at one time or
another. Usually the less savoury ones let him back after a token cooling
off period. But the standard joke at the time was: 'there's wee Geordie
off to London for a pint'. He was barred from so many bars in Glasgow
it was probably the only place people thought he would get served
with a drink.

Back in the scrapyards another favourite haunt was one of the Clacken
bars. They were dotted about Glasgow and he was barred from most
of them. One of them barred him for life. Even in his later days when
he returned as a member of Alcholics Anonymous he was refused a
tomato juice, such were the memories of him. That stemmed from an
incident when he popped in straight from the scrapyard for his customary
daily drink. While waiting to be served he took a fancy to the jar of
pickled eggs on the bar counter. Forgetting the filthy state he was in
he dipped his hand in the jar and the thick oil on his hand turned the
vinegar jet black. The only way out of this predicament was to buy
the whole jar. But that meant using up his beer money and he thought
better of it. The furious landlord argued that oil-stained pickled eggs
were no good to him. Geordie Aitken agreed and promptly threw the
jar through the massive stained glass mirror behind the bar. Not only
was he barred for life but arrested and charged with a breach of the
peace and malicious damage. 'Here I was getting into trouble with the
police for the sake of a pickled egg.'

Away from the drink his working life was not faring much better.

His next attempt at gainful employment came by way of the city corporation's parks department, but it was to prove one of the most humiliating episodes of the drunken hardman's life. Here he was, a villain of the tough Glasgow streets, being told to push a parks barrow along those very streets he ruled by night. The cause of the swearing, drinking, fighting Geordie Aitken was not helped by the fact that his boss was a Jehovah's Witness. But as always he lied his way through and told him he was a clean living man. 'Everything in my life was a lie from the word go. I told him I did not drink, swear, fight or steal.'

Such was his conviction, and his by now polished art of lying that a delighted boss told him: 'You must be the only one that doesn't'. He was to find out different when the latest recruit to the city corporation's cleansing corps was sent out with the dreaded barrow, lawn seed, scythe and elderly workmate in tow. To show him the ropes an elderly man had been assigned to work with him. The theory might have been a good one but it played right into an uncaring Geordie Aitkens hands. The pair were dispatched to the renowned Edinburgh Road where just about every one of his night time gangster friends spent their days idly watching the world go by – and soon their esteemed friend and his embarassment of a barrow. Such was his ego that Geordie Aitken informed his frail, old companion, who had spent his working life on the parks department and who was now seeing out his days until retirement, that he was to push the heavy barrow. After a brief argument, in which the old man was told in no uncertain terms that the job was his, the pair finally set off along the bustling main street.

Geordie Aitken's giveaway corporation overalls were hidden under the bags of lawn seed. The plan was that if anyone saw them Geordie Aitken was only talking to the old gardener who then had to say his farewells and walk off up the street alone. The coast clear a young egotistical workmate would catch up with him further along the road. One of the stumbling blocks was that Geordie Aitken knew just about everybody and by the time the two workmen reached their destination it was nearly time to set off back down the road to the depot. 'I was that embarrassed to be with him that I terrified him into doing what I told him. Here we are with a barrow, bags of lawn seed, and a scythe walking along one of Glasgow's busiest streets which by night I thought

I ruled. The nearest thing to a scythe I had ever seen was the sort of weapons we used to hit people with.'

Under threat of not living to collect his pension the old man lasted the distance. The lawn seed, scythe and even the barrow didn't. They were duly disposed of for drink money on a nearby council housing estate. Having blamed a local thief, which wasn't exactly a lie, the pair of them kept their jobs. But Geordie Aitken's mind was on bigger things. If he had to endure this working hell he was determined to get plenty of drink money out of it.

A few nights heavy drinking were paid for courtesy of a brand new petrol driven lawnmover. Such was their value that they had to be signed out by the workmen. Knowing what the immediate future held for the gleaming Antelope lawnmower Geordie Aitken duly ordered his terrified workmate to sign for the machine and off they went. The heavy industrial lawnmower perched on a sagging barrow and the by-now frantic old man pushing it, usually fifty yards up the road from his colleague, who invariably passed one friend or another on their travels. Hours later, and the grass duly cut, the old man went off to the the park toilet to answer a call of nature, leaving the lawnmower in the care of his young charge. Within minutes it had vanished into a house on the nearby estate, from which days later it emerged a different colour. The old gardener's face also changed colour when he returned to find the costly lawnmover had disappeared and a bemused looking workmate proclaiming: 'You can't leave anything for two minutes. I had to nip to the toilet and when I came back the bloody thing was gone.' Any efforts to placate the sorry old man failed and he made the long walk back to the depot mumbling pitifully: 'I've signed it out, I've signed it out, that's my pension gone.' The tears touched Geordie Aitken so much he fleetingly considered pushing the now empty barrow for the old man. But only fleetingly.

Not surprisingly a new job was beckoning. Still with the dreaded parks department but supposedly out of harms way. A stint on the corporation's mobile squad. To thank his Jehovah's Witness boss for transferring him to hard labour the arrogant employee stood swearing at him for ten minutes just to make him mad. Here he was waist deep in filthy ponds and streams fishing out rubbish. The only good thing about his new job was that his workmate was equally bent when it came to drinking and thieving. He was thankful for a like-minded workmate because he now had to work harder at his scams as the corporation had introduced a new pay system. Thanks to the antics of the Geordie Aitkens of the workforce, the workmen were now paid at clocking off time on a Friday afternoon instead of the usual Thursday afternoon. 'Every Thursday we got paid I would walk off the job and was not seen again until Monday. And there were plenty of Geordie Aitkens working for the corporation.'

The infamous Easterhouse estate was the new workplace for the two conniving workmen. 'What a place. It was the wildest part of Scotland. People deserved a Victoria Cross or Purple Heart just for working there.' But the area held no fears for the two wild street-fighting tricksters who stopped at nothing to get a drink.

Geordie Aitken's job was to dredge the streams and load the rubbish into his colleague's dumper truck. That was about the only thing they had not sold off. And only because they needed it to go backwards and forwards. Complete with spanking, brand new waders he set off for his first taste of stream cleaning. But even this presented a way of making some extra beer money. Only minutes into their task, they decided to adjourn to the nearby Swinton Arms. Their only excuse was the snow on the ground. To ensure a worthwhile stay in the pub the pair successfully negotiated an arrangement with the landlord and were allowed to drink on credit which was to be squared up on pay day. Everyone knew Geordie Aitken liked a drink, and the barmen knew that by the time he left the pub he would be owing quite a lot of money. As quick as the wine bottles tops came off so did his brand new waders. He needed no prompting when a boozed up fisherman asked an equally drunken Geordie Aitken where he could get a pair. 'No problem, pal, size 6 you say? take these.' Standing barefoot in the bar he spent the £5 he got for the waders then reverted to credit. Getting back to the job held no fears for the sozzled workmen, despite the heavy snow lying on the ground. A piggy back off his mates through the wild streets of Easterhouse brought a few cursory comments but the pair where past caring.

As they set off back to work a staggering fisherman set off in the opposite direction proudly clutching his new yellow waders. Not surprisingly, the two men were also heading for the ranks of the unemployed. But not before one last act of defiance from each of them. A furious boss who threatened to fire them there and then, was duly left lying flattened in the snow. But Geordie Aitken wanted to exact a more widespread kind of retribution and promptly urinated in the men's tea urn. The next day he was given his cards and ordered off the site after picking up his cards. But his childish act was to come stright back and haunt him when the truth came out.

Happy to let everyone think he had been up to his usual violent tricks and revelling in his hardman image, he was content to let people think he had been sacked for attacking the supervisor. A strutting Geordie Aitken headed for the pay office to collect his cards but was dismayed to find a lengthy queue of workmen, many of them there for similar reasons. In idle chat the parks department hero informed everyone he was being paid off for yet again lifting his hands to authority figures. But the Glasgow hardman was soon to be even more embarrassed than he ever had been walking behind the dreaded parks barrow. On nearing the front of the queue he was stopped in his tracks when a inquiring wages clerk shouted in the packed office 'Hey Aikie, is that right you got sacked for urinating in the tea urn up in Easterhouse?' To howls of laughter a furious and belittled Geordie Aitken walked from the room feeling at his lowest ebb. He had become the laughing stock of his beloved Glasgow and he knew it. From the nearest telephone he rang his sister and told her to tell their mother that he would not be home that night.

He took a train to the south of England that same day feeling the loneliest man in the world. Once again drink was at the root of his problems and he was leaving his homeland because of it. But he was to discover that the building sites and bars of England did not differ that much than those north of the Border.

Following his ill-fated trip to Newmarket ten years earlier Geordie Aitken was again trying his hand in England. His attempts to become a jockey nothing more than distant memories he wondered what the manual side of life had in store for the wordly-wise 25-year-old Scotsman. He was not to have too happy a time on his second visit and, as he did in Newmarket, found his new English friends hard to mix with. He had tried it as a teenager and failed, and his latest stint down south was doomed to failure, too. Back home he was a tough streetwise villain, here he was only a dosser. Even by the time he got off the train he was drunk. In twelve months time he was to make the return journey by coach and by the time he had arrived in Glasgow he would be drunk again. In between the two trips he was seldom anything else as the sites offered him little solace. 'This was to herald a change in my life. A new job, new friends, new surrounding and a new start. But if anything things actually got worse.'

He had met up with three other Glaswegians on the train and on arriving in Herefordshire set about drinking. No attempt was made to settle in with the locals. He did get his new job, new scenery and new surrounding. His new surroundings came in the shape of one of the dirtiest dosshouses in the area. It was full of everything, lesbians, puffs, murderers and violent alcoholics. They could have been called the Quality Street gang. The twelve months he spent in England were all spent in similar filthy surroundings. It was all he and his fellow Glaswegians could afford. The less they spent on lodgings the more money they spent on drink. And that was their main reason for living.

Despite decent wages on the building sites he slipped further into drunken depravity. Herefordshire police were regularly treated to what their Scottish counterparts were used to.

By this time the 25-year-old alcoholic's possessions were a tin mug and a twisted knife, fork and spoon set. Not that they were used that often. Food took a back seat to drink and that in itself was to lead to major health and hygiene problems for the now-bearded and filthy Scotsman.

Because of his alcoholic habits Geordie Aitken, slumming it in the affluent English towns, suffered badly from malnutrition and even developed scurvy. Here he was, at the onset of the swinging sixties, suffering from a disease of yesteryear.

Complete with filthy, dangling black beard, and covered from head to foot in dandruff he knew he was hitting rock bottom. 'To think my childhood days were none too happy but what a state I was in then.' Despite accepting he was in trouble he did nothing concrete about his problems. Drink would take care of any worries. It was because of his sozzled states that he had problems, but life continued for the down-and-out drunk.

The carpets of the dosshouse were soaked in urine, vomit, and in

some rooms human faeces. The residents were none too bothered
where they answered the call of nature. Home to Geordie Aitken was
a stinking room with two camp-beds and a dilapidated wardrobe, not
that it bothered him. The only things he kept in the wardrobe were
his mug and eating utensils. They only came out when it was time for
the four alcoholic builders to tuck into their daily meal. A pot of
strawberry jam and a loaf of bread between them. Any method of
supplementing the staple diet was grabbed by the hungry men, legal
or not. They were allowed to get credit money in advance of their
wages to buy lunch but with this quartet it only went to help push up
the local brewery's profit margins. 'The gaffer used to think we were
dining in top class restaurants because we never asked for less than ten
pound a day in lunch money. And that was in the early sixties.'

That spent on beer, it was back to Geordie Aitken's favourite pastime
to help provide the food, thieving. But just as in the wages office of
the parks department he was left ridiculed and burning with embarrassment after being caught stealing pears from a woman's tree. His
pathetic state was hammered home to him when the frail old woman
refused to call the police but told him to hang around for ten minutes.
She reappeared with a massive parcel of sandwiches and told him to
sort his life out instead of being an excuse of a man. 'I could have
handled the police but it hurt deeply when she told me it was disgraceful
to see a young Scottish man in such a state that he had turned to
stealing pears from a tree. It only hurt so much because inside I knew
it was the truth.' But in the grip of alcohol he couldn't change and,
far from sorting himself out, sunk deeper into the mire. Amazingly, he
was still being offered work on the building sites, because he was
prepared to put his back into it.

Every time he was given a fresh start he blew it through drink. Deep
down he was a proud man but the drink had him and brushes with
the law and authority in general still followed his drunken binges. Food
was still a luxury and life at the dosshouse was getting worse. Bathing
was now out of the question as most of the taps had been ripped from
their sockets to let the drunken thieves get at the lead and copper pipes.

Geordie Aitken and his fellow dossers now, themselves, urinated on
the sodden carpets, they were past caring. They soldiered on in the
face of depravity with the lure of a decent pay packet every Friday,

and the belief that Geordie Aitken was still being ridiculed in his home city.

In reality nobody cared, but his ego would not let him forget. One day on the building site they hit rock bottom. Everyone else always had something to eat during meal breaks but the drunken quartet just sat there waiting for the buzzer so they could get back into the job. An English workman, idly chatting to them during one break, laughed so much at their antics and colourful stories that he dropped a huge slice of pork pie into a pile of building sand. This time the four men were not the first back to work when the buzzer sounded. Seconds after the English man turned and walked away the four scavengers jumped at the pork pie and washed it clean under a building site tap before quartering it. 'His bait box looked like a Christmas hamper to us, but we did not want him to think that we were completely out of the game and kept our eyes off it as he talked to us. But, when he dropped this pie I actually thought it was Christmas. We waited until he had went then four grown men actually jumped a piece of pork pie.' As the days came and went in similar fashion so did his working career in England. With drink once again at the root of his problems.

He was thrown out of the dosshouse after drinking the rent money and being ordered to settle his bill. He returned from the building sites one day to find his prized mug, knife, fork and spoon left for him outside the locked door of the stinking room that had become his home. In a rage he decided to smash the place to bits and then burn the whole stinking dosshouse down. He managed most of his first thoughts but struggled with the *coup de grâce*. The place was so sodden the urine-soaked carpets would not burn. 'The place was waterlogged. It was actually that wet that it wouldn't burn. I went through a whole box of matches and my mate even went at it with lighted candles. Just because I had been thrown out I wanted to burn the whole place down. And with everyone in it if necessary.' Furious at being thwarted the demented pair attacked the structure with their hands and feet. The paper-thin compressed cardboard walls were no match for them. Holes were kicked and punched right through them to compensate for not being able to set it alight. They then strode defiantly out of the door past the cowering landlord. Knowing that police trouble would follow the men decided to pack up and head back to Glasgow. For once in twelve months the scruffy Scotsmen came away laughing. Having gone to the building site to pick up their cards and wages the foreman forgot, in the urgency, to debit the dinner money they had been borrowing every day in lieu of wages. A request for the £50 from each man to be returned met with a stream of abuse and the sound of running feet. Each of the four workmen scarpered in a different direction before meeting up at the coach station on their way back to their beloved Glasgow. But they could not even manage the coach trip home without trouble. By the time the bus pulled into Glasgow's Buchanan Street depot the frantic driver had already threatened to throw them off on four separate occasions. Had he had the nerve he would have gladly done it. One of them had thought he was back in the dosshouse and urinated down the aisle, another had taken a shine to a woman passenger and indecently assaulted her, while as a group they had sworn and sung throughout the trip.

Geordie Aitken's defence was his drinking.

A startled bus driver accepted it without question when he discovered the evidence – thirty-seven empty barley wine bottles. 'Here I was hitting the streets of Glasgow again and despite twelve months of work didn't have a penny in my pocket. What I did have, though, was an even bigger drink problem'.

Back in Scotland Geordie Aitken was about to embark on another trip. This one was to take him to death's door.

My spirit yearns for peace and joy
this ruined life is Satan's ploy
What has this life done for me
from filthy booze I can't get free

I get my kicks from this cursed drink
committing suicide I am on the brink
I am just a bag of skin and bone
Satan makes my spirit groan

I've many friends in mental wards
we sing our hurts with unmusical chords
My life has a filthy tale to tell
I am on the rocky road to Hell

I had my chance at Sunday School
Not to be the Devil's fool
I grew up with a mind of my own
now I have a heart of stone

Each day to me seems like a year
with hangovers from wine and beer
Shakes and sweats are my reward
because I walked away from the Lord

I knew Jesus when I was young.
He can save me from this heap of dung
Please, dear Jesus, hear my plea
remove the booze and set me free

I come to you as a child again
your death for me was not in vain
I've had my fill of Satan's power
give me your nectar heavenly flower

Put new breath into my soul
the breath of life can make me whole
Thank you, Jesus, for saving me
you open ear has heard my plea

Now I am free and born again
I'll share my faith with all kinds of men
My life's experience can be used
to save the souls that Satan bruised

Then all together in the heavenly choir
we will sing the songs with tongues of fire
Heavenly rays will light up the land
plus Gospel music from a heavenly band.

Booze

# CHAPTER 4

# Suicide Beckons

At least in Glasgow Geordie Aitken had some support and friends. His appearance was improved and from the outside he looked half normal. Inwardly, he was emotionally, spiritually and physically wrecked. Drinking and fighting continued and his religious fanatical beliefs still got him into trouble. But, ironically, his Protestant ideals also got him a job. Thanks to his Orange Lodge involvement he was offered a job at the city's massive Tennents Brewery. If ever in his early life he was to think there could be a God it was now. But his sister Rosemary adopted a more realistic attitude. 'Jesus Christ, Geordie, that's all we need!' she exclaimed when her drunken excuse for a brother proudly informed her of his new job. But he wasn't bothered what she thought. He promised he would keep off the drink and that, ironically, the brewery would be the best place to test his resolve. 'Here I was telling my own sister a pack of lies. I told her I would stay sober and change my ways, but in reality I was not even bothered about the wages. All I wanted was to drink the place dry.' That was the only truthful thought in his head and over the coming eighteen months he gave it his best shot. Still not believing he was actually going to work in a brewery he set off for Tennents where, he had been reliably informed, the man he was to see was as fanatical an Orangeman as he himself was.

'Uncover your arms and let him see your tattoos, and you'll be in' was the advice from a worldly wise street friend. It proved to be sound advice and the alcoholic was on the payroll of a brewery. He was asked when he could start and he offered 'Right now'. The brewery told him to come back the following day and for once the young drunkard stayed in his sister's house away from the drink. Within hours he would have as much as he wanted. 'It was unbelievable. Half the time I couldn't even walk straight and here I was being offered a job in a brewery no questions asked. If I was an alcoholic when I started I was a chronic, chronic alcoholic by the time I left.'

Working out of the brewery's Duke Street headquarters he soon showed a willingness to start early. But for the same reason as in his building site days. He was in there before everyone else just so he could steal. But now he was stealing his drink direct. He was in paradise. In the past he had to steal copper to buy drink, but now he could just steal the drink itself.

At 6 a.m. every day he could be found in the huge vat room where massive open containers held thousands of gallons of Geordie Aitken's reasons for living. But because of his drunken states the drayman found himself barred out of pubs while only delivering to them. Landlords either took offence at his being legless drunk or his fighting. Many of the pubs on his rounds were Catholic bars. 'This was heaven on earth. I was going in two hours early and half the time I was drunk before I should've even been starting work. If not, I certainly was by the time it came to delivering it to the pubs. They were only just opening but you would think I had been in them all day.'

The effects of the massive vats soon compounded his alcoholic addiction. He gleefully dished out the booze to any workmates who wanted it. 'This thing was like a swimming pool. There was a huge jug hanging at the side which I used to lower in and then dish out to anyone that wanted some. We were drinking gallons of the stuff and it wasn't even fermented.' Even while he was getting his poison for free, and earning a wage into the bargain he still had sidelines going to ensure he never ran out of drink money. One was to sell the gas pumps, used to flush beer through the pipes, to a local garage. A quick service job and they promptly resold as foot pumps to be used to blow up car tyres. Another scam was more basic, stealing bottles of spirits and cartons of cigarettes from under the noses of landlords as he passed the kegs of beer down to them in their cellars. Often he did this in front of startled customers as they stood drinking at the bar. 'They knew that if I was daft enough to do this, I would be daft enough to happily beat them up if they reported me.'

Once he returned to the bar after stashing his ill-gotten gains in the cab of the brewery lorry parked outside, and returned with a bottle for his startled drayman colleague – to ensure the shocked workmate would never report him to the brewery bosses.

Off the street and back at the depot things were getting hectic thanks to his now habitual binges. He was even barred from the brewery canteen for stealing bread rolls and slices of black pudding. He did offer to hand the food back. When he produced it from the inside of his beloved combat jacket, complete with cigarette ash and pieces of filthy fluff, he was told to keep his ill-gotten gains. But his career was on a slippery slope. Were it not for his Orange Lodge connections he would have been long gone. But his supportive militant bosses could not save his skin after two more drunken escapades while a representative of Tennents.

On one delivery the draymen started a riot in a Catholic pub that ended in its customary bloodshed. All because he had overheard a harmless conversation about religion. Out came the infamous tattoos, the chants of King Billy and that was that. The tables went up, the bottles flew and Geordie Aitken forgot about delivering kegs of Tennents lager. The landlord contacted the brewery, who smoothed things over, but unlike his former girlfriend Mae, they only gave him one last chance. He used that up only days later when once again drunk out of his mind he wrongly accused an innocent barmaid of stealing his pay packet and in demanding it back smashed up the pub. He later realized the pay packet had slipped through an overall pocket and he had mistakenly vented his anger on the nearest person. As, throughout his early life, bar staff were usually the closest people to him when things went wrong.

Even his orange-coloured guardian angel could not save him now. The boss did manage to get charges of malicious damage dropped and Geordie Aitken, although unemployed, did escape a prison sentence. But he continued to serve his life sentence of alcoholic abuse. On the day he was fired, eighteen miraculous months after being started through the back door, he walked out into the street of Glasgow half dead. And still wearing his brewery overalls. He had been asked to hand them back but after explaining they were the only clothes he owned he was told to keep them on. That was another lie, albeit a little white one. He did in fact own a pair of pyjama bottoms which he wore under the blue overalls. The bit about only having what he stood up in was true. Back on the streets and also on the cheap wine he was now convinced he was to be 'a scumbag until the day I die'.

On the streets he was a familiar sight in his tattered overalls, pyjama bottoms and shoes that were held together with pieces of string. But little traces of pride still remained in the broken man, and he even blackened the string of his shoes to make it look like laces. Not that it changed anything. 'I did not have much going for me but when I took a drink I felt proud again. I was living in a land of make believe and with the bottle things seemed normal.'

At death's door and an embarrassment to his family, without a genuine friend in the world and with his drunken head still in the clouds, he would not and indeed could not change his ways. But something had to give and it nearly did for good. Two botched suicide attempts were the closest Geordie Aitken ever came to giving Glasgow some peace and quiet. He was living on his beloved mean streets, in one of the world's toughest and most violent cities but could not handle the violence in the way he once could. He was still fighting after drunken binges but was now on the wrong end of too many hidings. Years of neglect and drunken depravity had taken their toll and most of the time he was not strong enough to finish what he had drunkenly started.

A fractured skull, often broken nose, and smashed hands were testimony to that. The days of standing over a battered foe were rapidly slipping away. He was the one who was now literally on the bottom. He was a physical and mental wreck living a filthy drunken existence and was not only killing himself but his family as well. They were often left to pick up the pieces of such incidents, like the one when a man tried to take his eye out with a can opener in a drunken brawl or the time he was left half dead with a screwdriver sticking out of his neck.

Home at this time was a field, a back lane, or yet another dosshouse.

Still only 27 he was losing his will to live. The drink had a firm grip on the madcap alcoholic and he convinced himself that the only way out was at his own hands. As a service to his family and the people of Glasgow in general 'I was acting like an animal and the people were treating me like one. All I could see ahead of me was a lifetime of hurt and I knew that the only way to stop hurting my family and people in general was to take my own life.'

He was pushed to the brink of suicide when an old school friend passed him in the street. He was now begging outside pubs dressed in the pyjama bottoms and what was left of the overalls. His one-time friend could only stare in disgust and label him 'an excuse for humanity' and hurry off down the street.

Memories of the old English lady who had given him a plate of sandwiches after catching him stealing pears from her garden flooded back. She had used the same words earlier and he had not managed to change. Even in his pathetic drunken state the truth hurt him again. He knew he had been given chances but had blown every one. One of those chances had been provided in the shape of his sister Rosemary but like everything else he ruined it after hitting the bottle. His frantic sister had let him sleep on her floor in a bid to get away from the depravity of the streets. She endured a lot during his days with her.

A woman neighbour felt the full force of the Aitken anger after he attacked her in the front porch of her flat, which adjoined his sister's for allegedly trying to get the family's pet dog put down. She claimed it was urinating on the stairwell but after he heard the woman had been pouring water on the carpet before telephoning the coporation just so that his dog would be destroyed he set out for revenge. After she answered the door to him he grabbed her by the shoulders, thrashed her about and then pulled off her prized wig. That he duly ripped into quarters and pushed through her letterbox before departing cursing and swearing. Rosemary managed to live with that but was devastated when he turned on his own.

He was back on the streets after she threw him out for taking a knife to her 4-year-old daughter's prized piggy bank. He even tried to justify it by saying he had put some coppers into it after coming in drunk. His disgusted sister ordered him out of the house and told him that if the piggy bank meant so much to him he could take it. He did, and the handful of coppers that were his 4-year-old niece's proud savings.

He had always felt at home on the wild streets of Glasgow but he was not so comfortable now that those same streets had actually become his home. It was on them that the begging, scrounging, and scavenging nearly came to an end in a filthy derelict warehouse. The mindless near-corpse of a man walked into the dark, dusty building with the intention of ending it all. He very nearly did but was discovered by police in a pool of blood and rushed to the city infirmary where two blood transfusions saved his life. At that time he could never understand what led the police to his half dead body. In later years he was to accept that it was divine intervention. His mother had given him a final chance after hearing how he was sleeping rough in a field. Despite his earlier brush with death he had returned to his old lifestyle. On returning to the family home he promised his mother he would never drink again. Days later he turned up drunk out of his mind. His mother fainted and in the following row he took a metal poker to his father.

With both of them still there he walked into the kitchen and took a serrated bread knife to his arms. Thanks to his parents who discovered him in a pool of blood he was back at the infirmary where doctors once again saved his life.

But he still would not accept, or admit, that drink was killing him. He told the surgeon that he was a glazier and that he had slipped while carrying a pane of glass. An unimpressed Glaswegian doctor walked away after asking: 'What kind of windows use blunt corrugated glass?' Geordie Aitken realized that not even his lying was saving him now. Back out on the streets he continued to drink and was now a resident of Glasgow's infamous dosshouse, The Great Eastern Hotel. 'Man, was this place something. It only housed the lepers of society.' Still alive but without a life worth living he sunk back into a drunken depravity that outstripped his days in the English dosshouse.

Despite the warnings, the close calls, and the chances he had been offered since the ill-fated working trip to England things had only got worse. The more drink he could get the better. Even if some of it was at the very best dodgy and at the worst highly dangerous. To fuel his addiction he was drinking the cheapest alcohol in the worst places. A gill of White Tornado and a pint glass of mixed cider and lager were his favourites. He first came across the potent but dodgy wine as it was being made in the back room of a Glasgow pub – in a sink. The main ingredients were methylated spirits, sugar and colouring. Geordie Aitken proudly helped christen it when his back-shop brewers decided on an acceptable label before making a big impression in hitting the shelves and bars. He got the name from a television advert for furniture polish. Its proud creators thought it was because it would be polished off by drinkers. It was duly christened White Tornado and did polish off quite a number of unsuspecting drinkers. Without having a real name it even earned itself a nickname: 'The busby hat'. 'After drinking this stuff you would get up the next morning thinking your head had been stretched. White Tornado by itself was enough to blow your cap off but I used to drink it with this cider that tasted that raw you would think it still had apples floating in it.'

Most of this suicidal drinking was done in an infamous Scottish bar. 'Tourists used to come and visit this place just to take pictures of the animals that used to drink in there.' Women were barred from the pub because of the constant violence and wicked behaviour of its wild regulars. Those regulars had to nip across the road to use the park toilet, because the landlord had his boarded up to stop the constant theft of copper piping and vandalism. But more usually die-hard drinkers would answer the call of nature where they stood without undoing their trousers rather than risk a fellow regular pinching their drink. 'It was like an old fashioned cowboy film with fights breaking out every five minutes and tables and chairs being hurled everywhere. A publican's answer to Sodom and Gomorrah. Many a sore face came out of the vicious bar and you could get barred for life one night then welcomed back the next. I loved it because these were my kind of people.'

Apart from a mental disorder the only other thing needed to get past the doors was money. And the hardened boozers weren't too bothered how they got it. Anything that could be sold was. Geordie Aitken did a nice line in dodgy everythings. His musical boxes bought in the Gorbals area of Glasgow, were touted as being smuggled in from Switzerland. The only drawback? 'The ballerinas looked like Irish navvies.' His disposable cigarette lighters weren't much better and had their own flaws. 'They tended to overheat and many a time exploded in someone's face.'

His drunken selling days came to an abrupt end courtesy of a savage beating dished out by a disgruntled customer. 'I got as many good hidings from selling dodgy stuff as I did through being drunk.' His practised answer now on yet another trip to the casualty department was that he was an amateur boxer and had just been in the ring.

When the wild men were not selling they were lying. One such stint ended in disaster, when Geordie Aitken got the shock of his life at being confronted by a massive crucifix in the local church. He was only in church because his friend had gone to borrow enough money from the parish priest to pay for his father's funeral. The only problem was that his father was still alive and had been talking to the priest. While the delicate discussion was going on a bored Geordie Aitken decided to have a peep around the church but on pulling back a curtain was confronted by the massive cross and the face of Jesus glaring down at him. He fled from the church leaving his mate to carry on with the 'funeral arrangements'. The priest duly threw his friend out of the church and scolded him for lying. He also gave him £5 to buy a drink. If out of ideas himself, a gasping Geordie Aitken often turned to friend Barmy Sammy. For the price of two drinks, one each, Barmy Sammy would do his famed impersonation of Jimmy Cagney. 'Sammy was tiny with a bald head, and looked like a garden gnome but if you closed your eyes and listened to his impersonation you would swear it was Cagney.'

Albert Todesco was another who always had a way of making money to buy him and his mate a drink. Both he and Geordie Aitken were alcoholic street-fighters. A plumber by trade, he would often go into a bar with his mate, order a drink then watch Geordie Aitken disappear into the toilet. Having duly vandalized the toilet and ripped the pipes from the wall he would rejoin his friend and wait until the water began seeping out. Many a grateful landlord took up the offer of a trained plumber's help. When not in the pubs the pair would be found outside them selling mussels and whelks picked locally and boiled in Albert's bath. Complete with the coal dust from the filthy bags they had been carried in. 'Most of our customers commented that our seafood had a special flavour. How right they were. It was the cheap soap that had been in the bath shortly before the whelks.' The more scams they pulled the more booze they drank. But the lifestyle of a dosser was catching up with an emaciated Geordie Aitken. He was now heading down the road to a mental asylum. Were it not for the perserverance and understanding of a sympathetic family doctor he would probably still be in a padded cell today. Instead, unwittingly he was going to come off the drink. He knew, and Doctor Jean McDonald knew, that something was going to give. He had gone to get something to make him eat. A furious doctor explained that it was only the drink that was stopping him from eating. That cut no ice with the alcoholic but her next statement did when she told him that she was treating his mother for nerves. His first feeling of guilt came when she informed him his mother was on the verge of a massive nervous breakdown and the likely cause of it was his behaviour.

He was only 28 and had already given her a lifetime of trouble. For once Geordie Aitken was not only mentally confused but emotionally uneasy as well. He didn't know which way to turn and instinctively started to lie.

When Dr McDonald told him to hold his hands out straight he sat there with them glued to his side. She grabbed them and pulled them out straight. 'My skin was leaking sweat and steam seemed to be rising from my forehead, she started drying my forehead and despite telling me that I probably had brain damage because of all the drinking and head injuries there was a way back.' That sunk in but the nail in the coffin came when she told him about the state his mother was in. 'When she explained it to me I burst into tears. Dr McDonald was telling me the truth and it was killing me.' As in the past home truths hurt deeply. He could handle life but could not handle inner emotions.

Despite the shock of actually hearing from a qualified person that his drinking was literally killing not only himself but his mother as well, a confused Geordie Aitken still struggled to beat the bottle. But in a very short time he was to stop drinking forever. Dr McDonald told him she was sending him to hospital for help. 'No problem,' he thought to himself, 'my mates can smuggle lemonade bottles in full of wine.' But the hospital his doctor had in mind was a psychiatric one. 'That stopped me in my tracks. I knew if I got sent there I might never get out and, even if I did, they would have hung a label on me. I was acting like a crazy man but I didn't want it to be official.' The only other option for terrified Geordie Aitken was Alcoholics Anonymous. But an even bigger shock than the one from his doctor was in store when he finally plucked up courage to go.

That came after what was to be one of his last drinks with one of Glasgow's oldest dossers. Things were changing within him and he was even starting to worry about the state he was in. Never in fifteen years of drinking had it ever bothered him. But in the company of the filthy elderly tramp he finally embarked along a path that would lead to

sobriety. 'The alcoholic had asked me if I had tried Alcoholics Anonymous and I just looked at him and said that those places were for the
likes of him not me.

'He turned on me and said that the only difference between us was
that he had actually lost all of his will to live but I was still young
enough to salvage my life. Other than that I was the same, filthy,
stinking, alcoholic tramp that he was.' That night Geordie Aitken
banged on the massive door of the central Alcoholics Anonymous
building with one of the biggest shocks of his young life in store. He
discovered that he had been going there for the last three months since
his meeting with Dr McDonald. He had usually been so drunk he did
not even know. When he went 'officially' for the first time that night
he pretended he was there on behalf of his brother who was waiting
around the corner too embarrassed to knock on the door.

The no-nonsense AA man who greeted him told him to stop lying
and accept his problems. He even called him Geordie. A broken Geordie
Aitken heard how the group had nicknamed him 'Beardie Geordie'
during earlier visits, that they knew of his problems and could help
him. He was not alone in being an alcoholic.

With tears in his eyes he entered the building for the first time
knowing what he was doing.

It was a step that was going to save his life.

Give me the live covering of Holy Ghost power
so that I bloom like a heavenly flower
Fertilize me with a growing sublime
to show Jesus' love in me everytime

The garden we need in this world of ours
is sweet-scented gardens full of Holy Ghost flowers
The seed we must plant is the word of the Lord
to grow in the hearts and bring sweet accord

Water us, Lord, so that we all may grow
that our heavenly scents are not only for show
Our colours are different but we have one aim
that Jesus our Lord is always the same

The soil at times can feel so like clay
that hinders our growth in things that we say
So toil the ground with a heavenly hand
go forth with Jesus throuhgout this cold land

So sweet bloom of heaven, Jesus by name
breathe on me deeply with Holy Ghost rain
Let the pollen within me taste O so sweet
may this flower bed Jesus grow at your feet

The Garden.

# CHAPTER 5

# Alcoholics Anonymous

With the nickname of Beardie Geordie, a shaking Mr Aitken heard the massive windowless door of the Alcoholics Anonymous building in West Nile Street, Glasgow, slam firmly shut behind him. Away from the outside world and its many influences he was here to win back his life. The first three days were hell on earth. After initial counselling his anonymous saviours told their new, nicknamed friend to go home and come back the next day. Beardie said that he wanted to stay and that he would gladly sleep on an upstairs floor of the building if it meant he had someone to help him through the sweats and convulsions he knew were soon to appear. He had experienced them once before in a prison cell and they had nearly killed him. He had imagined gorillas jumping out of the walls to attack him and when startled police ran to his cell found him fighting off his imaginary assailants with his shoes. Unsympathetic jailers had handcuffed him and when the gorillas returned later in the night he tried to fight them off with his head.

That night in the AA building the DTs came with a vengeance. Only this time it was a massive python that attacked him, curling itself around his throat. Unlike when in his prison cell he was not alone. Beardie Geordie's nurses were AA members they were motherly Duke Street Mae, and Freddy the Fly, an alcoholic Glaswegian safeblower. With the help of Fish Tank Harry, the centre's caretaker, they helped him through the DTs by sitting on his arms and legs to prevent him writhing from his wooden bed.

He sweated and shook so much that he could not hold a cup. His body fluids were replenished with milk bottle after milk bottle of cold water. The slim neck of the milk bottle was the only thing they could put in his mouth without the water cascading down his chest. His pyjama bottoms were peeled from him to reveal inside layers of sweaty filth and urine. In prising his tattered shoes from his feet his helpers thought he had developed gangrene. The panic only subsided when his putrid, blackened feet were scrubbed clean and feeling was restored to his numb toes. It was two days before he was back on his feet and caring for himself.

In a bid to beat the booze new AA members take a sponsor whom they can contact for help whenever the urge to hit the bottle takes them. Beardie Geordie took four sponsors. Meat Market Sammy, Freddie The Fly, Fishtank Harry, and Archie G, were the guardian angels given the task of guiding a half-dead and bearded alcoholic back to life. They eventually managed. They even persuaded him, and such was his determination to beat the bottle that he agreed, to sever his allegiance to the notorious Orange Lodges. Years ago he would have given his life for the cause but here he was turning his back on the violence in a bid to save that very life he would have gladly forfeited for the cause. That decision was made under the influence of something stronger than drink, AA member Meat Market Sammy was a devout Catholic. The sheep slaughterer pointed out that if Beardie wanted his help as sponsor, he would have to accept him as he was, faith included.

Now in his twenty-ninth year Geordie Aitken was having to learn about life all over again. He realized that he had never indulged in any normal teenage pastimes without being drunk. Here was a life beckoning without the bottle and it was hard.

He set out on the road to discovery with sponsor Archie G proving to be of invaluable help. He knew the ropes. He himself had been on the bottom and could speak from an experience that overshadowed Geordie Aitken's drunken escapades. The ship's steward once jumped ship in New York just to get a drink. An international wrangle was only averted when the British Consulate intervened and flew the alcoholic seaman home. While working on the world famous *Queen Mary*, he once stole everything he could get his hands on just to fuel his alcoholic addiction. He admitted to Beardie: 'I would have stolen the *Queen Mary* itself given half a chance.' He was now sober and ready to take Geordie Aitken under his wing. But Beardie Geordie's first steps toward a human existence were enough to nearly drive him back to the bottle. 'The physical compulsion had gone but the mental obsession with drink remained. I was thinking that I would never be able to do anything without a drink and often wondered if I would be better off getting drunk again. I was having to learn to live all over again and it was hard.'

Whenever he tried anything the dreaded sweats and shakes came back to haunt him. But a still streetwise proud man would not admit to being an alcoholic. Even though now he was partly reformed. Whenever the shakes took him he told people he had contracted malaria during his army service and it often resurfaced without warning. In a bid to be accepted into society he mixed with people who he thought were in a worse state than him. That included women and he picked on the worst specimens in the hope that they would not reject him. 'This girl was like a pig in knickers and even had a withered arm.'

Whenever the mis-matched couple went to the movies Beardie Geordie took an attack of the shakes and fled from the cinema. On meeting up with his street friends and explaining what had happened he was shamed into going back to the cinema. 'A good pal of mine said that he had a good mind to choke me for leaving the poor girl on her own. He told me that I was the last person in the world to pass judgement on a person's appearance when you considered the state I was in myself.' He did go back to the cinema but lied about what had happened. That particular relationship never lasted very long and his next romantic interlude was to last about the same.

This new flame came courtesy of the infamous Barrowland dance hall, the scene of serial killer Bible John's numerous murders. 'She must have been the fattest, ugliest girl in the whole of Scotland.'

Despite what Geordie Aitken thought she looked like it was she who gave him the push, after another 'malaria' attack hit him in the middle of the dance floor. 'We were at the dance and I was shaking and sweating. I had told her that I had contracted malaria in Penang during the war and had been medically discharged. She thought it was contagious and told me to get lost.'

Keeping him going and off the bottle, was a little piece of cardboard with the words of the AA on it. He read that whenever he looked at a clock. 'I used to check the time and say to myself "well done that's four hours without a drink."' Setback after setback, he put his faith in the words on the card: 'God grant me the serenity to accept the things

I cannot change, courage to change things I can, and the wisdom the know the difference.'

By the time the bearded alcoholic celebrated twelve months with the AA he was off the drink for ever. But he was still a streetwise villain and despite his abstinence could not give up his criminal capers. Half the battle was that he didn't want to. Without the drink his exploits became more daring and even enjoyable.

One lorry driver was to be on the receiving end on the day he pulled up outside a tenement block where Beardie Geordie and a friend were having a cup of tea. On seeing the lorry left unattended they bolted down the stairs. They lifted the tarpaulin and made off with one of the assorted boxes stacked in the back of the railway delivery lorry. Eagerly opening the box in the safety of his friend's flat they had discovered they had pinched two dozen shrouds for wrapping up dead bodies. 'We didn't have a clue what they were at first except that they looked like nightgowns with dickie bows on. We only found out by reading the labels.' In a bid to get them out of the house the conniving pair offered them to the local undertaker who took them for £2 each. 'When we telephoned him we told him that they were brand new and he replied they had better be or he would report us for grave-digging.'

One con that earned them a few quick sales was a con involving empty Hotpoint boxes. Midden cans were filled with bricks, stood in the new washing maching boxes, secured and delivered to an unsuspecting buyer at half the normal price of a washing machine. They did it three times before they were rumbled. That scam made the pages of the local newspaper, others landed Geordie Aitken in trouble. He was buying dodgy jewellery from fellow rogues and boxes from a reputable dealer. The cheap pearls he bought cost £1.50 and the boxes £4.50. By Geordie Aitken's reckoning that meant they were worth twenty-five quid. Or at least they were after he had explained to punters how his friend in the merchant navy was smuggling them in from Japan. One set he sold went to a respectable businessman just in time to make the perfect gift for his wife to wear at a high-class dinner dance. The doting husband noticed his wife's neck turning green. On examining the new pearl necklace the whole lot gave way and the pearls clattered to the floor.

Far from being invividually strung and lightweight the painted, lead balls stuck to the floor as if glued to it. Not one to mix in such circles the first Geordie Aitken knew about the man's embarrassment was when his hired friends caught up with him and dragged him off 'for a chat'. Another broken nose to add to the list. 'I wish to God I had never set eyes on those pearls. I nearly paid for them with my life.' Many times in the past he had been beaten up for selling dodgy wares but he had always been too drunk to feel it. Now it hurt and he didn't like it.

He soon gave that up but in the AA his life was going from one extreme to another and when he was not out thieving he was visiting Scottish prisons delivering the Alcoholics Anonymous message and words of comfort to their inmates. He was becoming an asset to Alcoholics Anonymous. Ninety per cent of the crime is committed by people under the influence of drink or drugs. 'If I had been caught for the crimes I had committed I would have probably become sober in prison. These people I was talking to could relate to me because they knew of my background and past violence. The only difference between us is that I was free and they were behind bars.' Prisoners flocked to the meeting halls whenever Beardie Geordie was due to speak about the evils of drink. Even those that were teetotal turned up. 'I knew all of the cons because I had grown up with them. They knew I was real and many used to turn up just to have a chat.'

But there was a positive side to his prison visiting and over the years Geordie Aitken has led scores of alcoholics away from the drink. In later years he was due to visit the prisons once again but this time as an evangelist. He would be as successful in that role as he was for Alcoholics Anonymous and was to lead scores of prisoners to Christ. He knew the alcoholic inmates were enduring every kind of mental torture by not being able to drink.

'I became a regular prison visitor and must have visited thousands of times. Many a time sobriety was established in people solely through humour, laughter and common sense. I would explain that the best way to stay out of prison was to stay off the drink.' Beardie Geordie knew that the fact the convicts were physically prevented from taking a drink did help them become sober. 'One of the worst things is becoming a dry drunk. You might not be physically drinking but there is mental obsession with alcohol. The only way you can get rid of it is by concentrating your mind on helping others.'

Many a convict has since walked free from numerous Scottish prisons sober, helpful, and reformed. Beardie Geordie used his street-level experience in his battle to help others overcome what he refuses to believe is an illness. Alcoholism is a three fold mental, spiritual and physical curse. 'With an illness you don't have a choice, but with alcohol you do have a choice.' Geordie Aitken had made his choice and he was fighting a curse. 'By this time it was a deep-rooted thing that I was never going to drink again. If I did I knew that within two or three weeks I would be right back in the gutter.' The tough Barlinnie Prison was his first port of call in his visiting days and he would go to the jail twice a week.

He cast his net further afield and was soon speaking to hardened convicts in the top security Peterhead Prison. Then it was on to Dungavel Semi-Open Prison. Wherever he spoke the message was the same. 'I visited nearly every prison in Scotland and met every kind of criminal. I gave them all a similar message. Every time I had been arrested I had been drunk. I never had any trouble with the law when I was sober. Drink and trouble walk hand in hand.' The common thread was the heartache, suffering and rejection the prisoners felt.

Geordie Aitken had suffered evey kind of emotional pain experienced by the inmates. He knew their minds and always left them with the words: 'it's about time we laughed – we have cried long enough.' Now a respected member of Alcoholics Anonymous, if not an honest one, his con tricks and thieving reached new heights. Only now the drink was not there.

In his early thirties the only difference between him and ten years ago was the alcohol and violence. Life actually became fun for Beardie Geordie and his band of AA friends.

As his life began to take shape and with his drunken days behind him a 33-year-old Geordie Aitken was beginning to live a normal existence, and he began looking for a girlfriend. Previous experiences had not put him off too much and he was to find true love in the shape of Glaswegian lass Marion Louden. But even in his early courting days, and four years sober, the demon drink came back to haunt him.

Often Marion would wonder why he never asked her out for a drink or spent a normal night in a pub.

Dressed in his best suit he would invariably meet Marion and suggest a night at the pictures or in the theatre. 'I was telling myself this is the girl for you wee man, so make an impression on her, be nice and speak polite. Quite a few times she would ask why we never went into a bar for a drink but I would tell her that I had once had an ulcer, brought on by worry and that the doctor had told me not to drink. The bit about the ulcer was a lie but the bit about doctors warning me not to drink certainly wasn't.'

But sobriety brought with it its own problems. Geordie Aitken, for the first time in his life, now had a conscience. 'I always felt guilty and scared that she would find out that I once had a terrible drink problem. But I also felt that I had to tell her the truth as I had been accepted into her family.' Shaking and worried he sat down on the settee one evening and blurted out the truth. Everything from his Orange Order beliefs right through to his wild drunken days. Far from being chased out of her life he got the reply that was to lead him to the altar. Marion told him: 'That is history, Geordie. It is the present and the future what matters now, not the past.'

'I was the happiest man on earth when I heard those words'.

The Glasgow overspill of Barlanark was to be where the happy couple were destined to live – only yards away from the Aitken family home. The parents that Geordie Aitken had grown up thinking hated him, were only too pleased to help him decorate and move into his new council home. Without a penny in the bank he saved up every spare penny of his wages during the six weeks leading up to the marriage. Now he had something to live for and he was not going to lose it. Here he was getting married and his parents were now talking to him.

Marion was working as a dental receptionist and with Geordie Aitken working full time for the city corporation his parents would often be seen at their son's council home decorating and preparing it for the wedding. His feelings of pride and independence were now coming from a sober head and not a wine bottle. During that six weeks leading up the registry office ceremony he slept on a camp-bed in the half-furnished house with a bayonet by his side. 'I was that proud of being independent and having something of my own, even if it was a rented council house, that I was terrified that someone would break in and wreck my dreams.'

When the emotion-charged big day arrived Geordie Aitken saw the things he had missed through drink. He was standing before a sheriff with a smile on his face and not, as in his old days, facing one to be dealt with for thieving and fighting.

In the background his mother cried tears of happiness instead of the customary tears of sadness. 'My mother was crying different tears for once. Not the kind she used to shed after seeing me lying in a pool of blood after a street fight, or hearing of my being in a gutter drunk out of my mind.' Even the pub reception could not spoil his happiness. As the guests guzzled their way through gallons of drink and danced merrily away Geordie Aitken contentedly sipped a glass of fruit juice and reflected on how lucky he was.

Their honeymoon was spent on the tough Barlanark housing estate and their marriage soon compounded by the birth of Audrey. The little bundle was to give Geordie Aitken a taste of what his own parents once had to cope with and made him realize that what he had once interpreted as their lack of love was nothing more than family responsibilities: nappies, crying children and the sleepless nights that accompanied them. Inwardly and outwardly he was contented but nothing would last for ever.

In a bid to survive on the rough estate and to provide for his family he was still pulling con tricks and mixing with his old friends. The drink had gone out of his life but he was still the same man.

As the years passed and their second daughter Beverley was born, married life became a hefty responsibility for the one-time loner. But he used his streetwise intellect to get the family through some dire financial straits. Because of his former drunken existence everything he now had was a blessing to him but Marion didn't always see things the same way.

'We were furnishing our house with cheap second-hand goods and even the very cots we got for our children were second-hand. I would rub them down with sandpaper and then Marion would paint them white. We survived, but life on the tough council estate was getting me down because I wanted our children to have a decent start in life and I knew that it was impossible in this man-made ghetto known as the Glasgow overspill.'

The family was later to move to East Kilbride but while in Barlanark Geordie Aitken had to provide the best he could. The novelty of marriage was wearing off and he was happy enough to return to his old conniving ways to provide for Marion and the two children.

To get them a new bedroom suite and fridge he headed back to the infamous 'Barras Market'. His intentions were well meant but his choice of furniture wasn't. He set off for the market clutching the £40 he had quietly saved up to buy the much-needed furniture. 'What a surprise for them,' he thought. He wasn't to be far wrong.

He returned home with his prized assets to a furious Marion and a street of laughing neighbours. 'I thought I had got a good deal when I arrived home with my mate and his van and I couldn't wait to show Marion the fridge and bedroom suite we had longed for. As we unloaded it everyone burst out laughing and asked me which unfortunate soul I was going to try and palm it off to. Marion's face dropped a mile when we began carrying it into our home and she realized it was for us. We carried it into the house with peals of laughter ringing in our ears and Marion ran in after us telling me to get that rubbish out of the house.'

His next attempt to provide furniture for Marion met with more success, mainly because it was actually what she wanted and not because she knew how he acquired it. He knew his wife had always wanted a simple kitchen suite made up of four stools and a formica-topped table with steel legs. His chance to get such a suite came at the grand opening of a new pub.

Knowing his old friends would be at the opening, although he himself would be content with a glass of lemonade, he set off for the new pub. 'I knew everyone who liked a drink would be there because the first round was on the house. I knew the place would be packed with my friends. Years ago we would have done anything for a drink and yet here was a pub actually giving it away. None of the old school would pass up that opportunity.'

While sitting with his mates his eyes descended on a brand new table in the kitchen area of the new pub, formica-topped with steel legs. Looking down he realized the stools that he and his two friends were sitting on would make a perfect match. Leather studded tops and tubular legs. 'Here was the exact thing that Marion had been talking about and what she dreamed of owning.'

Without hesitation he told his friends to go and sit at the next table as he was having their stools away. The first quiet moment he got, the stools were duly smuggled out of the packed pub and he vanished out of the fire escape. A return trip saw the coveted matching table also disappear in a similar fashion. In between trips he even stopped off at a local florists to buy a bowl of artificial flowers which he stood on top of the new kitchen table ready for when Marion returned from school with the children.

He headed back to the new pub but on arrival discovered that many of his friends had already left. He later discovered that they too had decided they wanted some new furniture. On the day that the new pub opened four tables and sixteen chairs were to go missing. Marion laughed as she heard the tale related in the streets as she made her way home.

She nearly had a heart attack when she discovered hers was one of the stolen sets and another of the now-commonplace arguments in the Aitken household followed.

Outside their home, things were not looking too good either for the lion-hearted provider. With the property had come a massive, but unkept excuse for a garden. It was theirs solely because they lived on the gable end of the street.

'I took a real pride in it and began to cultivate it so that the children could play outside. Compared to the concrete tenement blocks I had been brought up in it seemed like a breath of fresh air to me but in reality it was a complete eyesore.'

Weeks of hard work later, with the grass cut and the weeds pulled out, it took on the appearance of a playing field. Everyone began to use it but not for the reasons a green-fingered Aitken wanted. It soon became the local dumping ground.

'I thought I was doing some good but even that backfired on me in this rotten council housing estate. People began to walk across it and some would even stop to urinate up against the side of the house wall. One morning I awoke to find an old diesel engine from a bus lying in the middle of it. To this day I don't know how it got there but it was still there when we left Barlanark.'

Because of his pride in the garden and because of the distress the people who abused it were causing to his family he soon took to fighting with the usually drunken culprits. In the space of a few months he had gone from being nicknamed Green-Fingered Geordie to 'Killer Aitken'. Vicious fights were now a regular occurrence outside his council home because if anyone upset his family or, indeed, his neighbours the self-appointed vigilante stepped in to sort them out.

From his earlier days he knew only too well the trouble that drunks and street gangs could cause. Now he was on the other side of the fence but he still had a wicked temper and vicious fighting streak. 'We were trying to lead decent lives but it was so hard for us in this hell-hole of a place. Our marriage was suffering because Marion asked me not to get involved with these people but I thought that the important thing was tidying up our estate and warning these people off. I was never done fighting with people in the street.'

One night Geordie Aitken delved deep into his past when a gang of drunken youths refused to move away from his house where his young children were trying to get some sleep and he took a weapon to the goading gang leader after attempts to move them on peacefully failed.

'They were breaking wine bottles and screaming and swearing but when I told them to move away they just swore at me and challenged me to a fight. There was about twenty of them but I knew, from past experience, that if I battered the gang leader the rest of them would run away.' With that in mind he ran back into his house and grabbed the trusty Boer War bayonet which now hung over the fireplace, and headed back out into the street. Thankfully, the years had taken their toll on the bayonet and the blunt weapon did nothing more than knock his target out as he tried to plunge it into the back of his head. 'This madman came towards me swinging a huge wooden post to hit me with but with him being drunk on cheap wine he spun around after lashing out at me and missing. I hit him in the back of the head with the bayonet but to my good fortune it was very blunt and only left a massive lump. But it gave me the time to punch him stupid.'

That fight led to another police visit, who by now were warning Geordie Aitken against taking the law into his own hands as he was becoming paranoid about the gangs and was reacting violently towards them whenever they threatened his family or surroundings.

He was not the only one to suffer at their hands. His friendly neighbours were also humiliated and pestered. One family had to move because human excrement was often pushed through their letterbox. Others suffered at the hands of drunken arsonists. They, also, moved out of their homes but Geordie Aitken stood defiant. By night he was winning his war with the thugs and by day he was winning the battle to lead a sober lifestyle. He spent a lot of his time, when not working, at the 'Barras Market' where the crowds helped him regain a public confidence. Geordie Aitken's early sobriety also took him back into the spiritual circles and he discovered his early experiences of sitting watching his grandmother at her cottage in Stirling over twenty years ago had left an impression on him. With his wife Marion also interested in spiritualism, he and his sober mind were eager to return to the dark world of the occult.

Once, at a spiritualist meeting, he was picked out of a large crowd by a developed medium as 'having the gift'. That gift was one of extra-sensory perception, clairvoyance and clairaudience. He delved heavily into the subject and read scores of books to help heighten his awareness. Years later it was to be graphically shown that he did indeed have physcic powers.

While working on the building sites he had a premonition that a close friend and workmate was going to be killed in a horrific accident. Shortly after the premonition, his friend Joe McGee died from a broken neck after falling from a bridge on a construction site. A fascinated and involved Geordie Aitken travelled Glasgow attending various spiritualist meetings and was taken under the wing of a famous medium who confirmed that he had psychic powers. He was drawn deeper into the spirit world through a paranoid obsession with death.

During his drunken days he had never been bothered about death but now wanted to know what lay on the other side. As with everything else in his life he pursued his interest with a fierce determination. 'I wanted answers and these people were the ones that dealt with those who had already died.' To that end he joined a developing circle under the guidance of a developed medium. Often, during seances, in dark, cold buildings, he would see or hear from the dead. During one seance, in an old church his hair literally stood on end when an unseen choir of youngsters started singing the hymn Silent Night in beautiful voices.

'This was real and everyone heard it. It sounded as if it was echoing through a tunnel yet we all knew there was nobody else in the church except us.' He continued his descent into spiritual darkness when he was entered by two spirits. An amazing physical feeling was experienced which he was later told was the spirits of Indian chief White Cloud and Tibetan monk Yassa going into his body. 'I had the two highest spirits from the other side inside me.'

Further unexplained happenings were to convince the developing medium that there was life in the spirit world and he had been chosen as a gifted one. At one trumpet circle, where a luminous trumpet shaped cone is placed in the middle of the seance, messages were passed to members of the circle from the other side. Thirty minutes after the medium had gone into a transitic state the cone lifted and began to levitate. 'We almost rose with it out of sheer fear. But this was really happening. The cone actually hovered above us.' It stopped at one woman and a message was given to her from the other side. Moments later the cone stopped in front of Geordie Aitken and relayed the message that he had the gift of mediumship and how the two spirits had earlier entered his body. 'I now had the ability to contact the spirit world.'

On another occasion he was sitting in a circle attended by two strangers. He wanted a revelation from the other side about the identity of one of them. And he got it. The face of a dead minister, the Reverend Tom Allen, appeared above the head of the woman and Geordie Aitken was given a spiritual message and warnings about her intentions. It proved to be one hundred per cent accurate. The woman was a church of Scotland elder who had tried to infiltrate the circle in a bid to expose the group's occult practices. When Geordie Aitken revealed to the woman the reason for her attendance she jumped up, turned on the lights and fled from the room. He later discovered that she was an elder of minister Tom Allen's former church in Buchanan Street.

In years to come Geordie Aitken was to become a qualified medium while working in the Shetland Islands and was to have countless supernatural experiences.

After his conversion to Christianity his back was to be turned on yet another dark episode in his life. But at the time he commented: 'I make no excuses for it. It really was the occult.' The occult involvement was to feature prominently in his later life just as the more down-to-earth days were to figure in the not too distant future.

Away from the occult circles he was back to his best on the streets of Glasgow. Years on the great market attracted a now-sober Beardie Geordie.

To help him back into the public life he was offered work at the market by his good mate Jimmy Connolly. 'I took no money from him for three months as working amongst crowds was my trial.' Twelve weeks on and Geordie Aitken was capable of selling sand to an Arab and sun-tan lotion to a Pakistani and was soon earning a wage. Dodgy pottery from Stoke in England, was one of his first Saturday morning scams. 'The sugar bowls would not sit level on the table and the cups were slightly oblong with misshaped handles.' Such was the assortment that Jimmy and Geordie would get the pottery in tea chests and sit in a slum tenement block making up complete sets which were then packed in stolen boxes.

To draw attention to themselves the two market traders would dress up in Mexican hats and wear striped bath towels draped over their shoulders. They soon sold out of the 'finest English pottery around'. But trouble was in store when they returned to their pitch the following Saturday morning to sell off a batch of continental quilts. Queues of people clutching broken pottery awaited them demanding their money back. One woman explained she had been having a cup of tea when the handle fell off the cup leaving scalding tea streaming down her legs. Many others complained that their prized plates cracked in two as soon as they were put into hot water to be washed.

Geordie Aitken was also back on the building sites and, thanks to his sobriety, to become heavily involved in soup kitchen work. He gave up the weekend market work after two years. But the lure was too strong and after meeting an old stall holder at an AA meeting, he was soon back at the 'Barras Market'. He was employed by Tam handing goods through the crowds of people and collecting their money. Tam was on a wage and most of the cash went to a local Jew who owned the stall. But less was to find its way to the Jewish owner when Geordie Aitken started lining his pockets or, indeed, his shoes. Whenever he collected money from a punter in a crowd of people he would slip some pound notes into his pockets. Throughout the day he would sneak off, fold his money gently and put it in his shoes before returning to the stall. He reckoned the Jew was a greedy conman and felt justified in helping himself. But he also helped others. One Christmas Eve he stole seven bags of toys from the stall to dish out to needy children in his neighbourhood.

'I could not wait until work was finished so that I could deliver the toys to the needy children. I filled the biggest bags I could find because I did not want to miss any of the kids.' But the market also proved a sad place. 'My time was also filled with tears and joy because I would hear about one of the characters dying and that filled me with sadness because the folks at the market were like one big happy family even though we were a rough bunch.'

He finally gave up the market the day that Tam got conned out of thousands, and nearly lost his wife. The Jewish owner had given Tam £3,000 to go down to Manchester and bid for items at the auction. With a colleague in tow he set off for the train station but discovered they had two hours to kill. They went off to watch a pornographic film in a back street cinema to pass the time. During the film Tam's colleague offered to buy the ice-creams and disappeared. Ten minutes later a trusting Tam noticed that not only had the man left the cinema, but he had taken the briefcase, containing the £3,000 with him.

Tam's wife decided she was going to leave him because he had been to a pornographic movie but later changed her mind. The other man was later caught in an Edinburgh hotel, with only £100 of the money left. Tam lost his job and Geordie Aitken called it a day because of his commitments elsewhere. AA meetings were still a regular event and he relied on them to continue his alcoholic abstinence. But he also had another reason for attending the meetings in the company of his new friends on whom he now relied. 'Man, there was one of everything in the AA. The curse of alcoholism has no respect of people from judges down to Borstal boys.'

Jimmy Cropper, Sweaty Betty, Spoons Ernie, Billy the Sweep, Candy Miller, Eddie the One, F...ing John, Crimpolene Tam, Joiner Bob, Barlinnie Frank, Sheffield Ricky, Teacher Jim, Cadora Joe, Diamond Lil, Barber George, Chef Bobby, Slater Jimmie and Martin—Laird of the Bahamas were some of Beardie Geordie's new AA friends. As were his four first patrons, Meat Market Bobby, Freddie the Fly, Fishtank Harry, and Archie G. 'What a motley lot they were.' With their help Beardie Geordie was making a marvellous recovery and successfully fighting his addiction. He had also married, worked his way up to building site foreman but his criminal capers could not be curtailed.

The AA meetings proved a blessing in disguise for the thief. 'The best place in the world to fence anything is at an AA meeting.' He was still a street-wise hood and even had the blessing of his fellow members. As long as he stayed off the drink. 'I was still a gangster but a sober one. But I was told to get on and do anything I wanted as long as I kept off the drink. I was quite professional and determined. Before an AA meeting I would go out thieving, then sell the stuff at the meeting. What better place to get rid of stolen gear than at these meetings. Everyone that was there was a con of some description. Let's face it, the AA is full of thieves, cons and vagabonds. You can't be decent if you are an alcoholic.'

To ensure he eluded police capture a cunning Beardie Geordie would practise his thieving at home with a jeweller's tray and a pile of metal washers. Under the watchful eye of an equally bent cousin he would lift 'rings' out of the tray without being caught. His favourite ploy was to enter a jeweller's shop eating a bag of crisps and ask to see a tray of rings. He would slip one of the rings into his crisp bag with his little finger while talking to the jeweller. He never once got caught. But even when thieving he had a warped sense of decency. 'I only ever stole from second-hand shops because they were all conmen themselves, I felt like a Glasgwegian Robin Hood except that I was not giving any money to the poor.'

By this time the cash was rolling in from both the building sites and the unsuspecting back street jewellers. To ensure his income never dried up, and to complement his new dress sense Geordie Aitken practised speaking politely in front of a mirror at home. 'I only ever learned enough words to introduce myself to people.' Now dressed in his top-of-the-range clothes, sporting numerous gold half-sovereigns and with his pretend accent he easily conned his way into many shops. But his streetwise intellect lurked beneath the affluent exterior and he lived by basic rules. 'I never asked to see a full tray of rings, only those trays with some already sold. Take one from a full tray and you are caught straight away. It takes a lot longer for a shopkeeper to realize one had been lifted from one of the other trays.'

Camel coat swirling, and pockets bulging it was out of the back street shops and off to the AA meetings. 'Before the meetings started the people would buy the jewellery at knock-down prices. But there was a dual purpose to my generosity as it saved me having to sell the stuff on the streets.'

An alcoholic's glory days come when he gets his self respect back, but for Geordie Aitken it was at a price.

Working on the new Anderson Bus Station development, his elevated position of foreman had its own problems. Under normal circumstances the cunning builder would have been giving out his own instructions: 'Don't put too much cement in the mix lads because I've got buyers lined up.' But now he could only give the company's instructions. 'I was not entirely happy being a gaffer because it meant I had to stop stealing. Maybe it was just as well because with all of the materials that were being pinched it was not surprising that half of the buildings in Glasgow we worked on ended up condemned.' But his new found fame and responsibility did not stop him stealing outside working hours. Other spare time was spent helping out at the AA premises and putting his building skills to good use in helping to refurbish them and decorate them. His voluntary involvement on the helping side led him to the doors of

Geordie, off the drink, on Queen Street building site.

Glasgow's notorious Wayside Club. A dosshouse and club for the lowest of the low.

It was overseen by two nuns with a band of dedicated volunteers. Residents slept rough on newspapers on the floor and were fed through the hatch of the club's makeshift kitchen. The Wayside Club was to be Geordie Aitken's first experience of soup kitchens. In later years he was to become involved in numerous soup kitchens across the city and pioneer the Loaves and Fishes soup kitchens which served the homeless, drunks, dossers and prostitutes in the notorious red light area of Glasgow. The Wayside Club was in the top flat of a crumbling tenement block in the George Square area of the city. In another flat was a room where Geordie Aitken held his AA meetings. Once he had left his room and looked into the Wayside Club dosshouse, 'I saw filthy men crouched in the foetal position trying to keep warm lying on newspapers. The smell of stale urine, wine and meths hung in the air so you could almost taste it.' He decided there and then to do his best to help and embarked on soup kitchen work that in later years would be talked about as far away as America. 'My heart went out to those filthy shreds of humanity so much that I decided I would dedicate my life to helping the needy.'

Years later he was to find Christ and take a different message from that of the AA out to similar people. He would lie in bed at night thinking abut the dossers at the Wayside Club. 'The burden for the underdog became so heavy that I would lie awake thinking how fortunate I had been to make it through and how some of my mates failed to make it and had died through the curse of alcoholism.' He adopted the line that if Geordie Aitken could make it then anybody could. 'I would sit amongst the men on the newspapers and tell them about my own past life as a drunk so that I could plant some hope back into their hearts and spirits.'

Alternating between the AA meeting room and the soup kitchen Geordie Aitken spent most of his spare time at the Wayside Club. He experienced both joy and sorrow in the confines of one filthy tenement block. He witnessed drunks dying in their own vomit curled up on newspapers. 'I would think of them as kids running around the streets laughing and joking then seeing them die in squalor and poverty.' The joy came through seeing drunks come off their newspapers and attend

AA meetings. He grew to love the people of the Wayside Club. 'My heart still goes out to the dear brothers who never made it.'

Others descended upon the AA meetings but for many their only aim was to cause trouble. Volunteers at the Wayside Club were also beginning to lose control to a group of maverick alcoholics who were now trying to give the orders. Help was needed and Geordie Aitken had the credentials to help. A knowledge of the problems and a handy pair of fists. 'I would never forget where I got sober but some of these people were real rebels. The place was becoming the pits and attracting residents who could get under the belly of a snake wearing a top hat and holding an umbrella up.' Beardie Geordie revelled in his new role. Any bother and he handled it with relish. He had the wisdom and expertise, gleaned from his street-fighting days, to ensure the troublesome drunks who tried to wreck his AA meetings came off worse and thought twice about disrupting a Beardie Geordie AA meeting.

He was doing his best to bring people back from the brink and nobody was going to spoil it. There was too much at stake.

He had developed his own bouncing system which incorporated a method of ensuring the troublemakers never returned. He would rip the backside out of an argumentative drunk's trousers. Despite the alcoholism ruining their lives a reformed Geordie Aitken knew from firsthand experience that the last thing a drunkard lost was his pride. 'I developed this habit of ripping people's clothes after throwing them out of the club. They never returned to give me any more trouble. An alcoholic walking along with his bottom hanging out of his trousers, the lapels ripped off his jacket and with his bollocks kicked in is not a clever sight.'

At many AA meetings in the derelict tenement block Beardie Geordie and his band of bouncers were called upon to stand guard. 'Half the time the only thing missing from the meetings was a referee.' Those he did not batter and the ones who needed help, he befriended. One was Old Pill Jackie. He got his name because he supplemented his daily intake of methylated spirits with tablets. While working on the building sites his mentor often skived off work with arms full of sandwiches he had stolen from his workmates, to feed Pill Jackie and an army of other dossers. 'It was like the Pony Express in full flight.

Once Pill Jackie got these sandwiches he would run off to the dosshouse and feed his friends. It was like a feast day for them.' Even then Geordie Aitken had another reason for his commendable acts of generosity. Though for once it was a genuine non-profit making one. 'It was a privilege helping the drunks because little did they realize they were becoming an even bigger help to me. I was learning that there aren't any hopeless cases in the AA which then obviously applied to me. Everyone in the AA is a miracle. I have seen dossers at the point of death, and have seen them go on to lead full lives.'

He was becoming inwardly contented and outwardly respectable. His life was also becoming financially fuller, thanks to work and thieving. Every finger now sported a gold ring and his once emaciated body was constantly clad in designer suits and camel hair coats. Camel hair coats were a sign of wealth. But everything Geordie Aitken was doing, including his dress sense, was following his lifetime extremist values. Fighting and drinking had always been done to the extreme and now he was making up for the lost years in a different way.

Once the alcoholic gets off the drink the purpose for living returns and invariably an alcoholic will go over the top to prove it. 'Here I was by day a builder, and by night I looked like a Bombay money-lender.' But he was not the only one to go to extremes. As people pulled themselves further away from the grip of alcohol, so did AA meetings take on a new image. Albeit, a fantasy one. 'Even park cleaners used to wear camel hair coats to impress people. At AA meetings there used to be twelve camel hair coats sitting in a row.

'There were people with broken noses, scarred faces and gnarled bones sitting in their camel hair coats. It looked like a conveyor belt of tailors' dummies. We were looking like businessmen but it was all make-believe.' Dressing up to impress people became almost addictive to the AA men. But there were still countless things a 30-year-old Geordie Aitken had never done.

One was to place a bet. His chance came courtesy of a Saturday AA meeting when a reformed gambler told him two horses were running. Wee Geordie and Dire Straits. After going to the bookmakers, where the clerk had to put his bet on for him, the two horses came up trumps. He was £29 better off. 'The only other gambling I had ever done was with my life, and the only other time I had visited the bookies was to sell some stolen stuff to the punter who I knew had backed a winner.' Now he was off to the city centre to blow his winnings on a leather jacket. But the AA grapevine had done its job and on stepping out into the street he was confronted by three of his AA mates. 'I could see from their faces they were starving and decided to buy them a bag of chips from the winnings. When we went into the fish and chip shop their eyes lit up and I ended up blowing the lot on double helpings of fish suppers and pie dinners.' Not to worry, he thought, he could always pinch himself a leather jacket.

Beardie Geordie was still thinking and trying to act hard but deep down he knew his image was crumbling. Without the drink, as cunning as he was, he was not as wicked as in his early days. However, his days at the main AA headquarters were drawing to a close and he would soon be setting up his own groups in various parts of Glasgow.

His AA recovery message was different from that of the establishment and he was being labelled rebellious for not adhering to the strict daily programme. But he was off the drink and wanted to help others beat the bottle. The twelve step recovery plan and ninety day trial was not his way of giving up on the drink. 'For all the years I have been sober I never got past the first step.' His slogan was 'One day at a time'. He never thought about the spiritual side of things, just simply beating the bottle. 'It is no good telling an alcoholic to stay off the drink for ninety days by following a twelve point plan. The simple fact is that if you don't take that first drink then you can't get drunk.' To that end Beardie Geordie and Scrap Tommy set up a sub-group in a rent free Salvation Army hostel in Bridgeton.

After three months their meetings were packed solid. 'We did not have twelve steps to recovery just one, we did not want it to be complicated for people and just told them to concentrate on the first step. If they could not manage that they had to telephone us.' The group was now attracting people from the seedier sides of Glasgow, and amongst them came some of the AA's craziest characters. They were exciting, colourful, real people. Sometimes sober people would come along just to hear them talk. And talk of their exploits they could. Humour, passion and truth were the main ingredients of Beardie Geordie's Bridgeton group's recovery plan.

It was at the raucous meetings that Jimmy Cropper, Spoons Ernie,

Candy Miller, Barber George, Billy The Sweep and Martin The Laird of the Bahamas repeatedly won over people with their true stories.

Jimmy Cropper was an ex-inmate of the top security Peterhead Prison who had learned hairdressing while serving his sentence. After being freed, the distinguished looking gentleman, complete with snow-white handlebar moustache opened up an appointment only hair salon in the exclusive Royal Exchange Square area of Glasgow. The moustache had been grown to hide facial battle scars. He wore a swirling grey coat, dapper hat and carried an empty briefcase. He furnished the salon with second-hand bus seats, salvaged from a scrapyard and which underwent a miraculous transformation. He put an Italian name above the door announcing it was a swish continental-style salon. Inside, his receptionist was Miss Turner, who just happed to be Sweaty Betty the prostitute. His doorman was a hood he had met in prison and everything in the place was bent, including Sweaty Betty's gold jewellery. Amazingly, the self-styled Peterhead Prison barber enjoyed a flourishing trade, including many lawyers from the nearby criminal courts in the Royal Exchange area. But while Jimmy Cropper was cutting hair as best he could, his assistants were obeying orders and rifling coat pockets and leather briefcases. The shop was duly closed down after twelve months when the haircutting side of the business expanded. Jimmy and his staff had moved into extortion and blackmail thanks to the documents stolen from the coats.

As other AA members relayed their experiences so did people give up the bottle to a backdrop of laughter and tears.

Spoons Ernie was another favourite of the Bridgeton group. 'We were supposed to be talking about alcoholic recovery and there was Ernie playing these bloody spoons.' To show their affection the group members splashed out on a new set of instruments for him from the local hardware shop. Off they went on their travels like the group from *One Flew Over the Cuckoo's Nest*. But such was the camaraderie they all wanted to go. 'We looked like a shower of idiots going in to buy these two soup spoons for Ernie. The shopkeeper was at his wit's end by the time Ernie picked the ones he wanted and then demanded to play them before buying them.' The new spoons proved a good buy. They landed Ernie on a Scottish Television talent programme. STV was looking for street entertainers and the dedicated band of AA supporters put him forward claiming he had played in front of royalty. They didn't bother telling the producer it was the Royalty café and not, as he thought, Holyrood Palace.

'He was sober but he still looked like a tramp so the make-up people gave him the once over and dressed him in a dinner suit from the props department.' Spoons Ernie duly performed and got through the show looking as if he had indeed performed in front of royalty. But trouble flared when the show ended, Spoons Ernie had taken a shine to his new dinner suit and legged it out of the studio. A frantic floorman had to chase him down Hope Street and manhandle him back into the STV studios from which he later emerged in his customary tattered jacket and torn trousers. But his performance had inspired other Bridgeton members. In particular Billy the Sweep who decided to jump on the television bandwagon via a local newspaper.

Billy the Sweep was approached by STV after masterminding a story which was leaked to a Scottish newspaper. He claimed to be the sole surviving prisoner of war from a particular camp who had survived because as a child his mother had fed him on raw meat. He duly appeared in a Scottish morning newspaper, complete with a massive plate of raw meat. He tricked his way through that interview but came unstuck when approached by STV. It had not crossed his mind that he would actually be asked to wade through a plate of raw meat for eager viewers. 'Right then, Billy,' said the producer, in presenting him with the mountain of uncooked meat, 'you have fifteen minutes to show the viewers what you are made of.' The plate of meat looked more like one of Desperate Dan's pies and a gasping Billy could hardly get his fork into it. He managed a few mouthfuls before embarrassed studio bosses cut him off. 'And now for the weather,' came the impromptu announcement.

Candy Miller was an AA member who related in heartbreaking detail what lengths he previously went to in order to get a drink. Candy, the proud owner of a mourning suit would scour the obituary columns of the *Evening Times* newspaper to find respectable sounding funerals to attend. He would duly turn up, offer his respects, then drink his fill. The next day his suit would be returned to the pawnbroker's where it would remain until another high-class funeral came along. He often made the wrong choice. On one occasion his big red alcoholic's nose gave him away and furious mourners beat him up for his trouble. 'The sad thing about Candy was that when he died not one person attended his funeral and he was buried in a pauper's grave. His prized mourning suit was still in the pawnbroker's the day he was buried.'

Barber George had a novel way of getting customers eager for a haircut. With Beardie Geordie as his PR man he would scour the city's bars on a Sunday offering impromptu haircuts. Into the toilets the customers would go and sitting on a toilet seat would have their locks shorn. As the day wore on and the drink took effect, the haircuts became more erratic, sometimes even incomplete. On more than one occasion a customer would be left in the toilet after Barber George and Beardie Geordie were rumbled by landlords and thrown out. It was not uncommon for Barber George to take a break in the middle of a trim, order himself a pint and forget to go back. He usually remembered while setting up stall in the next pub down the street.

Martin, Laird of the Bahamas, was one of the group's strangest characters. His exploits matched his dress and he was remembered as much for his eccentric behaviour as he was for the orange dickie bow, orange socks, green shoes and Hawaiian shorts. Having been deported from the Bahamas for diamond smuggling, he knew he could never return to his island villa and wore the sunshine clothes as he walked the cold grey streets of Glasgow as a reminder of what he had left behind. But he probably lived that little while longer by being in Scotland. Often in the Bahamas he had drunk himself into a coma. At many of the AA meetings the last thing on people's minds would be getting off the drink. They only wanted to hear the group's characters speak of their lives. Yet without realizing many did give up the bottle as much for listening to the life stories of the group members as any daily recovery plan.

Beardie Geordie prided himself on working with street alcoholics and the lepers of society but even he had to draw the line when it came to being a sponsor for Sweaty Betty the Glasgow prostitute. 'I had never seen a woman sweat but it poured out of her. My nose had been broken more times than I remember but I could smell her. You could smell her before you saw her. The AA taught me there was no such thing as a lost cause, but I could not bring myself to be her sponsor in case I was called out to visit her.' At the other end of the scale many a famous and respectable member of society helped beat the bottle under the guidance of Beardie Geordie. But usually in the comfort of their own meeting halls not the derelict Salvation Army hostel or in a Glasgow back street.

The beauty of the AA is its anonymity, but numerous film stars, TV personalities and upper class members of society know the truth behind Beardie Geordie's words.

An amazing event, held every year, is the Blue Bonnet Convention, where alcoholics from around the world meet for a massive rally without a drink exchanging hands. At one such convention in Dumfries, Scotland, Geordie Aitken saw the warmth behind the sorrow and pain caused by alcoholism. 'It was like a festival but without a drink in sight. There were people there from every walk of life and every culture across the world. At night they sang and danced but not one of them drank.'

His work with Alcoholics Anonymous took on new dimensions when he met up with an American ship's captain at the King George V Docks in Glasgow. Still on the building sites and employed by various construction companies, Geordie Aitken was having a dinner break in a dockyard warehouse when he met the flamboyant Captain Bob Corcoran.

With Geordie Aitken was AA member Holy Gerry. He was so called because of his misguided religious beliefs. 'Holy Gerry wore a massive shining crucifix around his neck because he believed the bigger the cross the closer he would get to heaven.' The down-to-earth American captain invited the two men aboard his ship for lunch, eager to hear more of the idle banter they had been swapping. For once lunch was not a cheese sandwich, but a massive T-bone steak with all the trimmings. Hours later the men parted company with an invitation to America ringing in their ears.

With money coming in from the building sites, con tricks, and nothing being wasted on alcohol, Geordie Aitken made it his goal to save up enough to pay his fare. Staying as a guest of the captain he carried on his AA work across the Atlantic. In the month he was there he spoke at numerous AA meetings across New York, from back rooms of shops to sprawling meeting halls. He visited the Bronx and set up one of the first AA groups in the seedy back streets of one of the infamous areas of America. He was amazed at the squalor in the Bronx. But a bigger shock was in store for the reformed alcoholic when he visited the AA headquarters in New York and found among the membership records a file on his Bridgeton recovery group.

He started writing for the organization's magazine *The Grapevine*, about his personal experiences and those of his close friends. Those recovery stories were read in many American prisons and by countless AA members.

Now fourteen years sober, he had a lot to tell, and became a regular contributor to *The Grapevine*, after his return to Glasgow. Most of his letters were written from his sanctuary—the toilet cubicle he used as an office. As his letters and writings spread across America so, too, did others find their way back to him. 'People were getting in touch with me via the AA General Service Office in Glasgow, and I was becoming renowned for my work throughout the slums of Glasgow.'

Back in Glasgow his AA recovery work spread across the city. By day he was on the building sites but heading for a change. Having now given up his gaffer's job, Geordie Aitken was moving rapidly up the trade union ladder. As with his one-time Orange Lodge beliefs, fighting, drinking, and thieving, Geordie Aitken was still extreme in everything he did. That continued throughout his construction site days and was increased throughout his membership of the trade union movement. The battle cry of militant trade unionists was applied to give him another nickname away from Beardie Geordie. He became 'One out – all out Aikie' because of his hardline stance. Solidarity was the key word of the trade unions and if one man had a gripe everyone was expected to support him. 'I was that militant that places where I worked ran the risk of being closed down every day.'

The shop steward was, as usual, about to call for a strike, when he received a telephone call from management that was about to change his life. His employers offered him a chance of a sought after job in the Shetland Islands away from the filth and squalor of the sewers he was presently contracted to maintain. He could not understand their reasoning except to think that they were sick of his militant union activities and wanted him out of the way. He had thought right. His frantic employers wanted an answer immediately, but the family man had a duty to his wife and children and felt that they would want him at home. At least they would want to discuss the 42-year-old's career move before dispatching him to the wild islands. A quick telephone call to his sister, who alerted his family, gave him an answer. Wife Marion, exclaimed: 'you beauty—off you go.'

His family happy, his employers happy and Geordie Aitken slightly bemused the contract was signed. 'That was me on my way to the Shetland Islands. At the head of the queue of 200 men desperate to work out there and only hours after being offered the job.' A short aeroplane trip to the massive inshore building site heralded three and a half years of experiences that Geordie Aitken would never forget. Neither would the local inhabitants of the rough and ready islands.

When I look upon the Cross
for my gain not my loss
It reminds me of Christ my King
who saved me from Satan's bin

Satan's bin stinks with sin
in the form of drugs, sex and gin
What a smell erodes the air
from Satanic forces that do not care

I stayed in that bin for quite a while
living my life in Satanic style
The clothes I wore were garments of hate
the dirty bin was my fate

Then a voice spoke in my ear
come out of this bin have no fear
I am the way, the truth the life
I'll save you from your hellish strife

The bin you stay in is your own choice
in this bin you can't rejoice
The only way out from your bin
is ask the Lord to do his thing
He will save you from a pit of shame
just cry upon the Saviour's name

With a mighty swipe he will open the gate
of the bin that was your fate
He will burn up all your sins
Jesus Christ he always wins

So follow Christ one and all
your life in the bin you won't recall
It's in the past to be forgotten
its very memory smells so rotten

Fate

# CHAPTER 6

# Perils of the Occult

Geordie Aitken at 42 had gone to the Shetland Islands to work but he was to encounter much more than bricks and mortar during his time in the wild islands. He took on so much and got so involved he was to be sent home with a mental breakdown four years after he first flew out.

Still very much affiliated to Alcoholics Anonymous, Geordie Aitken had a ready made market of alcoholics. He also got dragged into the islands occult practices and endured many frightening incidents. By day, he had his own job to do and to see to the needs of his trade union members. By night he had his work with the alcoholics and his involvement with the dark satanic circles. Before too long day was mingling into night and his life became nothing more than a continuous hard slog.

Such was the scale of alcoholism that he helped pioneer an Industrial Alcoholism Unit which won the praise of companies and employers based in the area. He had realized there was more to be gained by counselling a drunken workman than by just simply sacking him. Companies soon reaped the benefits of the innovative scheme and paid the former alcoholic a weekly wage to ensure his work continued with the unit. Inside and outside the camp he fought doggedly to get people off the drink. Alcoholics were to be found both inside the work camps and also amongst the hardy islanders on the outside.

Outside work, and with the help of others, he set up one of the first ever Alcoholics Anonymous meetings in the Shetland Islands which to this day now attracts over 1,000 members.

Geordie Aitken, a high-ranking trade unionist, hard working builder, counsellor and spirtualist medium, even started working with alcoholics in the camp hospital. Often he would sit throughout the night holding hands with a drunken workman in a throwback to the days at the AA building in Glasgow where he himself had been gently nursed through the dreaded DTs. Such was the scale of the problem that sometimes his much-needed and sought-after advice came too late. On one occasion he was called from the union office by workmen unable to rouse their colleague from behind the locked door of his room. Geordie Aitken broke into the room to find the big Irishman dead in his bunk following an almighty binge. Covering him was three days worth of vomit, urine and faeces.

Such was the working day of Geordie Aitken. Had there been twenty-five hours in a day the AA workaholic would have struggled to get through his tasks. 'I never got a minute to myself. Apart from having my own job to do I was also responsible, as their trade union representative, for the welfare of over 1,800 men. Into the bargain the majority of the workforce had an alcohol problem.'

As he was to find to his cost, so did the majority of the local islanders. Often he would be called by the police to visit the local cells to counsel a drunken prisoner.

As he was still up to his thieving and con tricks one such visit by the local constabulary had him break out in a dreaded sweat that had nothing to do with alcohol consumption. Panic set in when a burly constable nudged him and uttered the words every criminal fears: 'we have reason to believe,' but went on to add, 'you are the guy that has pioneered the AA meetings' Having breathed a silent sight of relief the counsellor agreed to visit the local hardman who was in their custody after half killing his equally wild wife in a drunken stupor.

The local Lerwick man was in the cells facing an attempted murder charge and police were struggling to placate him as he came out of his drunken state. When Geordie Aitken arrived the police had the man hosing down their Panda cars just to keep him occupied. Geordie Aitken took him back to his cell, sat and talked and then saw the wild man break down and then burst into tears. 'He admitted there and then that his bottle had gone and he was terrified. Everything he had ever done had been while he was under the influence of drink. Here he was now, sitting in the cell knowing he had gone too far and he felt alone against the world.'

With Geordie Aitken on the islands nobody with a drink problem would ever be alone. He had spent too many years in the alcoholic wilderness to want other people to suffer as he had done. On condition that the islander agreed to attend AA meetings and promise to try to solve his drink problem, Geordie Aitken offered to write a letter of support to the beckoning trial judge. In that letter he explained about his past life, how the AA had saved him and that he would personally be kept informed of the man's attendance record and be there to help him combat alcoholism.

'It must have inspired the judge because he was only given three months, but on condition that he attended, and worked with the AA, to combat his problems.' It worked for the local hardman and word spread like wildfire what had happened. That drew out countless other alcoholics and drunken trouble makers who decided that if the AA could help that man it would be able to help them. With the backing of Geordie Aitken they were helped into sobriety.

Nobody escaped Geordie Aitken's net. Those who needed help got it. But those who wanted to help were also roped in to become part of the spiralling AA movement on the islands. He soon had his own little workforce, within the AA walls, and enlisted the help of other builders to offer a mobile counselling service to the camp's many alcoholic workers. Many a night they would visit drunks in their tiny rooms and sit by their wooden bunks guiding them through the lonely darkness with flasks of hot coffee and reassuring words. But far from easing Geordie Aitken's workload it only released him to go into the villages and help the locals with their problems. While out on the streets not even the local Catholic priest escaped inclusion.

Father Donachy gladly helped Geordie Aitken and his band of dedicated helpers to combat what he knew was a massive problem within his congregation.

But still Geordie Aitken's streetwise mind worked overtime and he came up with an idea to make some pocket money for himself while helping the villagers.

Even the unsuspecting priest was roped in to help. With Oil Slick Cathy in tow, Geordie Aitken launched his idea under the guise of 'therapeutical treatment'. He worked out that the thousands of beach pebbles lying on the rugged coastline would make ideal paper-weights. Especially for AA members, purely for therapeutical reasons, they had painted a AA slogan on them and varnished over the top. Many a midnight trip was made from the parish church by the trio, with Father Donachy gladly pushing one of the heavy wheelbarrows. He was under the impression that he was collecting the pebbles to create a social life for the area's alcoholics away from the evil drink and happily sat up through many a night washing and polishing the pebbles in the church house. That was true, but a cunning Geordie Aitken and partner-in-crime Oil Slick Cathy, also knew that they would be able to sell the varnished pebbles at a hefty profit. And make profit they did. Until they became unstuck. Or at least until the quaint little messages became unstuck.

Trouble flared after buyers realized they were being had when the cheap felt-tip markings wore off and they were left with a blank beach pebble. Obviously, Geordie Aitken denied any knowledge of skullduggery and stated such a convincing case that the local newspapers even ran stories about the mysterious disappearance of the markings. But everything illegal he did was justified, in no small way, by the amount of good he was doing amongst the alcoholics and the islanders. At least that's how the entrepreneur viewed things. Having yet to find God he had nothing to worry about, he reckoned. That was still four years away and he still had plenty to occupy his mind at present.

Throughout the early and middle stages of his life the last thing on his mind was Christianity. In his early days he was convinced that God existed only in the lives of church-going 'middle-class phoneys'. In the ensuing years he gave up caring altogether.

What he did believe in was spiritualism and the world of mediums and spirits. He was to later learn what a dangerous world it can be.

During his stay on the islands he developed his skills and became an accomplished and recognized medium often experiencing paranormal occurences. It was only, in years to come, when those turned into filthy Satanic experiences that he realized the full horrors of the psychic world. But in his early days he used his psychic powers to help others. Once he laid his hands in the icy North Sea to banish a disease at a fish farm that was threatening the stock and the farmer's livelihood. Following the ceremony not one more fish died.

Following his arrival on the islands he had joined a home circle because, despite there not being any recognized spiritual churches in the area, the islanders were deeply involved with the occult. Back at the camp he began having a series of strange paranormal experiences. Homes for the workmen were massive accommodation blocks standing on stilts. His particular block housed 250 men.

One night Geordie Aitken awoke to see the luminous faces of twelve old women peering at him out of the darkness. When they finally disappeared he heard the sound of heavy breathing and his bed started shaking violently. He thought it was being caused by passing lorries shaking the stilted accommodation blocks but, every time he tried to reach the window, the noises and shaking stopped. As soon as he returned to bed they started again. This continued throughout the night but next morning not one other person said they had heard anything.

Months later the vibrating bed and noises came back but this time with a vengeance and he was to go through a terrifying out-of-body experience. As he lay there feeling paralysed, and unable to lift his arms to pull the light cord he felt as if he was being catapulted out of his body. 'I could see my sleeping body lying on the bed but my spirit was being taken on a journey.' That spirit was taken to an old red-brick building, with tall chimneys and spacious lawns which Geordie had never seen before. Once inside, an old lady, with saliva dripping from her mouth, appeared at the end of a long table and glared at him through a distorted, frightened face, seconds later a huge metal chandelier fell from the ceiling and crushed her to death. Five other old women looked on in fear as a snarling Dobermann dog entered the room and terrorized them. In a bid to show these old women that his spirit was strong he put his hand into the snarling dog's mouth. 'I could actually feel the hot saliva on my hand when I put it in the dog's mouth to show these frightened old women that I was protected by spirits.'

Two days later Geordie Aitken received a postcard from another medium. On it was the very building of his out-of-body experience. 'When I saw this postcard the hairs stood up on the back of my neck and I just froze.'

During another out-of-body experience Geordie Aitken was taken back in time. 'It was like an epileptic seizure. I got catapulted out of my physical body and was flying through darkness. I was taken back to early 1800s Glasgow and hovered above the Maryhill area watching bustling crowds happily living their lives. Then it was as if a shutter came down and I was shown what modern technology had done to the same area. There was pollution and filth everywhere.'

Another paranormal experience, in the same accommodation block, led to the sleeping quarters being evacuated and eventually exorcized by a Catholic priest. This one did not involve Geordie Aitken. Three men, in a room across the hall from where he slept, were experimenting with a home-made ouija board when trouble flared. It later transpired that they had called upon a spirit to reveal itself. And it did. In the shape of a ferocious Viking. In their panic the three men all bolted for the same door and the head of one of the men went through a glass panel. While in hospital he related the story to Geordie Aitken. He spent seven days in hospital while his two colleagues were flown home in shock. They never returned to the islands.

They had started off with the 'Is there anybody there' routine and the glass tumbler they were using spelled out 'Yes'. It then spelled out the name Olaf and the men asked him to show himself. 'A mist appeared and a Viking came up through the floor boards. The men were that frightened they all ran for the door at the same time and one of them had his head pushed through the glass.' While lying in his room Geordie Aitken had heard the commotion and after leaping from his bed had seen the door smashed to pieces and blood splattered across the framework. He also saw the upturned ouija board and smashed furniture. Because of his obvious interest in the occult he sought out the injured man and learned the full truth of what had happened in the room. Following this incident a priest was called in to exorcise the block. 'This priest sprinkled holy water around the building but scarpered pretty quickly. You could feel the icy presence of something in the block.' Geordie Aitken was soon to be personally involved in the serious, heavy side of spiritualism.

He had his first experience of automatic writing in the presence of a woman worker. 'It is as if you are in a deep sleep and a spirit guides your hand.' One night he and the woman sat in the canteen to try out the writing. Shortly after Geordie Aitken went into a trance-like state his arm began twitching and the pencil he was holding began writing. The message was garbled, but after being arranged into a readable form, away from the gaze of the startled woman, it relayed a message of how this woman's brother had been killed in a horrific work accident while driving a post office van. It also contained a plea from her dead brother to give up drinking and not to take her own life. The woman immediately broke down and told Geordie Aitken how she was a secret alcoholic and had been actively considering throwing herself from a cliff to end her anguish.

An experience of poltergeists came shortly after when Geordie Aitken, on home leave, visited the house of a friend who was a developing medium. The friend had previously shown him a treasured brass wishing well which always sat proudly on his fireplace. He was devastated when it disappeared. Days later the wishing well was found twelve feet above the floor perfectly balanced on top of a wire curtain rail. 'It was not only impossible for anyone to reach up and put it there but for it to balance on a thin rail without falling. Yet it sat there perfectly balanced.'

Geordie Aitken had always used his psychic and spiritual powers to help people and comfort them. Now he was becoming afraid of the dark Satanic powers that were at work. In later years he was to call upon his powers in the name of Christ in a series of frightening, disgusting and bizarre experiences.

But even before those days he was beginning to doubt his psychic calling and which way his paranormal life was leading him. 'A fear was coming into my life because I was getting more bad experiences than good experiences. I had been used for healing in the past but now I was frightened. I had lain my hands on many people and they had been cured of physical ailments but now I was experiencing terrible apparitions which were the work of Satan.'

In years to come, after his salvation through Christ, he was to return to the islands and pit his psychic powers against evil in the name of the Lord.

He was to say of the spiritual world of evil: 'occult practices are an abomination in the eyes of God. The experiences are nothing short of horrendous.' With a now divided belief in the paranormal and ever-increasing fears about what was really happening he threw himself even further into his pioneering work with alcoholics. Not only did his already hectic lifestyle continue but he took on new challenges. Actively involved in the welfare of the workers he began organizing social events in the camp. In a throwback to his army days he helped a boxing club and arranged cabaret evenings and social events.

Away from the camp he added to his workload by raising cash for local needy children. He and a workmate hit upon a novel way of collecting money from the hardened regulars of the island pubs. They went in speaking a language the boozers could understand. While one carried a plastic bucket for cash to be put in, the other wielded a heavy baseball bat to pressure people into donating. As with everything else, Geordie Aitken came to the conclusion that because they were doing some good they could be excused the badness involved. The end always justified the means. The end result of the fundraising trips was that the men collected thousands of pounds for sick children.

Geordie Aitken began speaking on the local radio station and had his messages broadcast across the remote island courtesy of the BBC. But everything was beginning to take its toll on a burnt-out Geordie Aitken. In the time he had been there, he had helped countless people both in the camps and in the villages. Now he was getting less than two hours sleep a night and still trying to do his own job in the heavy construction trade. His close friend, Dr David Gaskell, with whom he had worked very closely in the camp hospital, knew something was wrong. But a defiant Geordie Aitken refused to give in or admit that he was struggling to cope. By now he was taking refuge in solitude and his only comfort was sitting at the top of barren cliffs looking out over the icy North Sea. It was his only refuge place. He knew his previous lifestyle and current workload were catching up with him but he needed to keep his job. He had a wife and a family and needed the money.

He soldiered on helping people who, by now, were probably in a fitter state than he was. Despite his commendable courage, people were beginning to realize, and so was he, that he was losing it. 'I was becoming very depressed and even thought about throwing myself from the cliffs that I used to love sitting on top of.'

It got to the stage where he forgot his wife's name, the names of his children, and at one stage even forgot his own name. Inside, he was broken but he kept up a proud exterior for all his worth. Throughout these dire months Dr. Gaskell could see the state his friend was in and kept a close eye on him without him knowing.

Despite not wanting to, the doctor knew when the inevitable happened that he would be left to pick up the pieces and what that would do to Geordie Aitken. The man had soldiered on by his side voluntarily helping those who were past helping themselves. He knew how much it would hurt the proud volunteer to become one of those hopeless cases who needed help. He had spent four years helping others overcome their problems but very soon he was to be in need of help himself. The proud fighting man was broken. The final score came when the half-demented Geordie Aitken half killed a fellow builder who had been tormenting him for months. Because of his voluntary work, and the high regard in which he had found himself being held in, he had previously ignored his taunts.

He had turned his back on the sectarian jibes of the strapping Catholic workman, putting his job and his AA membership before any trouble. But over a few days he realized he could not take any more. A plan formulated in his now-deranged mind to actually murder his tormentor and bury his body in a plastic sheet under the stilted accommodation blocks. Ironically, it was his frenzied state of mind that saved him from murder. His patience snapped and he lost his temper before he finalized his murderous plans.

One morning as his tormentor sat down to breakfast, a half-crazy Geordie Aitken screwed a plate full of steaming porridge into his face. While his tormentor was on the ground screaming in agony Geordie very nearly caved his head in with his fists and feet. 'He was left looking like something out of the *Phantom of the Opera* because of the steaming porridge burning his face but I was past caring. I continued to attack him and would have probably killed him if I had not been dragged off. That was the end for me and not even Dr. Gaskell could do anything more to help. He knew I had to get taken off the island immediately.'

The heart-breaking part of the whole escapade was actually having to go to see his close doctor friend, as a patient with obvious emotional problems, having once worked side by side with him and having earned his genuine respect. From the days when they worked the wards and shared moments of both sadness and happiness he had returned a broken man to see the doctor. Sentiment aside, he knew it was all over. What he didn't know was that in years to come he would return to the

Shetland Islands as a Christian evangelist and deliver a different message. But, at that moment, in the private room of Dr. Gaskell, a washed-up Geordie Aitken burst into tears, took the shakes and poured his heart out like a child. He did not notice that the caring doctor also had tears in his eyes.

After the forced diagnosis he was given one hour to pack his bags, under supervision, in readiness for the first available flight home. In his pocket he carried a sealed letter from Dr Gaskell who had told him to take it straight to his own doctor the moment he arrived home. Half aware of what was in the letter, a desperate Geordie Aitken ripped it open, read it, and immediately decided that it would never reach his doctor. Throughout the flight Geordie Aitken cried all the way home. 'The guys on the flight who knew me were thinking that I was round the bend. How right they were.'

Geordie Aitken was leaving the Sullom Voe Oil Terminal after four years of helping others but was now himself a broken man. The contents of Dr David Gaskell's letter revealed just how broken. Through tear filled eyes Geordie Aitken read about himself. The letter stated: 'this man has worked for years helping people with deep alcoholic problems and also social misfits who cannot handle their own lives. He has been doing this work outside his own normal working hours and now he cannot handle his own life and problems. My advice, as camp doctor, and also as his friend, is that he should be under strict medical supervision as he is on the verge of a massive mental breakdown.'

Back in Glasgow he was given only weekly sick notes as his doctor wanted to keep a constant check on him knowing that was the only way he could get him back to the surgery every seven days. He didn't want him out of his sight for more than one week at a time.

'He wanted regular contact with me in case I tried to take my own life or indeed someone else's for that matter.'

Coupled with the weekly medicals and appointments were the sedatives he was eventually prescribed to control his emotions and mood swings. Even the smallest noise would irritate him and he would fly off the handle. On a good day he knew how much pain he was causing his family. On a bad day he didn't care.

'I couldn't settle down or relax and the least thing would irritate me to the point where I wanted to smash the whole house up.' Things got so bad that he even took to hiding in his garden shed or under the blankets in his bedroom where the curtains were invariably pulled shut.

'Once in the hut the door slammed shut behind me and in a panic I kicked it open and rushed into the house sweating and shaking and dived into my bed. I would lie in the bed in complete darkness with the blankets pulled up over my head. This stinking breakdown was killing me because I could not cope with the constant fear and the endless tears. Often I would clench my teeth until my very jaw ached.'

Things got so bad that he even forgot what day of the week it was and even the names of close friends who called around to see him. More tablets were duly prescribed because his agitated state soon stopped him sleeping and even eating.

'I never knew the mind could do so much damage to me mentally and physically and also spiritually as I was still harbouring this death wish. Sadly, my family were beginning to feel the effects of my breakdown as my suffering also became their suffering. Why should this stinking breakdown happen to me as all I had done for the last fourteen years was help people. Why me? I thought in my crazy mixed up mind.'

As the months rolled agonizingly on he became terrified of even leaving his own home. He was in a lonely void that brought back memories of his drinking days. 'Loneliness is just a word to some people but I can assure you it can be a spirit-breaking reality to others.' Because of his earlier alcoholic days he would often suffer loneliness. 'It is the curse of all curses because when you suffer you suffer alone. Most suicide cases have went through so much loneliness that they can no longer walk hand in hand with loneliness so they take their own heart-breaking lives.'

Usually, when drunk, Geordie Aitken would stand alone because he was too busy wallowing in self pity and propping up a bar to bother about conversation. The more cheap wine that went down his throat the worse he got. 'Many a time when I staggered along the rough road of the boozebag I would always look down as I had no cause to lift my head up, and count the paving stones while looking for cigarette ends. I knew every paving slab by name by walking the head down pattern for so long.'

Often he would reminisce about the happier days in his life when he walked those same streets either as a proud child or a courting teenager. 'In my drunkenness happy memories would come flooding back but then the cursed loneliness would come upon me and the salt-tasting tears would flow like a river down my dirty cheeks and how I would wish I were dead.'

Despite the drink having been out of his life for nearly fifteen years the same suicidal lonely thoughts had resurfaced. In a bid to combat his living hell he set out to confront his fears by taking a train into the centre of Glasgow. But even that seemingly simple exercise ended in anguish.

'I purchased my ticket with a shaking hand and sweating brow as I was that afraid of just simply standing in a public place. The journey was a nightmare because I thought everyone on the train was watching me while those unseen ones behind me were waiting to hit me over the back of the head. I got off the train miles before my stop and walked home with stiff shaking legs and crying like a baby through anger, hurts and frustration.'

The fact that he had once been confident enough to address packed meetings and speak in public only fuelled the fiery hatred he had for this nervous breakdown. 'Now this yellow-livered excuse for a man could not even travel on a train because of this breakdown and I hated myself to the point of constantly wishing I was dead. For a very long time now I had forgotten how to laugh but I had become an expert in crying tears of heartache and hurt.'

Then the physical pain started. Often the doctor would be called out when Geordie Aitken suffered the symptoms of a heart attack. Indeed, they were the dreaded panic attacks which left him gasping for breath. 'I would panic that much that I would be left gasping and struggling to breathe and doctors were injecting enough stuff into me to knock a horse out. Little did I know at this time but this hell was actually a product of my sick mind.' Geordie Aitken was, at this terrible stage in his life, aged only 46.

Things got steadily worse and he knew that something had to give. All his life the street fighter had pushed himself to the brink yet somehow had always managed to pull himself back. This time, however, it was going to take something stronger than a big heart to save his life.

That something was to be God.

In later years he would use this episode in his life to lead people to the Lord and show that the 'filthy curse' of loneliness could be beaten. 'The marvellous thing about suffering is that it helps to humble us enough to ask for help. How I wished, at that time, to be normal again as I honestly thought there was no road back for Geordie Aitken. But God in his mercy proved me wrong after I called out to him in desperation for help. I can assure anyone who suffers from a breakdown or the filthy curse of loneliness that there is a road back via God. I am living proof of that today but my thoughts still lie with those friends who took their own lives because of loneliness. Their deaths were not in vain: from their loneliness and my own loneliness I learned so much.'

That was how Geordie Aitken was to reflect on the deaths of his friends after his conversion but, when they had died, years before he was saved, they were heart-breaking episodes in his life.

During his years with Alcoholics Anonymous Geordie Aitken met scores of people fighting to beat the booze. Some succeeded but some failed. His friend Geordie was one who failed and he paid with his life. While one Geordie kept off the bottle another returned to it. Having vowed that he was off the drink he was taken back in by his parents who thought he was sticking to his sobriety. But one night they telephoned Geordie Aitken after finding their son lying face down on the settee at their home. They greeted Geordie Aitken with the words: 'we think he's got the flu because he is awfully cold.'

On pulling his friend from under a blanket in a bid to rouse him, Geordie Aitken was horrified to find his friend was dead. Under the settee he found an empty wine bottle and an empty sleeping pill bottle. At that time he was only 26 but because of his drinking did not have any friends. 'His funeral was well attended, but how I wished that the people who attended it had showed him some friendship while he was alive so that he might never have taken his life at such an early age.'

Another man who died by his own hand, only in more horrific circumstances, was another friend from his Alcoholics Anonymous days. In keeping with the anonymity enjoyed by the organization Geordie Aitken will only refer to his former friends by first name to save their families from any added heartache. Jimmy, a married man, with a young daughter and wife whom he adored, hit the bottle after his wife left him. Geordie Aitken regularly accompanied him to AA meetings where he was trying desperately to get sober in a bid to win his wife back. Things appeared to be going well until the day that Geordie Aitken realized Jimmy had stopped attending meetings. Having heard that Jimmy was visiting family in London, Geordie Aitken never bothered checking on his mate. But after two weeks passed without a word he did check on him.

The sight, and stench that greeted him when he arrived at his friend's home will haunt him for the rest of his life. 'Myself and a mate went around to his flat to see if he had come back and if he was coping. After getting no answer we looked through the keyhole but the bolt was still in from the inside and I could smell a terrible smell coming from the house. We kicked the door in and as my mate headed for the bedroom I headed for the living room and to my horror discovered Jimmy. He was sitting in his fireside chair, completely dressed, but his skin was shrivelled up and almost black and the stench from his body was overpowering. He had two dogs and one of them was also dead but the other was alive. All around the room were tins of opened dog food as, in his love for his dogs, he had left them plenty of food so they would not die.'

That sight was enough to make anyone physically sick. But Geordie Aitken suffered even further mental torment when he noticed a piece of paper above the fireplace. Even in planning his own death Jimmy had been thinking of his good friend and what he had done for him. The paper read: 'Thanks Geordie for all of your help but I can't go on living without my wife, your pal Jimmy.' Geordie Aitken has shed rivers of tears for Jimmy since that horrific day.

While counselling for Alcoholics Anonymous Geordie Aitken met a chronic alcoholic called Rosemary. Many times she was weaned off the bottle but sadly always went back to it. Despite once staying off the bottle long enough to get a job and once even being admitted into hospital to dry out.

Geordie Aitken has happy memories of the days he and other AA members would take fruit and reading books to her in hospital as she set out on yet another recovery journey. The happiness was short lived when Rosemary was found floating face down in the River Clyde having decided to end it all. 'Ironically, in the times she was sober, she actually helped many people to get sober and many of them are still alive today thanks to wee Rosemary, but she never told us what made her continually go back to the drink. I think she knew, as well as anyone, that there can be a number of excuses made for going back to it but there's never a constructive reason. Her ashes might have been spread in the Garden of Remembrance but the memories of her are spread in the minds and thoughts of her friends who still love the wee woman.'

Geordie Aitken knows that he himself was pulled from the brink of suicide so that following his conversion he would work amongst the people who needed him most.

'People talk about hell in a verbal sense but I have been there and believe me hell is real. There's a hell on earth but it comes from within the person. The spiritual hell is unbelievable and the Devil would even rob you of taking your life. The Satanic powers are that real, through alcoholism, that he would take you to the brink of suicide and yet take the nerve to do it away from you. You are left at a crossroads and not knowing whether you want to live or die. I was a radical at everything but when it came to taking my life I was always just at the precipice of doing it. There is always this calling to come back into reality and I believe now, as an evangelist, that at the times I tried to commit suicide, Christ called me back, so that he could use the experiences of Geordie Aitken to take me back into the hell of the alcoholic, the hell of the drug addict and to take me back into the prisons. The prisons where the guys are not only behind bars but are also caged in spiritual prisons. There's no parole, no remission for good conduct and no release from a spiritual prison until God takes you out of it. When you are in a spiritual prison there is no good in you because you have lost the will to live and you only regain that will to live when there is something good happening to you. That something is God.

'If a person is suicidal I can understand how they feel as I have walked that road and I thank God today that I never succeeded because the hand of God was with me even then to save my life. I have suffered today as an evangelist as I have suffered the same suffering as the people I am dealing with. I have shared their suffering and can only thank God for letting me live to do that.'

My testimony proves that Christ is alive
the life that I led was a mess
At the gates of Hell my soul had arrived
by playing this worldly game of chess

The moves I made were stupid and sick
on Satan's sin-chequered board
I was the pawn that did inflict
with devilish treasures to hoard

This chessboard was made by tradesmen from Hell
with wood so different from the Cross
The king I used I knew so well
was not for my gain but for my loss

Then all of a sudden a new King appeared
in a light that lit up my board
With power and might my heart had been spared
from Satan's sick treasure hoard

Jesus is the name of my new chessboard King
I move so rightly with him
Always go forward and do the correct thing
your moves in Jesus must win

Thank God I am finished with Satan's old board
it's now back in storage in Hell
To burn and rot with his devilish hoard
as I love my sweet Jesus so well.

The Chessboard

# CHAPTER 7

# Salvation Through Christ

When a 46-year-old Geordie Aitken found Christ in 1983 there were no hallelujahs, hymns and happy people present. In the stark reflection of the way his life had developed, he was sitting alone in one room of the family home in Glasgow. The rest of his family were in hiding. By this time his wife Marion and their three children had taken to finding refuge in their bedrooms away from the ill-tempered and depressed loner. They kept their distance because they knew he would snap at the slightest thing. Life in the Aitken house was far from Christian; at this time it was sheer hell.

But this particular evening was to change their lives for ever. For months he had known he was at the crossroads, and that life, yet again, had become unbearable. He knew it, his family knew it, everyone knew it. Once again, as in his demented drunken days, his thoughts had often turned to suicide. He knew drastic action was needed but what he didn't know was that this drastic action was to be taken from above.

He was alone deeply rooted in the depths of despair and watching his beloved little TV set when it happened. 'By this time life in our house was like something out of a Charlie Chaplin movie. Everyone was walking about not speaking. The rest of my family would even go upstairs to get out of the road of me, the madman.' As the madman sat in the dark, watching a choir singing 'How Great Thou Art', four simple words were to lead him to Christ.

'I had done everything possible, committed every sin in the Bible, and despite being sober for nearly seventeen years I knew that sobriety alone was not the answer. It would take something else to get me out of this mess.'

Alone in the world with only the TV choir for company he asked simply: 'Hey, Jesus, could you do me a wee favour? If you are as alive as the words in this hymn say you are could you come into my life?' At that moment Jesus did come into his life.

'At that exact moment a beautiful feeling came upon me and I felt a spiritual heat moving from the top of my head through my whole body down to the tips of my feet. The knot of hatred loosened within me and was replaced by a spiritual presence. I had received a blessed assurance from the Lord that my life had just started and I accepted the Lord as my personal saviour. Through the words of that hymn 'How Great Thou Art', I went to Christ as a street corner boy ready and willing to start my life all over again.' But far from being a time of great family rejoicing and celebration his spiritual transformation was met with the now customary apathy his frantic family showed him. When the born-again Geordie Aitken dashed up the stairs to tell Marion of his conversion, the long suffering wife suggested calling the police. 'You're off your nut, you idiot. You've finally flipped this time. After your lifestyle you expect me to believe you're a bloody Christian. You need treatment you stupid sod.' That was a proud Geordie Aitken's first experience of the joys of Christianity. He accepts now that he might have summed it up too briefly for the woman who had endured years of torment and anguish, when he delivered the blunt message: 'Hey Marion something strange has happened.' What's new, she had thought, before launching into her tirade and vowing to have him certified come first light.

That night, Geordie Aitken, though confused and bewildered, slept with an inner peace for the first time in forty-six years. Excitement, trepidation, and bemusement filled his mind and body. But so did something far stronger.

Any illusions of what Christianity meant were to be continuously shattered in the coming weeks and months when he discovered that it was not only Marion who was to have difficulty in accepting what had happened. Her disbelief was to be shared by scores of others. All he was going to experience was heartache and rejection. But, deep inside, he knew the Lord was at work. 'Right from that very moment I was repenting. I was not just saying sorry but really meaning it.'

In the Aitken household things had turned upside down. Marion couldn't comprehend what had happened and still kept the telephone number of the nearest asylum close at hand. But the couple's three young children were loving every minute of it. This nutter was pro-fessing to be a Christian. 'Over the months I had stopped being their dad and as far as they were concerned I was just "It" or "Him". What time is It in tonight? What will It want to eat? Will It being going out later and will he be arguing when he comes in? This was how my own family saw me.' But this new lease of life had given his children, Audrey, 9, Beverley, 6 and little 5-year-old Adam a new pastime. Watching the Mad Christian.

Once, while praying, the children crept up the stairs and saw him kneeling by the bedside mumbling. Not knowing of prayers they thought he had started talking to himself and stood, peeping around the bedroom door, blowing raspberries and laughing at him. Geordie Aitken had only been kneeling by his bedside because he thought people had to look reverent in order to pray. To escape the ridicule of his children, Geordie Aitken told them he was only looking under the bed for his slippers. They gleefully explained that he was already wearing them, and that he definitely was a nutcase. 'They thought it was great. They were now convinced I was mad and all set to call the doctor in. Here I was with a broken nose, scarred face, covered in Protestant tattoos, and generally in a right mess, trying to look reverent simply by kneeling down and clasping my hands. I felt like a dirty stinking phoney and would have been more at home sitting praying on a toilet seat.' But from that moment, after lying about his reasons for kneeling by the bedside, he swore never to make excuses for his Christianity again.

He drew on Christ for a boldness to make him stand up and be counted. In the early months his boldness was to be repeatedly tested to the limit. Nobody would accept the former alcoholic and hardline Orange Order fanatic could have a Christian thought in his battered body.

His first public test came when he met up with his thieving mates who were planning a burglary at an industrial unit. In declining to join them, he explained that he was finished with crime and that he had given his life to Christ. When they picked themselves up from the floor, and wiped tears of laughter from their eyes, they, too, were reaching for the telephone number of the nearest psychiatric ward. They couldn't understand it and, to be honest, Geordie Aitken couldn't either. 'Here I was telling my gangster friends that I was a Christian when I didn't even know what a Christian was myself. I knew nothing about it, I thought Calvary was the name of the American soldiers who rode horses and fought Indians in cowboy films. I knew of Jesus Christ but actually believed that his parents were Mary and Joseph Christ. Everything about this Christianity was new to me.'

To overcome it he decided the best way to learn was to read his Saviour's 'autobiography' the Bible. But such was his confusion over Christianity that he promptly decided to pinch one from the nearest bookshop. To do that he had to find out what Bibles were used. He wanted the one that was used by the local Baptist church worshippers. Off he went, dressed in a stolen leather jacket to hide his Orange Order tattoos to get the name of a Bible before paying a visit to the nearby Church of Scotland bookshop to furnish himself with one.

'I was still a thief, I thought you could take Jesus into your life but still steam in.' He was to learn different, but he was able to learn that he himself was different. Churches would not accept him for what he was and his interpretation of Christianity. 'I did not want to become a theological zombie but someone with the will to live.'

Geordie Aitken wanted to be out on the streets proclaiming the message of Christ not sitting on a polished church pew once a week on a Sunday morning. He soon discovered that not many 'Christians' shared that idea. On his first full visit to church the wary Christian stood outside and hid behind a tree as the faithful congregation filed in. Plucking up the courage to go in, tattooed arms duly covered, he took his seat on a church pew. 'When I went in everyone looked at me as if I had three heads.' Moments into the service, a shaking sweating Geordie Aitken took a panic attack and was about to flee from the church when an elderly stranger laid a firm hand on his shoulder and told him to sit still and see the service through. That man was to become a human saviour to Geordie Aitken. The Reverend Bill Creighton was to help him through his early conflicting emotions and give him the courage to continue along a Christian path. 'I had entered this church in God and in his mercy he had sat me beside this man. I could have sat anywhere in that church but for some reason I sat next to the man who was to become a heavenly godfather to me. Christ laid the foundation of my salvation but the Reverend Bill Crieghton was one of the builders.'

Bill Creighton was an ex-boxer from Belfast who had given his life to God many years ago. The ex-boxer knew the ropes and also knew exactly what Geordie Aitken was going through. Unlike Geordie Aitken, the Irishman had found Christ in a more public arena. While entering the ring for a big fight in Belfast he suddenly stopped in his tracks, took off the gloves, and turned his back on the fighting game. He was ordained in the tough Shankill Road area of Northern Ireland before embarking on a lifetime of God's work. He spent twenty-five years working and preaching along the Amazon River before finding his way to Scotland at the age of 78. Now he was sitting next to a terrified Geordie Aitken and about to embark on another mission of God.

'I was sitting in this church sweating and terrified but he gently put his arm around me and told me he was my friend.' He began visiting Geordie Aitken at home and taught him the Bible.

Months later Geordie Aitken was baptized at the age of 46 in East Mains Baptist Church in Glasgow, under the watchful eye of proud Reverend Bill Creighton. But as the months wore on Christianity became a heart-breaking lonely chore for the born-again Christian. The only support he got was from Bill Creighton. 'I had the faith but I didn't have any support. I became very, very lonely. I had severed all of my past ties and my family still thought I was mental. The people at the church made it obvious they did not want me there and I felt like a stranger.' Without the assurance of the Reverend Bill Creighton a confused Geordie Aitken could have easily given it all up. 'Sometimes I wonder if Christ really exists in the lives of some church people. I was told that the Baptists were the cream of the Christian people and filled with love, joy, and charity. During my stay I never experienced any of that from the people who sat upon the church pews.'

His everlasting impressions of his early days at the church are of long-faced, self-righteous people. He struggled through his early months with the belief: 'If I could come through the past life I had led then surely I could overcome this.' But he wasn't going to. He was always wrestling with his beliefs that the congregation were more interested in themselves than in their fellow men. 'I had never encountered so much snobbery in my life until now.'

His fears that God existed only for good people and not the Geordie

Aitkens of the world were heightened by the actions of several church-goers. One church elder refused to pray with him. 'I had asked him to pray with me because it was a difficult time in my life, and I was going through a very hard time as a Christian. But his answer was that I was now a Christian, I should be able to pray for myself.' Many a time when Geordie Aitken was walking to a service in the pouring rain, other churchgoers would drive past him on their way to church. 'They would drive past me in their fancy cars but when I looked up at them they would turn away as if watching something else and drive straight past.'

He was also always left out of home visits by the congregation and ignored in their social circles. He was never invited to any of the video nights and when he asked why was told: 'Sorry, Geordie, we thought one of the others had invited you.'

'It sure was a very lonely walk at that time being a Christian. Not only had I never been invited to any of their homes but neither had any of my family.'

By this time Geordie Aitken was doing anything he could to be accepted by the church. Digging drains, gardening, decorating, anything at all that would elevate him into their company. But he later realized that was not his way. 'I was still a people pleaser not a Jesus pleaser.'

He lasted in that church for two years. During that time he never received one home visit from the congregation or the minister. His only visitor was the Reverend Bill Creighton. 'When I prayed, my prayers would upset the congregation because I would pray for the prostitutes, drunks, homeless and suicide cases while the churchgoers only prayed for themselves. Geordie Aitken was, and always had been since the day he entered their church, a thorn in their respectable sides.'

The crunch came one hot summer day when Geordie Aitken was toiling in the church gardens. After removing his cardigan the militant Protestant tattoos incurred the wrath of an elderly woman churchgoer. In later years those tattoos were to become an important part of his evangelical work. But on this particular day they caused only trouble. His pent up frustration exploded and he turned on the self-righteous churchgoer and vented his anger after she labelled him an insult to Christianity. 'I told her that I could not remove the tattoos and that they were a part of me and my Christianity. She was wearing a ridiculous hat that made her look like a mobile fruit shop and I proceeded to tell her just that. I called her a middle-class phoney who was using the church for her own benefit and that she didn't have a genuine Christian thought in her head.' The woman shrieked and was joined by a frantic minister and band of church elders who leapt to her defence without asking what had happened. They unanimously decided, without hearing from Geordie Aitken, that far from being a Christian, he actually 'had the Devil in him'. They had never liked him and now they had their chance to get rid of him. Unknown to Geordie Aitken, standing watching this angry exchange was an American evangelist, Jeff Sindelar.

Jeff had been hitch-hiking around Europe and had met up with a Scottish couple who had given him somewhere to stay. He had been out exploring Glasgow when he stumbled across the Baptist church where a fight was about to start. Far from daunted at what had just happened Geordie Aitken actually offered Jeff a hot meal back at his house because he thought he was a dosser.

That chance meeting was to play a major part in Geordie Aitken's developing evangelical life. Unknown to him Jeff Sindelar was shortly to return to America and relate his story to church leaders.

One of them Benny Lee, was later to invite Geordie Aitken to the United States and become a close friend. But while, thousands of miles away, Jeff Sindelar and Benny Lee were talking of the 'Scottish Christian' a still bemused Geordie Aitken had more important things on his mind. He was a Christian without a church. He was now finished with East Mains Baptist Church after two years. Following the angry exchange with the woman, he got a telephone call from the church minister asking to meet him. He was dubious but went along. 'As Christians we must always go the extra mile and this I did with God's help. In my pre-Christian days I would have punched a few of these churchgoers in the mouth because of the way they had treated me and my family but because of my walk with God I could never do that now.'

On arrival at the church Geordie Aitken discovered that the minister had known all along of the ill-treatment. 'He tried to speak but burst out crying and asked me to forgive him and his congregation for the way I had been treated. He admitted nobody had visited me because they had not been interested in me or my family.' Geordie Aitken walked out of the church, with apologies ringing in his ears, and having forgiven them. Over the years he has visited the church with no malice towards them. Just pity 'much to my dismay that church has not changed one little bit. All I can do is pity them and pray for them.' Despite the minister's apology Geordie Aitken still did not have a church, and in his early Christian days thought you had to be a member of one to be a Christian. He was later to learn different and that his true calling was on the streets and in the prisons. Those were to be his ministries.

In between he tried to find refuge in the Church of Scotland. But that was to end as acrimoniously as his first church experiences. Again he encountered a coldness and rejection. He found it to be rife with snobbery and class distinction overseen by a hierarchy of church elders. Once he was stunned when he discovered a young preacher was obeying the orders of the elders by allowing a tarot card reader to set up stall at the church summer fayre. It had been agreed by the church congregation committee. 'The preacher was a good man of God but lacked the boldness to take a stand against things that were not of God. I asked him why he was going against God's will allowing something from the occult at the church fayre and he said that he was not allowed to go against the congregational committee's decision.'

From his earlier experiences with the occult Geordie Aitken knew the full horrors it could wreak. 'There were many people who took their lives because of their involvement with the occult, tarot cards and such similar devilish things but the church was allowing it to go on in its own grounds.'

Geordie Aitken discovered that beneath the church committee there were other groups. 'This place of God was full of Freemasons and women that belonged to the Eastern Star secret society. The only way you could be accepted into the congregation was by being a member of a society.'

With his Bible telling him that God works in mysterious ways Geordie Aitken believed he was being shown these aspects of the established churches so that he would leave the church pews behind and head for where his heart lay—the streets. That was where Geordie Aitken wanted to deliver God's message, to the prostitutes, drunks, homeless and jailbirds. He had never been happier than when he was helping the more unfortunate members of society. He had already, during his days with Alcoholics Anonymous, worked with the dregs of society and was now preparing to go back to them with a different message.

It was many years since he had worked at the notorious Wayside Club and soup kitchens and now, along with his reassuring advice, he had a Christian message to deliver to Glasgow's dossers and drunks. Since his involvement with the Wayside Club it had closed down, and he set his spiritual sights on the equally squalid Wyneford Anchorage Kitchens.

The soup kitchen was opened up in the Wyneford Mission Hall and had been called the Anchorage by its Christian founders, who saw God as an anchor for the drunks if they accepted God into their lives.

For a rejected Geordie Aitken it was heaven. Not because of what it stood for but because of what he knew he could do with the people who desperately needed it. This, he knew, was his true calling.

The Anchorage, a wooden hut in the working class area of Maryhill in Glasgow, catered for a population of drunks but was also in an area where many hard-up families could not afford to donate anything to it.

Geordie Aitken was also confronted by the problem of drugs and solvent abuse for the first time. He knew the life of an alcoholic but this particular area of Glasgow had serious teenage drug problems. It was also new to him that the people behind it were Christians.

During his days at the Wayside Club he had mixed in with the drunks and even been called upon to throw rowdy dossers out and revert to his wild fighting days. Here the dossers were treated with compassion and care. 'It was a joy to hear the Christian folk at the Wyneford Mission Hall praying for the drunks and drug addicts.' But by now, many people were turning from alcohol and fuelling their addictions on anything from hair lacquer to heroin. But away from the sadness there was also the humour which had followed Geordie Aitken even in his darkest days.

As with the AA groups the soup kitchen had its own characters. Once while stirring the soup in the tiny kitchen Geordie Aitken noticed something out of the corner of his eye. Ignoring it he continued with the soup until he saw it again. This time he turned to see a massive brown rat hungrily scratching about the floor.

As the soup stirrer ran from the kitchen shouting about the size of the rat, one disgruntled drunk, without lifting his head, shouted back at him, 'throw it in the soup.' 'Even in their terrible sufferings, the poor drunks would crack a joke that would make us laugh.' One resident swore down that he was Princess Margaret's nephew and promised he would take everyone from the Anchorage to a garden party when she next visited the Scottish palace at Holyrood to make a change from the soup kitchen food. He had the accent to back up his claims but the tiny group never made it to the palace. Harry committed suicide by throwing himself under a train.

With his new-found Christianity blossoming, Geordie Aitken not only worked the soup kitchen but also attended the Saturday night Bible classes and services. Of the two it was the Wednesday that proved raucous. But it took a few weeks for Geordie Aitken and Pastor Benny, a former alcoholic to realize why. Half-way through his preachings the crowd would start to drift away leaving him in full flow. 'They had come to be fed not to hear about the great man called Jesus. We used to give them their sandwiches and soup before the gospel message but once they had eaten their fill they would walk out.' In a bid to get their gospel message across the hardy duo decided to dish out the food and soup at the end of the sermon and hoped the drunks would not notice the ploy. 'Benny thought their spiritual food was more important than their physical food, and we decided that they would have to sit through the gospel message before being fed.'

Come the following meeting the usual crowd turned up at the hall in anticipation of their grub. Half-way through Pastor Benny's sermon chants of: 'why are we waiting, why are we waiting,' filled the dingy wooden hall. Undeterred, Pastor Benny continued preaching, and the louder the drunks shouted the louder he preached. But nobody lost that night. The message was delivered and shortly afterwards the drunks and dossers gobbled down their sandwiches and drank cups of steaming soup. 'These feeding nights were full of excitement because you never knew what would happen next.' But while he smiled through the heartache Geordie Aitken was suffering in silence closer to home. Now unemployed, and on state benefit, he himself was literally living on the breadline. Often he would take sandwiches and soup home for himself and his own family. But his personal problems took a back seat when it came to helping others at the Anchorage. Not everyone showed the same spirit. Even the Christian charity fell prey to desperate, alcoholic conmen.

In his day Geordie Aitken had pulled some callous stunts but now he was on the other side of the fence to people like Danny, the boyfriend of a hardened Glasgow prostitute. 'He could never pull the wool over my eyes but he conned people very easily. So many Christians have had an easy life and fell for his tricks.' Once he walked into the Anchorage, and told a Christian helper that his girlfriend had been arrested after fighting with a punter who had turned nasty on her and that he needed £10 to bail her out of the police cells. Shortly after Danny left with the cash, the prostitute walked in asking if anyone had seen Danny. She was concerned about him because he had not awoken her, where they slept rough under the Kingston Bridge, in time to get their free soup at the kitchen.

Across the hallway the Saturday mission nights were a law unto themselves. Often during a service a drunk would pipe up and shout and bawl at the top of his voice. Many, with the best intentions in the world would raucously join in with the hymn singing. But usually, to the disdain of the sober members of the hall, they would make up their own words as they were not too familiar with the hymns. Then off they would go to the darker side of life. One elderly man never got very far. He was hit by a car and left for dead at the roadside with his skull cracked open and his brains spilling out. Geordie Aitken and Pastor Benny knelt with the dying man until an ambulance arrived. He never regained consciousness or heard the simple prayers his two comforters made by the roadside as they knelt over him.

In months to come both Geordie Aitken and Pastor Benny were to move on to new pastures. For Pastor Benny, the former drunk and street-fighter, it was not what he imagined. Since becoming a Christian he harboured dreams that God had chosen him to work as a missionary in Africa. After his stint at the Wyneford Mission Hall, he was convinced that was where he was heading. But he was never destined to get out of Glasgow, let alone Scotland. He was to continue his Christian work in the less Amazonian setting of the city's main mission hall. Following the interview, Pastor Benny got the job he didn't want and set off to work with the city's destitute, with dreams of becoming an African missionary now firmly behind him. He also left plenty of tears behind. When he left many a drunk shed a tear along with Geordie Aitken. 'We thank God that Benny did not go to Africa, as he is still doing a tremendous job amongst the needy.'

Geordie Aitken stayed on for a few weeks after Benny's departure to look after the soup kitchen but he himself had to move on. Before he went he had one last task to peform for the mission hall. Act as Santa Claus for the needy children. But organizers had to wait until 27 December to hold their Christmas party as they were waiting for cast-off toys and unwanted gifts to share out to the children. Genial Geordie Aitken was chosen for the part because of his large stomach and not for his height. The costume borrowed from a local church would have done a six footer proud. For five feet two inches Geordie Aitken it trailed the floor like a wedding dress. Not to be outdone he tied the oversized coat around his waist with a rope. Complete with black wellington boots, two sizes too big, 'I must have been the worst Santa Claus ever seen in Glasgow.'

He entered the Wyneford Mission Hall with a bang, to chants of 'Hurry up' from the hardened children. Stumbling about in his massive cloak and gigantic wellies he managed to trip over the hem and enter the hall head first. The audience of 6 to 11-year-old street-wise kids greeted his entrance with laughter, but urged him on in a bid to get their long-awaited presents.

One young boy asked for a pair of boxing gloves with which to beat up his little school friend. When Santa Claus refused he hit back in a way that only a saddened 7-year-old could. 'You're not Santa Claus anyway. You're Geordie Aitken.' The youngster had noticed, under the wide sleeves of the Santa Claus outfit that the man had tattoos on his arm. He knew that helper Geordie Aitken had tattoos. 'So much for trying to kid a street-wise Glasgow boy.' Despite the poverty, pain and sorrow the Christmas party in the old wooden hall went well. 'This delayed party was a great success by just being ourselves. I will never forget those young kids as long as I have a breath left in my body.'

The Wyneford Hall is still running its soup kitchen and Saturday evening gospel nights.

Because of his new found Christianity Geordie Aitken had to sever his links with Alcoholics Anonymous. As in his days with the group, the drinking had stopped but members still swore, fought and thieved, and Geordie Aitken now had no time for such things. But he could never forget the important part it played in his life, and he knew it was not going to be easy walking away from it. His chance came when he was due to speak at a massive convention in East Kilbride Civic Centre, to an audience of 600 people. Over the past months the AA had thought he had been working at one of the various sub-groups across the city and they were not aware of his Christian commitment. 'I decided the best way was to tell them straight from the platform when I was called to speak, but what a commotion it caused.'

On his way to the rostrum the crowds were cheering, clapping and shaking his hand, five minutes later you could have heard a pin drop. Then many of them got up and walked out. This was not the rabble-rousing, fighting Geordie Aitken they knew, they were speechless, those who were not shouted: 'you're still an alcoholic and don't you forget where you came from and who helped you.' This was Geordie Aitken's last AA meeting, despite attempts by the organization's General Services Office to try to lure him back. He knew he could never return to that life, but swore never to give up helping alcoholics and dossers in an evangelical way. 'People at these meetings were still swearing, fighting and stealing and I could not manage that anymore. I told them that I had a new sponsor and that his name was Jesus. I walked away from it and never went to another meeting.'

But he was never to leave the alcoholics to suffer. He became involved with the Stauros Foundation which helps the less fortunates in society. Members of the group would visit drunks at their homes, and prisoners in jail to spread a Christian message. It was while with the Stauros that Geordie Aitken made his first trip to Northern Ireland and had his first dealings with the Christian Police Fellowship.

While speaking at one Stauros convention he was spotted by two policemen sitting in the audience, and after hearing his testimony they invited him to speak at one of their meetings. He was to be a joint speaker along with a Catholic man with previous IRA connections.

What a sight the UVF and the IRA fanatics made side by side addressing a hall full of policemen. 'I used to feel nervous at the very sight of policemen even if I hadn't done anything wrong. Here I was now about to stand in front of 300 of them.' But by the end of the meeting there was hardly a dry eye in the room. Many of the older officers were the ones who used to arrest him in his wild drunken days. One senior officer remembered him from his days when he was a traffic policeman on match days. He never forgot the day he saw a drunken Geordie Aitken throwing beer bottles at a bus full of rival Celtic supporters. As a Protestant Geordie Aitken was a devout Glasgow Rangers supporter. On that day the frantic policeman had been unable to arrest the hooligan because in those days there were no two-way radios, and he had been unable to leave his position in the middle of the busy road. But he told Geordie Aitken at the fellowship meeting he had reported him the minute his traffic duty finished. Geordie Aitken had always wondered how he got arrested the day after he stood throwing beer bottles at the coach.

Following the meeting Geordie Aitken forged strong links with the police in a bid to beat the twin problems of alcohol and drug addiction on the streets of Glasgow. He was regularly invited to meetings and even to the homes of both uniformed and CID officers. Often he would be asked by the local officers to speak to a convict as he lay in the cells.

For his work on the streets and in the community Geordie Aitken has been honoured by both Strathclyde Police and the East Kilbride Development Corporation.

Years after his first speech to the packed hall he was awarded a top honour for his work with Strathclyde Police's community officers. He still receives an annual invitation to the fellowship's Christmas Choir Service. But despite his work he was always scared that neighbours and friends would think he was an informer because of his close contact with the police. 'I still speak with the convicts and the gangsters and used to pray that they would not think I was a grass. At one time, I myself hated the police but here I was going to their homes and working hand-in-hand with them.'

Such was his upbringing that he still lives by the law of the streets. Following one choir service he was offered a lift home by Chief Superintendent Douglas Kelly as the rain lashed down. But half a mile from his home he asked the high ranking officer if he would let him out so that he could walk the rest of the way. 'He had his full uniform on and I was worried that the neighbours would deinitely think I was an informer, if he pulled up outside my door. But he knew what people were like and laughed as he dropped me off at the street corner in the pouring rain.'

With avenues opening up in all walks of the community Geordie Aitken found himself being asked to deliver his no-nonsense Christian message at meetings attended by people from dossers to dignitaries. Word was spreading like wildfire about this unorthodox evangelist.

His involvement with the Stauros Foundation also led him to Northern Ireland for the first time since his involvement with the Orange Order, and he learned about Christianity after witnessing first hand, life in the troubled Province.

During a rally in Ulster he met a fellow Staurist who showed him the real meaning of forgiveness—the wife of a Royal Ulster Constabulary chief superintendent who saw her husband gunned down by IRA terrorists. As he lay dying the devoted couple forgave his killers as the brave policeman's blood seeped into the street while his wife cradled him in her arms. His widow later prayed for his killers and with the help of the foundation visited his murderer in an Irish prison. 'This woman was a power of strength to me.'

Many more trips to Ireland lay ahead for the Scottish evangelist through which his message would reach across the troubled island, from hardened terrorists caged in prisons to troubled youngsters walking the wicked streets. Those visits opened up new ministries for the street-level evangelist, but between each one he was tirelessly working his own Glasgow streets.

'There were many roads opening up for me and here I was working twenty-four hours a day for Jesus.' By now, a serious foot problem had forced him on sickness benefit, and out of work for good. But he continued his work for the Lord and even tried to preach to the doctor who was treating him. He was taken into hospital to have cortisone injections in his damaged feet and testified to the surgeon during the operation. Such was his testimony that the doctor often telephoned him at home and invited him into his office to discuss the power of the Lord. Not content with that Geordie Aitken would minister to the queues of people patiently sitting in a surgery waiting room. 'I was there to be treated but we would spend ages in the surgery talking about my life and my work for Christ. The doctor was sceptical at first but he soon believed me after checking my medical record and seeing what injuries I had suffered in my earlier wild days. Whenever he was busy I would even witness to his patients in the waiting room.'

Further work in the region's hospitals was just around the corner for Geordie Aitken opening up yet more avenues.

Throughout his life Geordie Aitken had never mastered the art of driving, either because in his early days he was too drunk to get behind the wheel, or in his later life was too busy helping others, or like now, too poor to afford lessons. With Christianity behind him he tried a novel approach. He prayed for wheels. And he got them. But only two, not the anticipated four. His quest for a car finished, the Lord provided him with a mountain bike. Two days after praying for wheels, a friend arrived at his house asking him if he had any need for an unwanted bike. He gladly took it and at the age of 48 started to learn how to ride a bike. Even while mastering the art, and in later years when he had it perfected, his mountain bike was to lead him into many scrapes in the name of God. Having lowered the seat, so that his tiny legs could reach the pedals, he set off to visit a friend in Hairmyres Hospital, East Kilbride. The first miracle was that the roads were clear.

A passing policeman pulled him over and urged him to ride on the path for the sake of other road users. He left Geordie Aitken on the path, with the words: 'you'll be better off on the pavement before you cause a nasty accident. It's a wheelchair you want, mate, not a mountain bike.' The second miracle was that he arrived at the hospital in one piece to visit an old friend who was having surgery on varicose veins. In he walked with his bicycle pump, his treasured bike chained up outside, to greet his friend. The third miracle was that Geordie Aitken finished up sharing fellowship with a ward full of cancer sufferers and was invited back to the hospital by a tearful surgeon who witnessed the impromptu gathering in the middle of the ward.

'I had gone to visit my old mate but by the time I had started ministering with the cancer patients, he was hiding under his bed with embarrassment. When the surgeon and doctor walked in I apologized and said I would leave. The woman doctor told me: "No you won't, I have never seen anything like this in my life. If you ever want to come back you are more than welcome."' An evangelical Geordie Aitken didn't need asking twice. Many a time he was to return to Hairmyres Hospital, on his bike, look up the duty nurse, ask which patients weren't expecting any visitors and sit with them throughout the visiting times which would otherwise have been a lonely hour for them.

Whatever their circumstances and situation nobody escaped from Geordie Aitken. He was more at home with the street people of Glasgow but whoever needed his help, was guaranteed of it. Even if they did wear expensive suits, expensive aftershave and dined in top-class hotels. But they got the same Geordie Aitken as the man-in-the-street did.

For his evangelical purposes the five star Highland Hotel, in Inverness was no different to the Anchorage soup kitchen in Glasgow. It was at the Highland Hotel that Geordie Aitken was asked to speak to the businessmen through Gospel Fellowship. He knew his trusted mountain bike would not get him that far so the organizers arranged for him to be picked up from home. He was in his usual attire, a second-hand tracksuit and T-shirt, when the man arrived. 'He thought I had been working in the garden and gave me five minutes to get changed.' After a not too eloquent exchange, in which Geordie Aitken explained that this was how he was going to appear at the meeting the pair set off in the delegate's car for the long journey to Inverness. 'This guy's face was tripping him up and he hardly spoke a word throughout the whole journey.'

When they arrived Geordie Aitken duly marched in and was met with an amazing sight. 'I was used to speaking in wooden huts and church halls, but this place had deer heads mounted on the wall, a pipe band in their full regalia, businessmen in top-of-the-range suits and solid silver cutlery on the table.' During the speech he noticed that a distinguished gentleman kept giving him disparaging and disdainful looks. In his raggy tracksuit and crumpled T-shirt Geordie Aitken asked from the platform why he was looking at him in such a manner. 'My ministries are with the homeless, the prostitutes and the drunks. But we are all brothers in Jesus so never look at me in disgust. If you reject me you are rejecting Jesus.'

The humbled man, who Geordie Aitken later learned was a millionaire and an influential Scottish businessman, broke down in tears and gave his life to Christ as he stood in the massive oak-beamed hall. During the meal many others shared fellowship with their raggy little friend. 'We finally came together as people. There were four spoons on the table, three forks and two knives and I didn't have a clue what they were for. I was eating my dessert with the soup spoon and vice versa. The miracle about that evening was that in my earlier days I would have rolled all of the cutlery up in the tablecloth and pinched the lot.

The only thing Geordie Aitken left the Highland Hotel with was a standing ovation ringing in his ears. And the knowledge that some of the businessmen had given their lives to Christ.

While away from Glasgow on another mission, this time back to his more familiar surroundings, he led thirty people to Christ during a two week mission in Kilbirnie. One was an AIDS victim who heard him speaking in the local church. Having heard Geordie Aitken's testimony he asked for a quiet word with him after the sermon. 'I led that man to Christ sitting in his car outside the church.' The distraught man, who knew he was dying, explained how he had caught the deadly virus during an extra-marital affair, and how he had then passed it on to his wife. Geordie Aitken continued visiting the man in hospital as his condition deteriorated. 'It was a grotesque sight.'

The comforting evangelist once remarked tht it was sad to see the man in such a terrible state but the born-again Christian replied: 'don't be sorry to see me like this. I was lost and worried but now I know that the Lord is taking me home and there will be nothing but rejoicing when I meet him.' A tearful Geordie Aitken walked from the hospital and within days learned that the man had died. He also learned that he had asked hospital staff to play the hymn that was on TV the night that Geordie Aitken found Christ. 'How Great Thou Art' was played as the man's ravaged body was laid to rest.

His work in Kilbirnie was not lost on his close friend the Reverend Douglas Irvine. Douglas was a former British Petroleum lawyer who gave everything up to go and work with Sister Teresa in the darkest depths of Calcutta. He returned to his native Scotland where he became the minister of one of Scotland's oldest churches, The Auld Kirk, in Kilbirnie. His main ministries are also with drug addicts and desperate teenagers, and himself and Geordie Aitken have worked through many a dark day leading people to salvation. Vicious teenagers in Glasgow were also a target for evangelizing Geordie Aitken. One went from being a potential murderer to a Church of Scotland young evangelist. The church had started a group, Teenscene, to get the youths off the streets but could not cope with the rowdy youngsters. Organizers had heard of a 'bold, radical, preacher called Geordie Aitken' and contacting him proved a blessing in itself.

The troublesome Barra, was the leader of the vicious street gang who were ridiculing the work of the centre. 'He would have sliced you up as soon as look at you.'

When Geordie Aitken first met him he was facing criminal charges for allegedly attacking a man with a machete. Far from ending up as another convicted statistic he was to embark on a life of Christianity. But it cost Geordie Aitken his prized Bible. The one that a group of hardened prisoners had saved up to buy him in recognition of his work while prison visiting.

At first Barra would shout and swear at Geordie Aitken as he spoke at the Teenscene meetings. After hearing of his past lifestyle and the ensuing trials and tribulations he changed his ways. 'He thought he was too bad to come to Christ. But he said that if I thought anything about him and his salvation I would give him the Bible that I carried.' Geordie Aitken did. Barra went on to work with the Church of Scotland as a youth evangelist amongst the street gangs. He later married, had a son and still delivers a Christian message on the street. But that conversion also saved his mother and father.

The teenager's father was in a hospital bed suffering from cancer when he heard about his son and later met him in a different light. He was to tell Geordie Aitken: 'I don't care if I die, I have seen my son now and I am proud of him.' Months later he was to walk out of the hospital free from cancer to a transformed wife. Barra's conversion had also saved her. She had been a manic depressive, thanks to her son's wild ways, but following his conversion pulled her life together and is now firmly established back at her local church. 'It's beautiful when you see a changed life. These are the real miracles.'

Not every life could be changed but scores were improved. Following his work at the Wayside Club and Wyneford Mission Hall soup kitchens, Geordie Aitken pioneered another in the centre of Glasgow. This one was an open-air Tuesday night kitchen. It would stand as a proud embarrassment to the Glasgow bureaucracy. Only yards from the civic chambers, the makeshift kitchen fed hundreds of dossers, drunks and prostitutes once a week—often as civic dignitaries shuffled by on their way to a lavish reception in the massive local government buildings.

The soup pot even stood at the foot of the huge statue of Scottish hero Rabbie Burns in the busy commercially thriving George Square. Come rain or shine, and even police involvement, the team of volunteers would set up the kitchen in the shadow of the statue every Tuesday night at eight o'clock. Over a hundred needy people regularly attended the kitchen for a sandwich and a cup of steaming soup. Geordie Aitken would be thankful to the pouring rain that often soaked him and his volunteers. 'It sometimes came in handy as I would leave the lid off the soup and let the rain in. That way I could make sure there was enough soup to go round.'

It became a bigger attraction than the splendid civic chambers themselves and attracted hordes of snappers eager to capture the plight of the less fortunate before dashing off to their warm homes to escape the rain.

But with the tourists came the wrath of the civic leaders who found the soup kitchen an embarrassment to the city. They decided it had no place in the thriving city-centre of Glasgow. Especially when Glasgow was named the European City of Culture. 'Thousands of pounds were spent sand-blasting and millions on arranging the Glasgow festival. They could hide the old buildings with the sand-blaster but they could never hide the reality of the homeless and the hungry that lined up at our soup kitchen.' But the hierarchy did try.

One freezing evening the police were sent to disperse the dossers and order Geordie Aitken to pack up the soup kitchen. He refused. Uniformed officers threatened to call in a tactical support unit and physically remove the kitchen and the volunteers. On hearing the news a hundred dossers started chanting 'we shall not be moved.' As support for Geordie Aitken grew others filed into the square and warned police that if their little saviour was arrested, as promised, for a breach of the peace, every one of them would also have to be arrested. It never materialized. Geordie Aitken later heard that a certain high-ranking police officer had been keeping a distant, but very close eye on the situation. He later told Geordie Aitken: 'I know you didn't know at the time but don't worry. I would have never let it happen.' The soup kitchen was becoming quite a thorn in the side of the establishment but while queues of people made the weekly pilgrimage to it Geordie Aitken refused to budge.

Often revellers from the civic chambers would pass the soup kitchen and look the other way. 'As they passed our little oasis they turned their heads. Guilt must have been spoiling their appetite for smoked salmon and caviar. What a divided world we live in.' But not everyone turned their heads. Though it might have been better had one couple done that. One night a Rolls Royce pulled up and an elegant woman stepped out and approached the soup kitchen. 'I was amazed and stunned but reluctantly gave her two cups of ham soup thinking a generous donation would follow.' Without even a thank you the woman turned away, walked back to the gleaming car and drove off. The hoped-for and much-needed donation never materialized. To Geordie Aitken, letting the rainwater into his soup to make ends meet, it meant two less cups of ham soup for those who genuinely needed it.

Geordie Aitken had severed his ties with Alcoholics Anonymous because of the base pastime of thieving, fighting and conning that some members still indulged in. But back on the sordid streets he did not have as much choice despite his Christianity. On the odd occasion he had to revert to his street-wise intellect while running the George Square soup kitchen. Often a drunken menace would turn on a hapless woman or elderly man as queues formed for the soup. 'When a poor defenceless man or woman was attacked I would down the aggressor then ask the Lord for forgiveness.'

Geordie Aitken worked with the dedicated band of helpers at the George Square soup kitchen for years before moving into the notorious red light area of Glasgow. Every soup kitchen Geordie Aitken had been involved with had been firmly established before his arrival. Now he was to pioneer one of his own. His Loaves and Fishes ministry was to take his evangelical message into the heart of Glasgow's forgotten society. The Christian named it from the biblical passage where Jesus fed the five thousand with five loaves and two fishes.

Geordie Aitken was not to offer fish at his soup kitchen but he was destined to feed thousands of people, the drunks, homeless, drug addicts and prostitutes who roamed the back streets in the very heart of Glasgow. 'My days at George Square had come to an end but my work was just starting.'

The Loaves and Fishes soup kitchen was to become a registered charity and help thousands of people after being set up in 1988. But in its infancy Geordie Aitken, his wife Marion, and a small band of helpers were all that stood between many of the city's dossers and an untimely, hungry death.

For the first six months it didn't even have an official name. On his first night Geordie Aitken headed into the notorious red light district armed with a carrier bag of his wife's clothes and two flasks of soup that Marion had made. He took the bus. The clothes and soup were gobbled up within minutes and Geordie Aitken knew then that there was a need for his soup kitchen. He also encountered the people he was to become a saviour to over the coming years. Most of them would be prostitutes.

The first lady of the night asked him if he was looking for business. The business-like smile which appeared when he said 'Yes' soon disappeared when he added God's business. An exchange of 'f...ing hell, are you a goody-goody' followed.

But the evangelist's street-wise answer paved the way to years of friendship on the streets. 'No, hot lips, I'm a baddy-baddy, trying to be better.'

The hooker burst out laughing and Geordie Aitken had made the sort of conquest he had set out to make. She then took her pick of the clothes from the carrier bags, and took a drink of soup. Mysteriously, she was joined by four colleagues who did the same. As the five walked off, she turned and offered to help Geordie Aitken with his venture. 'My sister works in the local school and she can pinch a soup urn for you if you want.' Explaining that was not the Christian way, but appreciating the gesture, he headed for the bus stop, with a warmth in his heart and two empty flasks.

Marion Aitken, was by now well versed in the art of soup making. Many a time her husband had brought dossers to their home to be fed. She had duly put the soup on. Now she was still making the soup but her husband was dishing it out on the streets. 'Our home had become a haven for the refugees of society so to Marion it was just a part of normal life.' For months he struggled to find a name for his planned soup kitchen. But confident that it was to be the success it later proved to be, all manner of names flashed through his busy mind. One was the five star soup kitchen but it was ditched for being too commercial and not spiritual. 'The name came to me because I was adamant it was going to be the best soup kitchen in Britian.' He was not far wrong. While waiting to christen his venture he continued making the bus trip into the city centre with his carrier bags and flasks. With every visit he attracted more people.

Weeks later he was asked to speak at the Lady of Lourdes Catholic

Seen here with the prostitutes who always had time to share a joke with the evangelist.

First Loaves and Fishes van.

Church and duly turned up in his unkempt state. Wearing his T-shirt bearing the words 'Jesus Saves' on the front in bright red letters, and his Protestant tattoos adorning his arms he admits he didn't exactly cut a dash. One sister turned to him and politely asked, on reading his tattoos, whether he was at the wrong meeting. When he explained who he was and why he was there the elderly nun put her arms around him and gave him a little hug. After the meeting finished a stranger approached Geordie Aitken and offered him a ruined little Honda van for his soup kitchen work. He explained that he had gone bankrupt, and that he was getting rid of his assets. 'What an asset. When he offered the van to the Inland Revenue, to help cover some of his debts they told him to keep it.' Until that moment he had been travelling around in a car with his friend Tom. 'I told him about this great van which would help with the soup runs but he didn't share the same enthusiasm as me. When we went to see it he burst out laughing and said it wasn't safe enough to drive on a road.'

Yet, that little red van when repaired, helped launch the Loaves and

Fishes ministry. Now Geordie Aitken could take his vision out into the streets and help the homeless, drunks and prostitutes.

Full of anticipation he even had an official charity document drawn up with the help of a Glasgow solicitor. Everything had come together and he was now ready to hit the streets.

The street team consisted of himself, a man and a woman. The new avenues that were opening up for Geordie Aitken were to lead him into the hitherto unchartered areas of prostitution and drug abuse.

'We were set to hit the streets of the twilight people who lived in anticipation of their next fix.' But the prostitutes were to play a major part in his evangelical teachings. The message of Christ was as important to Geordie Aitken as the clothes, blankets and soup he dished out. He realized deep down that the street-corner hookers were as genuine as any women he had met and shed countless tears over their plight. But it became a two way thing and he earned the respect of many a hardened hooker. They also had their uses.

Many a time they would help to push his red van when it refused to start. 'The van was a joke as sometimes it would start but more often than not it just wouldn't budge. Often we had to push it along the road with the help of a couple of prostitutes. It was hilarious to see them pushing this van in their high heels and mini skirts while Tom and I prayed out loud for it to start. But nine times out of ten it would cough and splutter then start and keep going, at least until we parked up again.'

One night the van clapped out in the infamous Gorbals, leaving the three volunteers stranded. Geordie Aitken marched into the nearest police station and begged assistance from two strapping officers. 'When the two policemen came out they burst out laughing at the size of this matchbox van. One joked: "Push it? Just pick it up, put it in your pocket and get the bus home." After they had stopped laughing we got a push, and with another loud prayer we headed down the road with two hysterical policemen in tow. Amazingly, it yet again spluttered into some form of life and we managed to get home.'

But in with the laughter came the tears. The twilight world of prostitution was alien to Geordie Aitken and he was to discover the truth about the seedy world the woman lived in. He got to know the girls personally and won their respect for what he did. He and Tom must have been the only men on the streets of Glasgow who wanted them for something other than sex. It became a family affair on the mean streets. 'They were real down-to-earth people with hearts that went out to their mates. How I wish some so-called Christians could take a leaf out of their book when it comes to loyalty and concern for fellow human beings.' One of many who regularly attended the soup kitchen was June, a 23-year-old prostitute with a £160 a day heroin addiction to feed. On the first night she met Geordie Aitken there were tears shed all round. From Geordie his helpers and June as they stood praying together. 'June parted with tears in her eyes heading down a back lane with yet another perverted customer. We saw her for the next few weeks but then she just disappeared. I often wonder to this day if she is dead or alive.' He knows that many of June's street friends are dead. 'Most of the girls we have met have passed away in tragic circumstances. Many of them unintentionally overdosed by forgetting what drugs they had taken, then taking more on top.'

One year on and Geordie Aitken and his team knew every one of the girls on first name terms. Often when one would be locked up they would get word to the soup kitchen that they were in Corton Vale Prison so that he would not unduly worry about them. 'I used to be pleased to hear that they were locked up because at least they were getting a night's sleep, a bath, decent food and the chance to come off heroin.'

When they were back on the streets the Christian trio often had to listen to the graphic details of their twilight trade. 'If we wanted the street girls to listen to us about Christ then we also had to listen to them about their experiences. If I said to those girls that I loved them in Jesus then who am I to judge.'

The Loaves and Fishes scheme had now grown to about ten Christians who worked the streets. The group included a murderer who had given his life to Christ while serving his sentence. He had worked with a colleague as a butcher but when the pair had an argument one day he stabbed him in a fit of anger, and in his panic had cut the body up and fed him through an electric mincer. He would never have been caught had he not confessed to the killing.

He met Geordie Aitken while the Christian evangelist was visiting Scottish prisons, as part of the Christian visiting team. Geordie had said to him then that he ought to come and help with the needy whenever he was released. As soon as he was released he headed for Geordie Aitken's soup kitchen. 'John was a great blessing to everyone at Loaves and Fishes. He was a born-again spirit-filled Christian.'

The soup kitchen was also visited by many of his old gangster friends and hardmen who still ruled the mean streets. Often ten and twenty pound notes would be handed to a toiling Geordie Aitken. Within years the soup kitchen grew to become an integral part of the savage city's everyday street life. As it grew so did the need for a bigger and more reliable van. Geordie Aitken tried a subtle approach at the local Mercedes dealership in the affluent St George's Cross area of the city.

'I felt the boldness of Christ and went in to ask for a van.' But the hardnosed businessman had other ideas. Especially after he had given the would-be customer a cup of tea, guided tour, and thirty minutes of sales pitch. Only to be told that his customer didn't even have his bus fare home, but thought that he might have been given a van out of kindness. 'He must have thought I was some kind of eccentric, when I walked in saying I wanted a brand new Mercedes van. When he showed me the latest top-of-the-range model I said that it would be ideal for the soup kitchen. He thought I was into mobile shops and catering and that I travelled around the building sites and factories selling food.' When Geordie Aitken explained that he didn't have a penny but had thought the dealer might have donated one to his soup kitchen he was unceremoniously shown the door.

With that avenue closed the Christian volunteers raised enough funds to buy a second-hand Ford Transit van for £600 from a man who supplied churches with vans. Getting the van had proved a struggle but the publicity side of it proved disastrous. In a bid to save money Geordie Aitken reverted to his street friends for help. The van needed some artwork and sign-writing and he knew just the man. An alcoholic painter who would do the lot for £25. Geordie Aitken bought the black paint and had the van dropped off at the 'artist's' lodgings. Two days later he was due to collect it.

When he arrived he realized he had made a mistake in offering the job to his friend. On the back was the greeting 'Shallom', complete with two Ls, and a childish drawing of an arthritic chicken. It was the nearest the drunken painter had been able to get to the requested dove.

Geordie raised £600 for new van.

For good measure he had even managed to get Geordie Aitken's telephone number wrong. 'He had told me he had never seen a dove before. I told him that he must never have seen a chicken before either.' But the artist's antics proved a blessing in disguise. 'We were the laughing stock of the roads but I never realized what attention the wrong spelling of shalom and the pathetic looking excuse for a dove would bring. It certainly did the trick but I often wonder which poor soul got the telephone calls that were meant for me.' Undaunted the charitable group continued their work on the streets. The state of the van paled into insignificance once they were back amongst the prostitutes, drunks and drug addicts. As the van stood in various areas of the city the same kerb-crawling punters, would drive slowly past picking out prostitutes.

'West Campbell Street must be one of the busiest in Scotland for traffic because the cars would just drive round in circles. Most of the men were just looking to pick up the needle scarred broken bodies of the street girls. Many businessmen would drive past in their BMWs and fancy cars hiding their faces in case we recognized them.' Many of the perverted punters even offered to work with the soup kitchen staff just to leer at the girls in their skimpy clothes. 'I knew every move of the perverted customer. They wanted to work with us because many of the girls were near topless with mini skirts on. I would tell these guys to go and get lost and that I knew why they wanted to help.'

Those destitute, drug addicted girls had become his life and he was fiercely supportive of them. One in particular summed up the squalor of the streets.

Elizabeth was a beautiful young woman from an upper-class background, her mother a doctor and her father a solicitor. She had been introduced to drugs at art college and later turned to prostitution to pay for her addiction. The needle soon took its toll and the once beautiful society girl now stood at the hatch of the soup kitchen with a massive blood clot in her leg. The veins in her once shapely legs had collapsed through heroin injections. Gangrene set in and her life was only saved after surgeons amputated her left leg. But still she walked the streets.

The typical signs that Geordie Aitken and his dedicated helpers would lay out on the streets to proclaim their Christian message to the world.

On one occasion when Geordie Aitken was due to visit Northern Ireland to speak in prisons, Elizabeth had said to him: 'come home safe, Geordie, because the people of the streets all love you.' Two weeks later he did return home safe. But he discovered that Elizabeth had died in a dingy bedsit after injecting pure heroin into her body.

AIDs and drug abuse were rife amongst the prostitutes and Geordie Aitken very nearly paid with his life for trying to help the girls. The odd stranger would start to work the streets every now and again. Most of the regulars he knew, and they loved him. One stranger he didn't know and she didn't love him either. In trying to bring the drug-crazed hooker to Christ she suddenly turned on him and held an AIDs infected heroin syringe to his neck. 'I can send someone to heaven quicker than you,' she snarled. Undaunted Geordie Aitken said he was not afraid of death and that heaven held no fears for him. He would be happy to go to the Lord if that was his wish. He put his faith in God. The trembling girl dropped the needle, burst into tears and threw her needle ravaged arms around him. It was only hours later that he realized that he had been a millimetre away from an agonizing AIDs inflicted death and he knew that the Lord had spared him, to lead that girl to him. Which Geordie Aitken did on a hot summer night in Glasgow. Most of the girls who walked the streets and sold their bodies did so solely to finance drug addictions. But one woman did it purely for the money.

Mary, with a steady boyfriend, and once an office manager realized that there was more to be made on the streets than in the city centre rat race. Once she handed over £20 of her earnings to the soup kitchen

Geordie Aitken in typical pose handing out soup and clothes from his soup kitchen. The young girl on the right of the picture used to sleep rough in a toilet at Glasgow Royal Infirmary.

sparking a row between Geordie Aitken and one of his helpers. The young woman helping out had urged him to refuse the cash. But to Geordie Aitken the money was not the issue. He had been trying to lead Mary out of her squalid lifestyle for months. 'This girl said to me that we should not take Mary's filthy money, but she could not see that we were trying to win Mary over for Christ. To refuse her money would have been refusing her love for us. The girl would not listen so I politely asked her not to come back to work at the soup kitchen.'

One prostitute gave her life to Christ at the entrance to one of the back lanes where she would entertain her clients. Jean had approached Geordie Aitken saying she was sick of her filthy life and had been contemplating suicide. After listening intently to his testimony she, like countless others before her, burst into tears and threw her arms around him. She left the streets and after treatment in a drug rehabilitation centre returned to a normal life.

Even Geordie Aitken did not know the full horror of her story until he was approached one night at the soup kitchen by an elderly woman. 'She asked if I was Geordie Aitken and then threw her arms around me and thanked me for saving her daughter Jean.' The elderly lady told him how Jean had found her way onto the streets as a prostitute. Her doting father had been murdered years ago as he made his way home from work. Jean cracked up and rebelled against everything good. Once into drugs she also turned to the streets to feed her addiction having been caught in a deadly trap. For years she had cursed God for taking her father from her, but had accepted him into her life at the hands of Geordie Aitken.

One woman, away from the drug scene, had taken to the streets solely to make ends meet for her family. One night Rita asked Geordie Aitken why he worked the soup kitchens without pay. He explained that the best way to get rid of your own worries was to help others and consider their problems. Two weeks later Rita gave her life to Christ, left the streets, and was baptized at the local church, along with the two daughters she had been working the streets to provide for. She is now back on the streets but only to share her testimony with Glasgow's present day prostitutes. When not speaking to them she speaks to the inmates of Scotland's female prisons.

The soup kitchen not only attracted prostitutes but the resident population of dossers and drunks. Despite their own predicaments many of them learned a Christian message over a plastic cup of ham soup.

Andy, a former male nurse, who hit the bottle after his wife ran off with his best friend, often prayed for sobriety. Not just for his own benefit, but so that Geordie Aitken would let him work at the Loaves and Fishes soup kitchen. Until that time came Andy would be found sleeping on top of a heating duct at the back entrance to a Chinese takeaway wrapped in blankets provided by the soup kitchen.

Away from the soup and sandwiches, Loaves and Fishes also took blankets and clothes to the destitute.

Often after collecting cast-offs they would spread the clothes across the pavement and let people take their pick. Such a sad but heartfelt gesture brought much needed humour to the mean streets. 'It would be like an open-air market at times with all the clothes laid out. But I also had to stop many a fight because a lot of stuff came from the rich families, and the poor dossers would fight over it shouting: "get off, I saw it first." Even though they were literally down and out they still wanted the best gear. Life at the soup kitchen was never dull.'

But at times it was heart-breaking.

One man who benefited, albeit in the short term, was a schizophrenic named Charlie, who spent his days wandering the streets and local railway stations, dressed in

Derelict building. Home to six men sleeping on urine-soaked mattresses.

filthy rags, and living on whatever food he could salvage from a wastebin. One night at the Loaves and Fishes soup kitchen he got more than he bargained for. With his soup and sandwich already hungrily devoured, he was kitted out in new clothing. Forcibly.

Geordie Aitken and his dedicated team of helpers literally picked him up, dragged him into the nearest alley, kicking and screaming, and set about transforming him. Twenty minutes later he emerged in his new outfit—a suit, shirt and tie. But still stinking and with his filthy, unkempt beard covering his face. The soup kitchen staff were hoping the external transformation would lead to an inner spiritual transformation. But because of his condition he was beyond help. Years later, he was found dead on a busy Glasgow street.

'You could smell Charlie before you saw him. We dragged him into the back lane and stripped him naked. His foul clothes, covered in faeces and urine were thrown into a wastebin, and we even had to wipe him down with old newspapers before dressing him, from head to toe in new clothes.' When Charlie emerged from the alley, in his suit and tie, everyone at the soup kitchen clapped, cheered and prayed for him. They loved him because they knew his situation was not of his own making. He had been sent out of hospital to fend for himself as part of a radical and cost-cutting government plan to put mentally ill people back into the community.

'From the day he got out he never stood a chance. He had become institutionalized and could not cope on his own. It was horrific to see him wandering the streets barely able to communicate with people. He died as a tramp under the noses of many people on a busy Scottish street.'

'Old Charlie' was 40 when he died in the gutter. Yet there are still scores of others in the same position as Charlie, who have been put out into society and who will not make it. 'Charlie's problems did not stem from drink or drugs just an unfortunate mental condition. Such people are part and parcel of everyday life but nobody seems to be bothered about them. He died simply because of neglect and money saving government measures in what is supposed to be a civilized twentieth-century Britain. He died filthy, stinking, and starving in a gutter when he should have only really been half-way through his life.'

From the days when Geordie Aitken had set out on the bus with carrier bags full of clothes donated by his wife, and two flasks of soup tucked firmly under his arms, his dream of a much needed soup kitchen, in the red light area of Glasgow, had become a reality, and blossomed into an everyday part of Glaswegian life.

In its infancy he had established it by using his £2 a week pocket money to buy ingredients for the soup and a bus pass to get him into the red light area. When that was used up he would walk the streets and rake through fruit shop wastebins for old vegetables.

He even did that while attending Sunday morning services. Before one such service he had received a telephone call from a prostitute telling him she was going to commit suicide and that she wanted him to ask the church minister to pray for her. She had come across his telephone number, knew of his work amongst the prostitutes and hoped she could rely on him for help. She would not tell Geordie Aitken where she was but he still promised he would tell the church minister of the telephone call and her impassioned plea for help.

On the way to church he carried out his usual scavenging in the bins and arrived at the church after the service had started. By the time he found a safe place to leave his salvaged boxes of fruit and vegetables, most of them half stale, and found a seat the service had begun and the minister was into his sermon.

Geordie Aitken was a common sight on the streets of Glasgow with his battered soup urn.

Remembering his promise to the desperate prostitute, and not being one to go back on his word, he was hit by a blind panic. 'I had promised her I would speak to the minister but by the time I got to the service he was already in the pulpit and preaching to hundreds of people.' But having made his promise he knew he had to keep it. And he did.

Geordie Aitken stood up in the middle of the packed church and called out to the minister and informed him publicly of her plight. 'I knew I could not let that girl down as I was the only thing she had.' After explaining to the congregation about the message, and how the prostitute wanted the church to pray for her, the minister stopped the sermon and led the prayers for the prostitute.

In the next morning's newspapers it was reported how a Glaswegian prostitute had been found hanging in a filthy, derelict warehouse in a seedy area of the city.

Such were the incidents Geordie Aitken found himself involved with since taking his Christian message out to the dossers, drunks and prostitutes of Glasgow.

'We had many happy experiences but they were equally matched by the heart-breaking ones. At times, after witnessing the deaths and horrors of the streets, I wished I had never gone out into them. But we also witnessed quite a few miracles in the red light area and took Christ into a lot of lives. The lives of people who needed him most.'

Throughout his early Christianity Geordie Aitken relied heavily on his human tower of strength Duncan Donaldson, a wild fighting man who himself had been saved. He was to prove a blessing to the new convert but in his early days of new-found religion he was as excitable as it would be possible to get.

The eighteen stone giant once marched into a shop and ministered to a silent audience for a full ten minutes, before realizing they were tailors dummies. Even when the novelty of his conversion wore off he took an evangelic message into the streets with the zest and passion he once showed while street fighting. Geordie Aitken will never forget the part Duncan Donaldson played in helping him come to terms with his Christianity. 'He was built like an ox and in his old days used to fight bare-fisted. He once bit a man's jaw off in a fight and when I asked him what had happened to the bloody flesh he said he had eaten it.' Everything he once put into fighting, and he had thirty-three convictions for police assault alone, he now put into preaching. The days when he would bend nails with his teeth then squeeze them tight with his massive fingers were behind him when he took to preaching with Geordie Aitken. But he retained his wicked, down-to-earth sense of humour. If anyone called a spade a spade Duncan Donaldson did.

That point was graphically illustrated when both Duncan and Geordie were asked to speak at a local mission hall. Resplendent in his favourite T-shirt, complete with the message 'Under New Management' emblazoned across the front, Duncan led Geordie Aitken, himself dressed in T-shirt and arms covered in tattoos, to the door of the upmarket church. 'The minister thought we were a couple of drunks when we turned up. He had been told that we were evangelists, but he didn't realize what kind of evangelists we really were.' And things actually got worse for the hapless minister.

Inside the church, and about to give his testimony, Duncan heaved his huge frame onto the wooden platform to join the despondent minister and duly set the floor boards creaking. Without hesitation he looked at the minister and asked, in a booming voice: 'Excuse me, Reverend, but did you fart? Are you perhaps bothered with wind?'

Lost for words the red-faced reverend mumbled out: 'Indeed I did not. And if I had wanted to I would have gone into the toilet.'

But the uncouth exchange broke the ice at the meeting. 'Duncan was a great guy, not very high on intellect, but very bold for Jesus. The great thing about that exchange was that scores of people burst out laughing and many were later led to Christ.'

Despite their earthy behaviour their powerful preaching carried them on and into many churches and homes. Duncan Donaldson had been saved in 1964, and had a nine year start on Geordie Aitken in the Christianity stakes. Geordie Aitken might not have had his experience but he shared his passion for preaching.

One night at a house gathering, the two of them proved miracles do happen. One man formally dressed in a suit and tie passed a snide remark about the unkempt pair and singled out Geordie Aitken's haircut for special mention.

Geordie Aitken with the towering Duncan at his back, strode up to the man and asked him if he believed in miracles, and if he had ever witnessed one. The sneering guest replied that he hadn't and was he about to see one. The smaller of the two evangelists duly informed his tormentor that he was indeed witnessing one right there and then and explained that he had overheard the remark, and if he truly wasn't a Christian he would have broken his nose and jaw and left him for Duncan. The pair then strode off into the kitchen area of the house where their hosts had prepared a meal for the gathering.

As the dozen guests sat around the table waiting for the food to be served the host wandered back and forth with various dishes. Her first mistake was to put an enormous meat pie down near to Duncan. She turned her back to return to the kitchen for the accompanying vegetables and the hungry evangelist tore into the pie which was meant for everyone. Right into the middle of it went his fork and by the time the woman returned he was busy carving it up. On seeing her shocked face, and those of the other guests, he immediately realized his error and tried to patch up the pie with his fingers. Knowing that the other guests had lost their interest in the pie she told him to eat what he could, and she would rustle up a salad for everyone else. By the time she had prepared the substitute salad Duncan had cleared the plate.

Wherever the pair went misfortune followed but whatever the cause of it people were also saved. They were indeed saving souls wherever they preached. And they would preach anywhere, churches, houses, streets and even bus stations and car parks.

It was at the Buchanan Street bus station, in central Glasgow, that Duncan performed a similar miracle to that of his close friend, when he was insulted about his haircut. This time it was Duncan who was on the receiving end of a drunken agitator in the crowd of people who had stopped to hear the two evangelists preach. Not wanting any distractions to spoil his preaching, and feeling a little upset about being called names and having raspberries blown at him, he approached the man, grabbed him with one hand by the throat and lifted him three feet off the ground. He then asked the man if his jaw was sore before explaining that the miraculous thing was that it was only tender and not crushed. He politely told him that in his old days he would have battered him senseless and not only fractured his jaw but his skull as well. On being planted firmly back on the ground the shaking man ran down the street as the crowd clapped and cheered.

As usual, the two men carried on to lead more people to the Lord. One of Duncan's proudest possessions was a carved cross made for him by Geordie Aitken. But he had problems in getting to grips with it. Having completed the mahogany cross, Geordie Aitken could not afford to cover the back of it in green felt. So he used a strip of patterned wallpaper to line the back of the wooden creation. Duncan's eyes lit up when he was presented with the gift. But Geordie Aitken later discovered that it was the pretty wallpaper and the not intricate carvings that had taken his fancy. On a visit to his house he found the wooden cross proudly hanging above Duncan's fireplace back to front.

No amount of cajoling could get the big man to turn it around and display his little friend's handiwork to the world. 'That was typical of Duncan Donaldson. It took me months to hand carve that cross but Duncan took more of a liking to the pretty wallpaper on the back of it and that was that. There wasn't much point in arguing with the big fella once he had made his mind up about something.'

One of the things that he had made his mind up about, regardless of the consequences was a massive signpost which he planted in his garden bearing the words 'Jesus Saves'. It caught the eye of not only everyone in the street but also the local planning officials who liked people to ask for consent before erecting such things. Duncan Donaldson had the consent of the Lord and that was all he needed. Like the wooden crucifix it stayed exactly the way he wanted.

Both in his wild days and in his Christian days he got what he wanted. But when he died he got something nobody expected. Strathclyde police, whom he hounded during the early years of his drunken life, actually gave him a guard of honour and saluted as his coffin was carried through the Airdrie streets. An honour normally reserved for heroes. But to Geordie Aitken and everyone associated with Duncan Donaldson, he was a hero. To young and old alike in the name of the Lord.

Through his Christianity people realized that he had a heart big enough to match his massive frame. But the police send-off still came as a surprise to many people. In his drunken days he would often lie in a cemetery or graveyard and get drunk on cheap wine. Whenever police came to arrest him he warned them not to even think about it until he had finished the bottle. If they tried, all hell broke loose and often reinforcements had to be drafted in to help. The local officers even had special handcuffs made to fit his massive wrists. Many of his thirty-three convictions for fighting with police came out of the graveyard shift. He once told Geordie Aitken that it was the only place he could find peace. All he wanted was to be left alone to drink himself into a stupor, sleep it off then return home to his wife the next day. More often than not a police presence prevented that.

'Duncan Donaldson loved the graveyards because he said they were the only places he could find real peace. He told me that living people always seemed to give him a hard time but he could be at peace with those who had passed away.' Whatever his problem with Strathclyde police they publicly declared their real feelings for him when he died in 1992. The once under-pressure arresting officers stood in silent tribute to the man they genuinely respected. 'Duncan Donaldson helped me along life's way and was a real person. I wish he was still alive today.'

By the time of his big friend's death Geordie Aitken had been saved for nearly ten years and in that decade had shared many fantastic experiences with big Duncan. He knows he can never be replaced but takes comfort that he is happy with the heavenly father, and some day the two men will be reunited. 'I know that big Duncan is now truly happy, and it will be a marvellous day when we are reunited in the presence of the Lord.'

An angel held my hand one night
and took me on a heavenly flight
I passed the moon and silver stars
then whizzed around the planet Mars

We headed down the Milky Way
and saw some other angels play
Their robes were a lovely shimmering white
That could brighten up the darkest night

Then further into the Universe
silver dust we did disperse
Further on we flew with ease
behind us blew a heavenly breeze

Fragrance from some heavenly flowers
filled our nostrils for many hours
Oh what a joy was in my heart
this heavenly flight I was a part

Then we came upon this land
of crystal seas and golden sand
The grass was green, green as can be
exotic birds on swaying trees

My heavenly host was showing me
what like it is to be set free
From this flesh of skin and bone
with my angel friend I am not alone

So thank you angel for the flight
that helped to pass my lonely night
In my dreams I'll think of you
my angelic friend with eyes so blue

The Flight

# CHAPTER 8

# An Early Walk with God

With his new found Christianity he was to prove invaluable in all walks of life. In the coming years he would find himself talking to everyone from schoolchildren to social workers, and pensioners to policemen.

He would also, after moving on from his soup kitchen work, find himself taking his evangelical message to the prisons of America, Northern Ireland, England and also still across Scotland. But countless people, as well as prisoners, were to benefit from the words of the one-time violent alcoholic who had risen from the gutters and dragged himself from the brink of death to take to the streets and lead people to the Lord.

In his native Scotland his worth was being fully appreciated right across the board and close to home, in East Kilbride, Glasgow, he was to become a firm favourite with the local Catholic priests and in the region's Catholic schools. A far cry from his earlier Orange Lodge days when his main purpose for living was to hound and batter his Catholic enemies.

He became a regular speaker in the schools and churches that now housed his new friends in the eyes of God. One such school was St Bride's RC School, East Kilbride, where his first talk with the pupils came about in mysterious circumstances. The school's head of religious education, Chris Hughes, was looking for someone to speak to the children and had asked Fr Bogan and Fr Ryan, of the adjoining parish church, if they knew of anyone who would fit the bill.

Both priests were now friends of a certain Geordie Aitken and suggested to Chris Hughes that his no-nonsense evangelical message and his life's experiences and the hardships he had overcome might strike a chord with the pupils. They knew that Geordie Aitken could talk about life on the streets without equal. He would be able to relate to the pupils while still getting his Christian message across.

Geordie Aitken pictured with teacher Chris Hughes and pupils of St Bride's School.

The only problem was that they only saw him when he popped in, usually unannounced, for a chat and a cup of tea. They had not seen him for over a month and did not know when he would be visiting again. They knew his numerous ministries often took him out of the region and that he could indeed be evangelizing almost anywhere. All the two priests could do was advise Chris Hughes to keep a note of his name and the next time they saw him they would pass on the school's interest.

The very next day, Geordie Aitken, and his trusty Labrador dog, turned up at the church house in the grounds of the school for an impromptu visit. This was to herald a meaningful and constructive relationship with the staff and pupils of St Bride's School.

Chris Hughes remembers how after his first talk at the school he could barely get the pupils to go home. Such was the powerful message being delivered by this captivating speaker called Geordie Aitken.

'We are always looking for people to come in and talk to the children and one day Fr Bogan suggested Geordie Aitken would be perfect as he has a very lurid background but unfortunately he had not been around to see them for some time. The very next day he appeared with his dog.'

Things progressed from that day and Geordie Aitken now regularly talks to the appreciative schoolchildren and Chris Hughes knows he is getting an important message across to them. 'It is literally unscripted stuff and he is a natural storyteller. The first time he spoke at the school the bell sounded at the end of the day but not one person moved. Usually you have to stand back to prevent getting caught in the stampede for the doors.'

Such was his influence at the school, word soon spread throughout the building about this former hardline Protestant who now spoke from the Bible, that even those younger children at the school who had never met him offered to help him in his charity work. The school even chose him as the subject of its annual fundraising event and collected foodstuffs and goods that they knew he would ensure reached the homeless and dossers who needed them most. Regularly at Christmas times he would leave the school with dozens of boxes of donated tins and parcels.

'It would have been an insult to offer him money so we asked what we could do to help him in recognition of the invaluable work he was doing at the school. In typical fashion he asked us to help those whom he himself was helping. Every Christmas he now goes away with stacks of parcels and the reason we chose Geordie Aitken is because of his value to the school in speaking to the children. They love him and his work with the needy so much that many of them even offered to go out and help him on the streets. But, sadly, it would be too dangerous for them on the streets so everyone collects instead in the knowledge that the much-needed items will get to the destitute people who need them.'

Away from the earthy and dangerous streets of Glasgow, Chris Hughes also knows how important a Christian message Geordie Aitken can deliver to the pupils. Often he has been invited to speak at special school seminars in the company of local celebrities, footballers and star personalities. Despite sharing the platform with famous sportsmen and showbiz personalities he still delivers the same forthright message that he does to the children during school talks. The message that faith can conquer everything.

In the area where he preaches and addresses the children the sectarian divide is immense. Deep-rooted hatred between Catholics and Protestants still exists and Geordie Aitken uses himself as living proof that such bigotries and religious divides can be bridged. Chris Hughes has been in the audience, with hundreds of pupils, when the tough-talking Scotsman has stunned meetings into silence simply by showing the devout Catholics his tattooed arms depicting his one-time fervent allegiance to the Protestant cause. Geordie Aitken makes no secret of the fact that 'at one time I would have gladly burnt the whole school down—and with everyone in it.'

But Chris Hughes knows those sort of remarks only help him hammer his amazing conversion message home. 'It is so divided in Scotland that to see someone like him cross that divide is amazing. It is a miracle that someone like Geordie Aitken can even survive in a Catholic school. But for the pupils to hear about Christianity from him is fascinating. He speaks a language they don't expect to hear as Christianity to them is very formal.'

With two of his closest friends. Catholic priests Fr Bogan and Fr Ryan.

Geordie Aitken says his constructive work with the children is a two-way thing. 'Just as I can, hopefully, help them, then so, too, do they help me in my faith. Without their love and kindness my ministry for Christ just couldn't continue.'

In the nearby church house of St Bride's both priests know of the love and kindness Geordie Aitken talks about in his own down-to-earth way. Their meetings are more casual and informal and usually when the tattooed evangelist drops in to share their dinners with them. Such is the friendship that he is always assured of a warm meal and a warm welcome.

Fr Ryan, a tough Irishman, who spent five years in the notorious Easterhouse area of Glasgow as a parish priest, can relate to the street-level evangelism Geordie Aitken preaches. He still laughs about the time Geordie Aitken was heading home and passed a Church of Scotland meeting hall where a poster was announcing a forthcoming event to celebrate the work of Scottish folk hero Rabbie Burns. The poster read: 'Spend the night with Rabbie Burns for £1'. Geordie Aitken instinctively walked over to it, crossed out the wording and altered it to read: 'Spend the night with Jesus for nothing'. It is his active and down to earth approach that Fr Ryan knows is special to Geordie Aitken.

'There is something practical about his preaching which people can relate to. He makes faith alive for people and challenges them in their beliefs.' Fr Ryan also knows how important his work at the school is. 'The kids really get shaken up by him as they have never met anyone like him. You can see them looking around and asking "Who is this man?" He is brilliant for them because you can't have too many characters in the place.'

His colleague, Fr Bogan, knows from his teachings at the adjoining St Bride's school the full worth of Geordie Aitken. He simply compares him to a massive advertising hoarding that hangs on a gas tower on the approach to Glasgow. It reads: 'Glasgow is Alive'. Fr Bogan thinks exactly the same about Geordie Aitken.

'He is alive in his faith. We have a great time when Geordie Aitken is around because we know what we are talking about as he is so convinced of his faith. He has the gift of communication and his own faith shines through in a real-life way. It is easy to relate to him when his personality shines through in such a way.'

As it is with the schoolchildren of St Bride's, Geordie Aitken knows his own faith is enhanced by both Fr Ryan and Fr Bogan. 'Whenever I visit them I feel as if I am getting my batteries recharged. Just saying hello to these two men gives me a spiritual lift as I know they are returning my love.'

Whichever school he visits, be it St Bride's School, Taylor High School or John Ogilvie High School the welcome is always the same. Many schools in the area know his worth. Many Catholic churches also know the worth of the man who has taken Christianity out into the streets. It is on the streets that he feels most at home and uses his

Geordie often addresses schools and colleges.

old experiences of his days on those same streets to get his message across. Usually there is humour involved. Even if he is not involved personally he can use incidents and escapades to help him get his street-level message across in a humorous way. A way that people can understand and accept.

One religious escapade he will never forget is when a Monsignor from Rome visited the massive St Andrew's Cathedral in Glasgow. Weeks before the glittering service, orders were dished out during rehearsals as to who would do what and when. The job of welcoming the Monsignor, by kneeling down and kissing his ring, before escorting him down the cathedral aisle, was given to Geordie Aitken's lay minister friend Jimmy. As the big day approached and nerves started fraying, Jimmy, who already had a liking for the drink, decided to invest in some Dutch courage and duly bought a couple of bottles of wine.

Geordie with pupils of Taylor High School.

On the big day he slipped into the confessional box and polished both of them off. With the arrival of the Monsignor, Jimmy duly approached him and knelt gingerly down before puckering his lips to the massive Papal ring. No problem with that. But in trying to stand up again he lost his balance and toppled over backwards. In desperation he grabbed the Monsignor and pulled him down on top of him leaving the two men in a heap on the cathedral floor. For good measure the Monsignor's resplendent robes lifted up over his head leaving his underwear in full public view. Most of the congregation looked on embarrassed but a few could not contain their laughter. To a backdrop of giggles the two men made it down the aisle but not in the expected manner. 'They proceeded to carry a mumbling and apologetic Jimmy out into the back of the cathedral while four men carried the startled Monsignor into one of the vestibules by his arms and legs.'

Wherever Geordie Aitken went something invariably happened but the events were not always humorous. Away from the churches and school of Glasgow he continued to work amongst the needy people in the dosshouses and back streets of the evil city. One such place that he often helped at was the dire Talbot Centre where the 'lepers of society' lived. Here were the worst cases of alcohol and physical abuse it was possible to encounter.

Today the Centre has taken on a new image but when Geordie Aitken would visit its residents they would be lying on urine-soaked mattresses dying slow agonizing deaths. The realization of how easily he could have been one of them had he not been saved by the Lord, dawned on him in graphic detail one day when he went to the centre with some food and clothes and to pray with the homeless drunks who called it home. The building itself, formerly a theatre, had been condemned and would have been demolished were it not for the suffering souls it provided with a much-needed place to sleep. It stank with urine and faeces, the overpowering stench emanating from the 100 or so men who slept on the rows of plastic mattresses. One of those 100 men was to make Geordie Aitken realize just how close he had been to extinction in his own earlier drinking days. Lying on one of the filthy, sodden mattresses was his old school friend Robert. The chronic alcoholic was lying half-dead after discharging himself from hospital following an emergency operation to remove a blood clot from his brain. The hospital packing was actually still inside his head.

'It was like a pre-Victorian workhouse with many of the men lying crying their eyes out and covered in vomit, urine and faeces.'

After spotting his old friend Geordie Aitken knelt by his mattress and cradled his head in his lap and prayed for the hopeless case. It was then that the full horror of Robert's situation hit him. 'As I cradled his head I noticed the big piece of wadding in his head and he told me he had discharged himself from the Southern General Hospital because he had been choking for a drink. That man's life was at stake but he had signed himself out after surgery and with the packing still in his head, just for booze.'

Shortly after his visit his friend died a stinking lonely death after choking on his own vomit. Many others in the Talbot Centre were in similar states but for some it was because of circumstances out of their control. In with the drunken dossers lay schizophrenics who had been discharged from hospitals and left to fend for themselves on the mean Scottish streets. 'These people had once been looked after in hospitals but had been released and were now lying on urine-soaked mattresses in a stinking dirty dosshouse in Glasgow.' On the streets of the city Geordie Aitken experienced the highs and lows of life. Usually they were the lows but he continued to preach at gutter level.

His only respite from the everyday horrors of his home city came in the shape of a 600-year-old abbey in the Scottish wilds. To this day Geordie Aitken still finds comfort, takes a well-earned rest and recharges his batteries in the company of the monks and brothers who live at Nunraw Abbey. Having roughed it in the back streets of Glasgow and worked knee deep in vomit and excrement he was understandably apprehensive about his links with the Catholic monks who inhabit the abbey. 'I had never even seen a monk at firsthand before and when I did meet my first monk I thought the man was a member of the Ku-Klux-Klan.' But whatever he initially thought he soon realized the invaluable Christian works that the monks of Nunraw Abbey do with problem people. Not only do they have an outside dormitory for drunks and dossers whom they feed, but they also welcome everyday working people to the abbey where they can find Christ and spend some peaceful moments alone.

People from all walks of life visit and stay at the picturesque abbey as guests of the self-sufficient monks. The main abbey now houses those who go on a retreat there while the 'new' Sancta Maria Abbey is home to the monks and also provides them with a place of solitude and a place where they can speak in confidence with their visitors. That itself was part-built by an army of Scotsmen and Englishmen living on a camp on the site and made up of people from the lower levels of society. The new abbey was opened on 22 August 1954, in front of a crowd of 13,000 people happy to be at the grand opening despite the rain, mist and mud that greeted them. The Cistercian monks repeatedly and publicly proclaim their gratitude to the 'good men who came in the summer months and gave their long hours of voluntary labour.' But it is also the older abbey which draws crowds of people to the Scottish wilds. Many have come away enlightened and happier after a visit to Nunraw Abbey.

Despite his initial misgivings, one of the greatest blessings to come from Geordie Aitken's conversion was his introduction to Nunraw Abbey. Not least because he was probably the first Orange Order man to be accepted by the Catholic monks as a friend. He was introduced to the monks eight years ago by devout Catholic Brian Roberts.

Brian, an ex-boxer, befriended Geordie Aitken following his conversion and after talking about the abbey at a Christian meeting he

Nunraw Abbey.

promised to take Geordie Aitken, complete with his spiritual transformation, to the abbey.

The pious monks were alarmed, at the very least, when the stocky tattooed evangelist started visiting them. But he soon won them over with his unique brand of street-level evangelism and later discovered that Brother Stephen, who was to become one of his closest friends, actually had a similar background to himself. He hailed from Glasgow, had once been a street bookmaker and admittedly, at one time, had been heavily involved with drink. He had visited the abbey over forty years ago to get away from the streets of Glasgow and has never been out of it since.

Such was the peace and tranquility that he decided to stay. Even a 'rescue' mission by his brother failed to bring him home. Indeed his brother ended up staying at the abbey as well. The former commando saw what his older brother had seen and decided the life suited him. He took the name of the patron saint of Glasgow and has been known as Brother Kentigern ever since. Both of them are fine exponents of the Christian doctrines and also firm friends of Geordie Aitken. Such was the rapport between the monks and Geordie Aitken that he even tried to join the order and live at the abbey. Jokingly the monks told him, in reference to his heavily tattooed arms: 'Maybe if you get two arm transplants.'

Although not on a permanent basis he was accepted into the monastic way of life and helped out at the abbey in whatever way he could to show his gratitude to the monks. When at the abbey he would, and still does, help out with decorating and refurbishment work, and when back in Glasgow collects food and clothes to take to the self-sufficient monks on his next visit.

Once, he and his friends took a van load of tinned stew up to the abbey. Packed solid, his Transit van from the Loaves and Fishes soup kitchen made the trip to the remote abbey where lines of monks helped pass the boxes of stew along a human chain into the abbey. 'We had been given thousands of tins and stew and thought it would come in handy for the monks. They are prepared to help anyone and always

With Brother Kentigern (right) and Brother Steven. Nunraw.

need the extra. When we got there the monks lined up and helped to pass these tins into the monastery. It was like something out of a *Carry On* film watching them all lined up, all shapes and sizes in their brown habits, manhandling all of this stew.' Despite the funny side of things he knew there was a deadly serious trust and respect behind their friendship.

Despite often going to the abbey for a rest he finds himself involved with the people who go there on retreat and more often than not he will be found counselling and comforting people during his short breaks at the abbey. Often a planned two-day break will last a week if his services are needed. 'My introduction to Nunraw Abbey was very fruitful by seeing God's love at work amongst the monks and also because it allowed me to exercise my own love for the needy. God had taken me to this beautiful abbey to meet many hurting folks who suffered badly with drink and depression and I also met people who had lost the will to live and were contemplating suicide.'

A prime example, only one of many which Brother Stephen can testify to, of Geordie Aitken's down-to-earth evangelism came at the abbey when he encountered a troubled looking middle-aged woman who would not join in any communal conversations but who just sat and stared at the ceilings. 'The rest that I thought I had gone to the abbey for did not materialize as within the abbey walls there were many problems within the visiting residents.'

One such woman with problems was 40-year-old Jane. Having noticed her obvious depression Geordie Aitken set out to cheer her up but his first attempt to break the ice ended in disaster. 'All she did was sit and stare at the ceiling with a very heavy spirit and in trying to figure out what was bothering her I sat beside her and said hello. All she did was give me the most evil look anyone could ever give and then complete silence.'

He later prayed to the Lord to give him the words of wisdom needed to comfort the suffering woman but realized it was not so much heavy counselling and theological verses that she needed but just simply cheering up. Mindful of his pious surroundings, Geordie Aitken took the bull by the horns, sat next to the woman and said: 'Hello, gorgeous, how are you today?'

'I half-expected her to cut me in two with her tongue or give me another icy stare but instead she gave me a small smile before looking back at the ceiling.' Undeterred, and actually half-encouraged by the slight response he tried to start up a conversation. After the woman quietly told him that she liked to look at the ceiling while thinking things over he instinctively told her that he often did the same thing. Despite sitting in his religious surroundings he told her that the thing he thought about most was winning the football pools, becoming famous and having scores of beautiful blonde woman sitting at his feet as he lounged lazily on a plush sofa. He knew it was a lie, and not the sort of conversation the woman would have expected in a monastery but he gambled on his down-to-earth conversation getting her attention.

The earthy conversation did indeed do the trick and the woman was soon talking and laughing with him. By the end of the week Jane was out of her depression and actually joining in the communal fellowship meetings and for the first time in months actually laughing and smiling.

Geordie Aitken was later to learn the full extent of his actions, and just how invaluable he had once again proved to be, when he discovered just what was behind the woman's depression. Her husband had left her for her best friend and she was pregnant at the time he walked out on her. Shortly after that, while she was still carrying the child, her other child was killed in a motorcycle accident. She had gone to the abbey, in later years, to blot out the memories and laughter was the last thing on her mind as she became lodged in the realms of manic depression. Yet by the time she left Nunraw Abbey she was looking forward to life in the outside world, rejoining a church and meeting new friends.

Through his down-to-earth manner, and persistence, Geordie had won the woman back from the depths of despair and led her to the Lord. During her stay at Nunraw Abbey the woman gave her life to Christ and Geordie Aitken later heard that she had fulfilled all of her intentions and was living a happy life back in Edinburgh. 'The tears that Jane shed at Nunraw Abbey were heavy and plentiful but they were tears of cleansing and joy as she gave her life to Christ.'

Whether inside or outside the abbey Geordie Aitken always had time for people and their problems. Outside the main abbey building is a small hut which the monks have kitted out for dossers and drunks to use. Often on his walks around the sprawling grounds Geordie Aitken would pass the unfortunate souls and see in them a reflection of his earlier drunken days. In offering up his prayers to the Lord for leading him away from his past life he also takes every opportunity to minister to the drunks.

'Many, many alcoholics stay at the abbey either to dry out or find solace in Christ and I have managed to help a few of them stay sober. I tell them to join Alcoholics Anonymous but if they don't want to do that then I tell them they should join themselves to Christ as he definitely has the power to sober up the worst drunk in the universe.'

But Geordie Aitken knows that whatever help he is during his short stays at the abbey it is the monks who offer such help every day of the year without fail.

'The most important thing is that the monks are not interested in what denomination people are. How I wish others would take a leaf out of their book when it comes to loving the unloved. Although I may not agree with doctrinal issues I certainly agree with their love for Christ and other people and how they don't worship money, fancy clothing or any kind of material gain.' The respect and pride that Geordie Aitken has for the dedicated monks is reciprocated by them.

Brother Stephen knows the full value of the little Glaswegian evangelist. 'He can certainly get a message across to people and one that is very important. He is a fiery man who will not let go and his faith is a very basic and simplistic one which people can understand. He also has a tremendous sense of humour and he can perk anyone up and often cheers many people up during his visits to the abbey. When it comes to faith, and an interpretation of it, he is certainly different.'

Word was soon spreading throughout the abbey about this one-time bitter and violent Orangeman who had found Christ and who was now spreading his message. Often the secluded monks would ask to see his militant tattoos and then tell him what a trophy of grace he was and how much they loved him in the eyes of the Lord. He would spend many long hours in conversation with the monks in a bid to strengthen his faith. Usually, he would walk among the rolling hills with them, and often as he was learning they would be left laughing as he recounted his colourful past to them. One of the older monks, Brother Andrew would sit for hours talking with Geordie Aitken. It was one of the darkest days at Nunraw Abbey when Brother Andrew passed away. The solemn ceremony still brings tears to Geordie Aitken's eyes. The monks are buried without much ado by their fellow monks in the grounds of the monastery, their graves marked only with a simple, small white wooden cross.

'Brother Andrew taught me a lot about my faith and I used to return that by having him laughing heartily at some of my drunken escapades. We would spend hours walking in the woods just chatting like two friends. When I compare those days with my earlier drunken days I realize just how much I have to thank God for. The simplest things like just talking and walking with the monks hold some of my fondest memories. Although Brother Andrew is a great loss I know I will be continuing my conversations with him in heaven and that he is there at this moment waiting for me.'

He also knows that as he continues to push himself to the limit through his evangelical work in various parts of the world there is always a welcoming bed awaiting him at the abbey and a hot meal with the dedicated monks who live in it.

'Many prayers have been said for myself and my family by all of the monks at Nunraw Abbey and also by many of the people who have visited there. I thank God for all of them as I know that many of their

Monks' graveyard. Nunraw Abbey.

prayers have been answered. We should take Nunraw Abbey as a starting point for revival as the love of Christ is definitely there. Let the rolling hills that surround the abbey sing the praises of God and let the voices of angels be heard above the moans and groans of the suffering people that descend upon the abbey. It is my honour and privilege to know the monks, past and present, of Nunraw Abbey as there is so much love amongst them. The time is here for all Christians to unite in God, love and mercy so that together we can make this selfish world a much better place to live in.'

The faith and hope that Geordie Aitken gleans from the monks at Nunraw Abbey helps him on his travels and in his deep belief that a simplistic faith in the Lord can overcome problems and alleviate suffering. Everyone he meets with the spirit of God in them serves to strengthen his own faith and fuels the fiery love he has for his Saviour. The abbey is typical of the simplistic faith he believes in and which leads him into contact with everyday people away from the established churches with once rejected him.

Since his conversion he has travelled back to many of his old haunts and has been forced to relive the horrors and suffering that he once inflicted upon himself in his dark past. Whether that suffering is experienced in Scotland, Northern Ireland, England or America he knows that people all suffer the same and that their main hope of survival is through the Lord. In most of the places where he had once roughed it, drank, fought or even worked he was destined to return as a Christian.

Years after his conversion Geordie Aitken was to return to the Shetland Islands with a different message from that of his membership of Alcoholics Anonymous and his involvement with the trade unions. His previous experiences had left him a broken man but now he was returning as a spirit-filled Christian. He set off for a two-week mision to the wild islands with the Reverend Jim Martin, a Scottish church minister, to witness to the hardy islanders in and around the Lerwick area and in many places where he had once delivered a message of sobriety. Now he was delivering an evangelical message.

'To think that an ex oil bear, who would have once fought with his own shadow, was now heading back to the Shetland Islands with a message of love via the Lord. My two weeks evangelizing for Christ on the rough island streets proved very fruitful indeed as many folks came to know the supernatural powers of the living Christ through my own testimony and through my love and concern for them.'

In a throwback to his earlier occult days, Geordie's spiritual strength was tested to the limit. Not only did he mix it with the alcoholics and drugs addicts but also with the demonically possessed. One night he was challenged by a young witch who arrived at the meeting he was due to address in Lerwick with the Reverend Jim Martin and the local minister Reverend Raymond Cowie. The 23-year-old witch had earlier been seen worshipping in the local graveyard and calling out in the name of Satan. With two terrified teenagers in tow the woman marched into the packed hall where the islanders held their Lighthouse Fellowship meetings and publicly challenged Geordie Aitken about the power of Christ.

Apart from the macabre and extraordinary sequence of events what Geordie Aitken will never forget is the woman's ice-cold blue eyes staring into his as she tried to delve into his very soul in front of a stunned crowd.

'She came to challenge me publicly in the power of Satan against the power of Christ. She was a beautiful young woman but she actually stood there hissing like a serpent and staring at me with those steely cold blue eyes and screaming "I challenge you in the name of Lucifer."' During the supernatural showdown the evangelist's whole body shook as he faced her across the packed meeting hall. On either side of her sat two young disciples, also silently glaring at their spiritual foe. 'I felt my whole body vibrating but on the outside I was holding up bravely. I was like a martyr willing to go to my death for my faith.' As she stood hissing and spitting at her Christian enemy Geordie Aitken bellowed out: 'I rebuke you in the name of the Lord Jesus Christ and I challenge you through the power of the Holy Spirit and will prove to you and others that the power of Jesus Christ overrules every power to come out of the darkness of Hell.' With those words he pointed an accusing finger at the snarling woman and, as can be verified by the two ministers and the packed hall, watched as the young witch stumbled backwards and fell silently to the floor. A trembling and sweating Geordie Aitken prayed out loud as he stood over the woman: 'Lord, please touch this wee girl and bring her into the kingdom of heaven but Lord let her rest in your spirit until such time as you are ready to awaken her.'

An agonizing thirty minutes later the trembling woman rose to her feet and walked towards Geordie Aitken before throwing her arms around him and bursting into tears. She tearfully asked Geordie Aitken to help her and asked him about his faith. She begged him to sing his favourite hymn to her and within seconds, the theme of his conversion, How Great Thou Art, was reverberating throughout the packed hall as the stunned congregation joined in the singing. 'Through that very hymn I had the joy of leading this young woman to the Lord.' The transformed witch later joined the Lighthouse Fellowship meetings and became a part of the Christian community. During his two-week stay on the island she told him how her mother had also been a witch and also of the horrors she had endured through her Satanic beliefs.

'The girl used to be sexually assaulted by male spirits from the other side as she lay in her bed at night. Her mother had actually experienced the same things and this young woman had even once told people how enjoyable it had been. That shows you the filth that some of these things are all about but it also shows you the power of Jesus in overcoming these things, Jesus also works in a supernatural way but not in the filthy ways of Satan.'

Away from the supernatural Geordie Aitken continued in a more spiritual manner and preached on the streets to the island's drunks and drug addicts. 'I went over there for two weeks to win over the drunks and drug addicts for Christ. The Shetland Islands is an open port for drugs and the area is beset with severe drink and drug problems. I was working the streets, where I am more at home, and many people came to the Lord. I have never really evangelized in big fancy churches except when I have been invited to speak about my past life. At many nominal churches they would only want to know about the filth in my life and didn't really want to know about the miracles of Jesus, the present and the future.'

On those rough and ready island streets he ministered to drunks, homeless, drug addicts, and even a gang of wild Hell's Angels bikers. 'There were a lot of rough teenagers that came to the Lord because they would say to me "if Christianity is what Geordie Aitken is all about then we don't mind having it. We want real people like him."'

Many of the islanders had self-inflicted drink problems but one woman had a harrowing tale to tell after being introduced to Geordie

Aitken. The bloated, repulsive alcoholic arrived at one of his sermons in Lerwick Baptist Church and drew his atention by screaming and shouting at him as he stood ministering from the tiny pulpit. The next day she approached him in the street, in a drunken stupor, and asked him about his work for the Lord, before collapsing in a drunken heap. He later discovered it had been a ploy to get him back to her home because moments after he helped her back to her house she stripped naked and stood in the middle of the room. He refused her advances and told the pathetic looking woman to get a grip on herself and think about trying to salvage her life. But the real heartache behind her seemingly wanton behaviour was to come out when Geordie Aitken told his friend the Reverend Jim Martin of the woman's behaviour.

The minister told him that the woman tried the same trick with many of the islanders and anyone who approached her house from the local postman to the village milkman. He also told Geordie Aitken what had driven her to do it and why her mind was in such a state. Years ago she had been a beautiful career-minded air hostess who had been introduced to social drinking and partying by air crews during their many stopovers in foreign parts. The drink finally took hold of her and she developed an alcoholic addiction. Ironically, having been introduced to drink through her work her heavy boozing ultimately cost her her job.

Back in her native Shetland Islands even worse was in store for the now redundant air hostess. Once, while in her customary drunken state she had been smuggled onboard a Russian factory ship for 'a laugh with the crew'. It turned out to be anything but funny when the container ship set sail, with her still on board, and at the mercy of the ship's crew. She was eventually put ashore in Germany wearing only a tattered dress and a Russian overcoat. After stumbling around and being taken to the British Consulate she was flown back to the Shetlands. Not surprisingly her drinking binges worsened and she became a regular sight rolling around in the streets.

'I would never have imagined her as an attractive career girl as by the time I met her alcoholism had taken a grip on her. It gets hold of you very quickly, mentally, physically and spiritually and she was the walking proof of the damage it can do to you.'

Geordie Aitken continued his ministering but to this day does not know whether he ever got his evangelical message through to the former air hostess or what eventually became of the stricken woman after his departure from the island. That departure, like the one seven years earlier, also saw him leaving the islands with tears flowing down his cheeks. But this time they were tears of happiness and far removed from those of his mental breakdown. The tears flowed after dozens of the hardy islanders headed down to the jetty to see the wee Scotsman off in an impromptu show of faith. 'Word got around that I was leaving and scores of people came down to wave me off.'

His emotions erupted into cascades of tears when the crowd of people started singing the 23rd Psalm, The Lord is my Shepherd. 'It was a heartbreaking experience for me. Here I was a dirty ex-drunk once into violence and thieving and now a Christian evangelist with a crowd of people who have known me for only two weeks openly expressing their love for me. There were many people on that ship who were not Christians who also stood crying at the sight of all of those people singing the psalm. It is a memory I will always cherish and never ever forget. It is etched not only in my mind but also in my spirit. Changed days indeed from those when I had worked in the Shetland Islands. Here I was a born-again, spirit-filled Christian and it is all thanks to Christ for taking me back there.'

He also knew it was thanks to Christ that he laid to rest his earlier Shetland Islands occult experiences. His working days on the islands had seen him involved with the occult and his return visit had also centred around his paranormal powers. But this time he had proved that good would always triumph over evil in the name of the Lord.

'Satan is very powerful and it can lead to almost anything if you get involved with the occult and its dark world. I would advise people never to get involved with spiritualism or the occult. You find places that go under the name of Christian Spritualist Churches but I can assure you that they have nothing to do with Christianity. These churches have the greatest calling of all because everyone dies sometime. When loved ones die those that are left cannot face life without them and try to find out if they are in heaven or on the other side. A medium can come up with a phoney message which gives them some hope but to find out in later life that it is all Satanic nearly kills some people.

Indeed there have been many, many suicide cases among people that have been involved with the occult.

'Jesus tells us that our future is in the palm of his hands when he says: "In my father's house there are many mansions and I go there before thee to prepare a place. If that were not so I would have told you."

'We don't have to go to mediums to find out the score if we know our futures lie somewhere else. They lie with our Lord Jesus Christ in heaven if we give our lives over to him in even just the simplest of ways.'

Having given his life over to Christ Geordie Aitken was to be used in countless ministries. Following on from his mission to the Shetland Islands he was to travel across the Irish Sea. Over many years he would speak to the people of Northern Ireland and those languishing in its jails. Far from the paranormal he was soon to be involved with the paramilitary. Once again in an attempt to show that good triumphs over evil when you walk with the Lord.

Ulster, Ulster, your blood has been spilled
many, yes many, men have been killed
Where is the answer for peace within you
of a land that flies the red, white and blue

There is a heaven above which covers your land
not the emblem of Ulster, Ulster's Red Hand
When will your war finally end?
give Jesus your suffering, your land he will mend

Let Ulster flourish with a heavenly hand
not the flute, the drum or accordion grand
Men in prison who fought for the cause
clap hands with Christ, in heavenly applause

Walk towards the Cross called Calvary's tree
and let this world know your Ulster is free
Get rid of the gun, the sword and the hate
let's all lead this land through the heavenly gate

And in the Christian years to come
no more playing of hate with the flute and the drum
Let heavenly trumpets blast out the call
to the tune that Ulster is free from it all

Your children will sing with joy once again
when Ulster produces heavenly men
So come on dead churches I am talking to you
get rid of your rules let Jesus shine through

Open your doors let all types come in
not self-righteous snobs soaked in their sin
Let our Saviour rule by his written word
not stinking traditions that are so absurd

Ulster

# CHAPTER 9

# A Solution for Northern Ireland

Despite the punishing soup kitchen work Geordie Aitken was also taking a Christian message into the lives of terrorists, prisoners and the unfortunate families caught up in the sectarian troubles tearing Northern Ireland apart. An accomplished prison visitor in Scotland, the street-level evangelist found his calling in the high security Irish jails that held hardened prisoners.

That avenue was to be opened up by a former Scottish CID sergeant he met at one of the Christian Police Fellowship meetings. But it was also going to take him into the very heart of troubled Northern Ireland. Away from the infamous prisons he was also to become involved with the families and children caught up in the horrendous violence.

In time he was to sit and minister in the same prison room with one-time rival Catholic and Protestant factions now housed in the notorious Maze Prison.

To this day governments and politicians are trying to find a way to end the bloody violence in Northern Ireland but the blunt speaking Scottish evangelist believes the only answer to the problem is through prayer.

The one-time sworn enemies would often sit side by side and listen to the testimony of the man who had found God. Prisoners, some jailed for murdering their fellow men in the name of religion were also to find salvation thanks to Geordie Aitken. One convicted gunman told him during a prison visit: 'I wish now I had become a Christian before being sentenced to life.' Many knew the foolishness of their ways but at the time of committing their crimes would have willingly given their lives for the cause whichever side of the fence they happened to be on.

'It was a great joy to me speaking to these men because my background was not much different to theirs. We were all street-wise kids from deprived backgrounds whether it be Glasgow or Belfast.' After initially writing to the gunman, his letters were soon being read by scores of prisoners locked up in the Maze. He had been asked to contact the prisoner and take a Christian message into the lives of the inmates by the Scottish detective. The gunman was serving fifteen years for armed robbery having tried to raise funds for his terrorist masters. Following his release he immediately travelled to Glasgow to look up Geordie Aitken and thank him for his help and is now living a trouble free Christian life. During his sentence he had asked Geordie Aitken to write to him on a regular basis and also asked his permission to share the letters with other inmates in the Maze Prison. Geordie Aitken agreed to both requests and soon his letters were being read by Catholics and Protestants alike. They in turn began writing to the Scottish evangelist to share their experiences with him and at one stage he was writing seven or eight letters a week back to the prisoners. The inmates remarkably pooled what little money they had to pay his ferry fare across to Northern Ireland so that he could personally visit them.

Geordie Aitken crossed the Irish Sea with the message: 'We all have the one Saviour whether we are Catholic or Protestant.'

Many of the men he was to meet in the late 1980s have now been released and are leading peaceful lives unconnected to the Irish troubles. But one man, who might never be released, still writes regularly to Geordie Aitken. He was jailed for his part in sectarian murders and told that he should be locked up indefinitely. Now in Maghaberry Prison, in Lisburn, Northern Ireland, he is a devoted Christian and brotherly friend of Geordie Aitken.

In many of his letters he has written how:

'I know I can't live without the Lord for what is our life without Christ. Nothing but bitterness and hatred and all of the things that go with sin. I have been down roads, Geordie, that I don't want to go down again. We are both on the pilgrim's road, which we freely admit is not easy, and there have been times when I have said to myself that I can't live like this anymore because I am a failure but even in those times I find that God takes my hand and says "let's go on". I wish I could get back to Jesus for I know I am not living the way that I should be living so please pray for me, Geordie.' Before his salvation the writer of such letters thought the answer to all of his troubles was

Geordie displaying tattoos.

a bullet. Now he knows there is a different answer to the trouble in
his country and that the answer is Christ.

'There is a great cry for peace in our land, Geordie, but for many
people there can't be peace at any price. But, Geordie, talking is better
than killing. Some of those against peace are our ranting politicians
who talk a great fight but never get their hands dirty. But we know
Geordie that true peace is knowing the Lord as he is our true peace
alone. Please pray that one night we may all know this peace.' The
writer of these letters urged Geordie Aitken not to name him in case
certain factions, with revenge in mind, held it against the Scottish
evangelist for befriending him. He classes him as a true friend and does
not want to see him inadvertently dragged into the troubles because
of their shared love of the Lord.

'I love you, wee man, with all of my heart. I would lay down my
very life for you and I don't say such things lightly. The friends that
I have are very precious to me and even in my past life I was always
like this because once I gave a man my friendship I would have fought

for and protected him. You have given your life to caring for the down and outs and have worked your guts out to help people.'

Writing to the inmates and visiting them in various Irish jails proved that the sectarian divide could be bridged through faith. On many occasions hardened killers shared fellowship with the Scottish evangelist. 'It was a mighty miracle of God's grace that Catholic and Protestant sat side by side sharing fellowship. I felt so at home with these spiritually alive Christians.'

When not in the prisons Geordie Aitken spread a spiritual message to young and old alike on the troubled Belfast streets. Whether it was Glasgow or Belfast he never felt more at home than when working with people on the streets. Children, sickened by the daily violence that besets the Shankill Road area of the city were to be the proof of that.

Walking down the notorious street he saw a group of children playing in the streets and gutters which over the years had witnessed countless bloody deaths. Proudly clutching £15 which he had been given for speaking in a Belfast Baptist church he decided to treat all of them to a meal in a hamburger joint. 'I could see that the strain of the troubles showed on their young faces and decided to use the £15 to take the wee vagabonds down to the McDonald's burger bar.' With

Geordie in Shankill Road area of Belfast.

the consent of their parents he marched his little army of eleven children
away down the road. The only condition slapped on them was that
they all sang a hymn as they marched along. For once the troubles
seemed to be miles away. Off they went singing: 'Jesus loves me this
I know, for the Bible tells us so, little ones to him belong, we are
weak but he is strong'. They even kept it up as they entered the burger
bar. 'Most of the customers were laughing but I also noticed a few
tears.' But after telling the children to order what they wanted, he
found the bill came to more than £15. 'They ordered up the goodies
but to my amazement I found I was short of cash. I explained to the
manager what it was all about and without any hesitation he said he
would sort out the difference. After my team ate their fill we all headed
back into the bomb-torn Shankill Road area singing the hymn. As
Christ said suffer little children to come unto me. Surely the kids in
the troubled areas of Northern Ireland have suffered all their young
lives. May the saviour that blessed me bless all of the little children in
Northern Ireland.'

A Northern Ireland youth club.

As he lay in bed that night, the guest of a Belfast family, he struggled to find a way to bring happiness into their lives on a larger scale. Having hit upon an idea of taking a party of them to Scotland as a break from the sectarian violence, he told the children in confidence his plans. He promised them a trip of a lifetime. But as he made that solemn promise he knew he didn't have a penny in his pocket with which to make his dream come true. But it was to come true. Fourteen were to make the trip and have £25 each to spend. 'I didn't have a penny but I knew a big Jesus who I knew would supply me with the money if I had a childlike faith to step out in my challenge.'

Back in Glasgow he set about fundraising. 'I was determined to carry out my promise to my wee friends in Belfast knowing the money had to be raised come what may.' And it was raised, even gangsters from his earlier wild days donated cash to the appeal. Money poured in from all walks of life from shops to school children. Shortly before the planned trip he hit the required £1,000 mark and for fourteen children and four mothers the trip across the sea was on. One small girl later told him that her mother had bought her a suitcase in an Oxfam charity shop to ensure she made the trip. The family had never owned one because they never imagined being able to take a holiday.

With the help of a Scottish bus company Geordie Aitken headed for the port to greet the Sealink ferry when it docked from Northern Ireland. 'I travelled about ninety miles and it was worth every inch of the journey to see the children coming off the ferry with beaming smiles shouting "Uncle Geordie".' That was the start of many tears of happiness that were to be shed during the holiday. They stood at the Stranraer Harbour and openly prayed to God in full view of the rest of the passengers. Geordie Aitken was not the only one who shed a tear. The singing children boarded the bus and headed for the Maranatha Christian Holiday Centre in Biggar. The singing never stopped throughout the journey. Visits to Edinburgh Zoo, McDonalds and the Lord Provost's office in East Kilbride, were planned during the seven day holiday.

At the zoo Geordie used his street market expertise to get the children in for a reduced price. It should have cost £90 to get the party in but after a preliminary telephone call to the zoo a price of £20 was agreed. 'I explained about the trip and how many of the children had never

Glasgow's Lord Provost Stewart Crawford with visiting children from Belfast.

been to a zoo. Miraculously, the director of the zoo was an Irish woman and she agreed to let us all in for £20.' When they arrived the zoo director herself welcomed them and gave them a guided tour. While the little children watched the animals a tearful Geordie Aitken watched them. 'They certainly were a happy bunch and I spent a better time watching them impersonating the monkeys than I did watching the animals.'

Geordie Aitken then asked Lord Provost Crawford if he could arrange a brief trip to the East Kilbride Civic Chambers. He arranged more than that and the happy party spent hours in the plush building where they were allowed to sit in the council's debating chamber and fire off questions to the Lord Provost. Before they left he presented them all with a Scottish souvenir. Then it was off to see Geordie Aitken's old enemy the police. Only this time he walked into the police station without a worry, head held high and to a welcoming party. Plus a party of ecstatic Irish children. Puppet shows, parks and plenty of sightseeing trips followed leaving Geordie Aitken a contented but tired man. 'The kids sure did burn me out but it was worth all of the aches and pains. The world would be a better place if more people burned themselves out helping others rather than sit worrying about themselves.' One of the saddest days of his life was when the party headed back to Stranraer and the waiting ferry at the end of the holiday. They had managed to buy the kids some sweets and lemonade for the return journey but the goodies could not make up for their leaving. They parted with the tearful children and four women singing, from the deck of the departing ferry, 'Will ye no come back again'.

The Scottish party left on dry land, shed their own tears. 'My heart was breaking and the tears were flowing like a fountain from everyone's eyes, including many of the ferry passengers, as the children waved from the ship right up until it disappeared into the horizon of the Irish Sea.

From that moment a distraught Geordie Aitken vowed to try to help other Irish children visit Scotland.

'I felt very heavy in my heart and spirit knowing the kids and their mothers were heading back to the troubles in Belfast. How I wish I could bring every Irish youngster and their mothers for a holiday, plus every deprived kid in the world. How I wish that I was a millionaire so that I could carry out my wish. If I ever manage to bring more kids over for a holiday then it will be some kids from the Falls Road area as I must bring both Catholic and Protestant children over.'

Despite the sadness at seeing them leave the holiday was to bring a lot of joy to Belfast. Mothers, fathers and community leaders were still talking about the trip months later. Even when Geordie Aitken returned to Belfast to continue his prison visiting the holiday was still the main topic of conversation.

One of the women, who had accompanied the children, now had something joyful to speak of. Instead of mourning her dead husband who had been killed by the IRA. While in Belfast she gave Geordie Aitken lodgings and he saw the difference in her and her young daughter. 'She knew I had been brought up on a diet of pork ribs and cabbage so most of the time my meals consisted of ribs, potatoes and cabbage piled as high as Edinburgh castle. After the heartache her family had suffered it was nice to see her smile. The wee holiday did her and her young daughter the power of good thanks to Jesus.'

While in Belfast many people turned to God thanks to the street-level preachings of Geordie Aitken. Many a time even he did not realize

the full extent of the sectarian troubles. One woman gave her life to
Christ after bursting into tears at the front door of her home in the
heart of Belfast. The couple's son was serving life in prison for his
paramilitary actions, and their daughter was a troublesome woman trying
to seek revenge for her brother and another member of the family who
had been killed in a terrorist attack.

'She was seeing me off at the door of the house when she asked
me to lead her to Christ. She had been hurting so much for years
because of the heartache the troubles had brought to her family. Her
son was in prison and her brother-in-law had been killed in a bar
explosion by the IRA. Her hurts had to come out somehow and they
sure did through her tears. It is terrible for the people involved in the
troubles as people can't forget when it comes to losing a loved one,
but death and murder affects both Catholic and Protestant families.'

Despite the horrors and heartaches of Northern Ireland humour also
followed Geordie Aitken on his travels. Margaret, one of the parents
who accompanied the children on the holiday to Scotland, had a run
in with the police that had nothing to do with terrorism. Travelling
along one of Ireland's main motorways in her old banger a gust of
wind lifted the bonnet and broke the catch. Determined to complete
her journey Margaret's friend Jeanie promptly sat on the bonnet to
keep it down. And off Margaret went. Startled RUC officers, not
surprisingly, pulled her over and asked her why her rather hefty friend
was sitting on the bonnet while she was doing 40 mph down a busy
road. She was let off with a caution but Geordie Aitken still wonders
how the pair finished the journey.

'Despite the troubles all around them there was a genuine humour
amongst the suffering people. Margaret once took a drink and when
she did was in many a fight but now she is a wonderful Christian
woman with three smashing daughters and a strapping son. Her main
worry is of their getting caught up in the fighting and I pray to God
that none of them ever do get involved in the troubles of that dear
country.'

During his visits to Northern Ireland Geordie Aitken preached in
numerous halls, churches and houses with people affected by the daily
violence. In his earlier wild days he was as vicious as any Protestant
follower of the cause and often violently clashed with Catholic rivals

in his native Scotland. The former hardline Orangeman now uses the tattoos, that once showed the world where his allegiance lay, to preach a different message. Many an amazed Catholic has sat and preached with Geordie Aitken and his tattooed arms. Every one of the thirty odd rebellious tattoos was a sign of his one-time fervent allegiance to the Protestant cause.

Just as he fought in a rough and ready way, he now preaches in a rough and ready way which is appreciated by many people in Northern Ireland who live rough and ready lives. 'My trips to Belfast were always fruitful because the love and kindness the people showed me would put some so-called Christians to shame. Give me down-to-earth Christians from hurtful backgrounds behind me and all of the country will witness a great revival.'

On every visit he was welcomed with open arms in areas of the country where the very mention of religion could be enough to spark bloodshed. 'The street folk of Belfast from working class background understood me and where I had been taken from through the love of Christ. I have had the joy of leading many people to the foot of the Cross where they have received their salvation in Christ. I still visit these lovely people whom I love very much and class as my Christian family.'

These people and Geordie Aitken believe that prayer is the only answer to the bloody sectarian troubles in Northern Ireland. He has sat in the notorious Maze Prison talking to killers from both sides of the religious and political fences and listened as they have talked of their conversions. He has also done the same on street corners and in the no-go areas of Belfast. 'My experiences in Belfast were both happy and sad. Happy to the point that I was visiting men who had become Christians and whose whole outlook had changed towards killing both each other and the many innocent people who need not have died. It is sad, though, meeting children who have been brought up knowing nothing but bullet and bomb rule.'

From the numerous experiences of Northern Ireland, one he will never forget is his first visit to the infamous Maze Prison. 'As I approached the massive doors of this hell-hole of a place my heart fell as I could feel the heaviness of the place eating into my very spirit.' He had been writing regularly to the men, and with his letters having been shared around the high security wings for others to read, there were quite a number of hardened prisoners from both sides of the religious fence waiting to meet him.

On his way to C Wing, in the infamous H Block, so called because of its physical shape, Geordie Aitken had to pass through a rigorous set of security checks before being ushered into the well of the prison. Then he and the other visitors, women and children visiting husbands and fathers, were put in a small windowless van for a short drive across the inner courtyard. It would have been quicker to walk but Geordie Aitken later discovered that the van was yet another security measure. 'The reason for the windowless van was so tht nobody could take any mental pictures of the courtyard which could possibly be used to plan an escape.' Once out of the armoured van the party of visitors were ushered along numerous corridors before coming into contact with the inmates.

Geordie Aitken, no stranger to violence, death, prisons and hardship, saw his heart go out to the families visiting loved ones. 'What a place for parents to have to take young children. But I know that they all want to see their fathers and that their fathers look forward to seeing them. Some men, locked away from the outside world, actually live for visiting days.'

The visiting itself was intense for Geordie Aitken because everyone had so much to share. 'I met all of the men who had written to me and Catholic and Protestant alike we all shared our life's experiences and fears for the future of their country and their families. If only the people of Ireland could live until a ripe old age rather than worry about an untimely violent death.' On his way out one hardened criminal, who had found the Lord during his internment, asked him if he would visit his elderly mother who herself had become a Christian following her son's conversion. Geordie Aitken had no sooner left the Maze Prison than he was heading for her home. 'She was so proud of her son's conversion that she actually became a Christian. I promised her that I would continue to pray for her and her son. Despite her happiness and pride she had tears in her eyes when I left. Yet another product of the stinking troubles in Northern Ireland.'

Getting clearance to visit the prisoners himself was no mean feat and the fact he did will never be forgotten by many people in Northern Ireland. He was doing what one Irishman wanted to do but couldn't.

Arthur Williams, of the Stauros Foundation, a Christian organization
helping alcoholics, drug addicts and prisoners, had been trying for years
to get into the Maze Prison to take his message of help and comfort
to the inmates but had always been denied access. Geordie Aitken was
the key that unlocked the high-security doors. 'Arthur had tried for
years to get in but didn't have any contacts to enable him to do so.
As I was established I was able to get him in. A Scotsman getting an
Irishman into an Irish prison sounds far fetched but it shows that the
Lord truly does work in mysterious ways.'

Following the prison visits Geordie Aitken spoke at Stauros Foundation meetings to follow up on the joint message the two men had
been spreading inside of the prison.

Over the years the compliment was to be returned with the Irish
contingent speaking at meetings and rallys in Glasgow. With them they
brought their own brand of humour and advice. Their choir was called
the 'Wasted Years' and they always opened the meetings with a musical
rendition by way of the choir's name. The Wasted Years was always
their introductory song as it served as a reminder to them and the
Geordie Aitkens of the world where we were now and where we had
been taken from.'

Arthur Williams, who now takes the Stauros Foundation message
to various countries was himself a man who once liked a drink and
who, before his conversion shared thoughts similar to those Geordie
Aitken once held about Christianity. Both of them had seen plenty in
their earlier days and could now preach a similar message.

Arthur Williams was saved by his local doctor whom he had been
visiting for a long time in the hope he could do something about his
drinking but they told him there wasn't much they could do. Then
one day an elderly doctor told him there was someone who could help
and when Arthur enquired who, the doctor told him 'Jesus Christ'.
He got down on his knees in the very surgery and the doctor led him
to Christ via the Cross. Following his salvation Arthur Williams mas-
terminded the Stauros Foundation in Northern Ireland and devoted his
life to helping people overcome their problems. Stauros is a Greek
word meaning at the foot of the cross.

Away from such recognized organizations Geordie Aitken was just
as happy on the streets, and indeed in cafés and even caravans. In one

Belfast café he helped lead a wild fighter and drunkard back to the Lord after he had lost his faith. The man had heard about Geordie Aitken's visits to the Maze Prison and from the underworld circles he mixed in he had also heard that the trusted and respected Scotsman had a message worth hearing. In the busy café, in a Belfast main street, the man poured his heart out to Geordie Aitken and told him of the wicked incidents he had been involved in. He had just been released from prison and after hearing of Geordie Aitken and his powerful testimony wanted his help to find the Lord again. In full view of other diners the little group sat there with tears rolling down their cheeks as the hardened ex-convict gave up on his life of violence and pledged his life to the Lord.

Also away from the political and religious divide Geordie Aitken offered comfort to alcoholics and depressives in Northern Ireland.

One frantic family, after hearing him speak at a mission hall, urged him to speak to a member of their family who was killing himself with drink and who had left them to live a hermit's existence in a stinking caravan in a desolate field. As ever, he needed little urging and was soon sitting in the sodden caravan with his arms wrapped around the depressive drunk.

Over the years Geordie Aitken has visited Northern Ireland numerous times and on each occasion has led people to the Lord. He still writes regularly to the troubled people offering them hope and comfort and reassuring them as they continue to strengthen their faith, while also taking the Lord's message into the streets. His deep faith, which they can see is for real, keeps them going in theirs.

Through his deep beliefs in the Lord, Geordie Aitken has won the hearts, and in many cases, souls, of many people across troubled Northern Ireland. People whose very lives have been shattered by the sectarian killings that plague the country. He has spoken to people many others thought were beyond redemption. He is as comfortable in the living room of a house in the notorious Shankill Road area of Belfast as he is in a secure church hall on the outskirts of the violent city where killings and bombings are an everyday part of life.

He goes about his evangelical business to a backdrop of armoured vehicles and machine-gun carrying soldiers and policemen patrolling the wicked streets. The very same streets that he is at home on.

Since his first visit to the troubled country he has tried to bridge a divide that governments and politicians are still struggling to bring together. Many people in Belfast believe he has a chance of success because he speaks a non-denominational language that both Catholic and Protestant factions can understand and he takes his message into the high-security wings of the infamous Irish prisons housing killers who have taken the lives of their fellow men in the name of religion. Some of their crimes are too horrendous to detail and many of the people cannot even be mentioned for fear of reprisals against their families and friends.

Even as Geordie Aitken takes his message of hope and comfort to the people of Northern Ireland the savage killing continues. Away from Christian circles some killers will never be forgiven and the very mention of their names in certain areas of Belfast is enough to spark an onslaught of bloodshed. Their actions have touched many on both sides of the divide and left a trail of heartache in their wake.

One woman who was widowed at an early age knows exactly what the sectarian violence means. She also knows exactly what the work of Geordie Aitken means.

Betty Harris, born and bred on the infamous Shankill Road area of the troubled city, was once herself a staunch Loyalist. Now she is a devoted Christian taking the Lord's message out into the hearts of those still fighting under the banner of religion. She derives a lot of strength from Geordie Aitken. Betty Harris, a mother of two, lost her husband Hughie to an IRA bomb in 1975 on the Shankill Road. For many years she continued to drink in a bid to wipe out the memory of the fateful night her 21-year-old husband became another statistic in the savage war raging across her country. Then four years ago she gave her life to Christ. 'I once said that I could never become a Christian because I was too bitter and hated the people that did that to my husband. If it meant hating the army or the Catholics then that is what I did.'

Betty Harris, reared in the Church of Ireland, gave up on church services at the age of 13. During her formative years she lived through some of the worst violence seen in Northern Ireland and hardened to what was happening around her on the streets of the Shankill Road area. The untimely killing of her husband had left her to bring up her

Betty Harris lost her husband to IRA bomb.

9-month-old son alone and after another relationship which lasted three years ended, she then had two children to bring up on her own in ravaged Belfast. She managed that with Christianity far removed from her thoughts. Then in 1990, with the children aged 15 and 11, she finally found true happiness in the shape of Christ.

In the months leading up to her conversion she had been attending mission meetings in a local church with a friend and after one such meeting she had returned home knowing deep inside that something was happening to her. But she did not know exactly what. 'After returning home I just got down on my knees in the middle of the floor, burst out crying, and asked God to help me. My daughter thought I had been drinking and over the coming weeks people began to think there was something wrong with my mind because I stopped going out to the pubs and clubs and lost interest in all of the things that had once seemed so important to me.'

Then Betty Harris had to discover what giving her life to the Lord really meant. 'I thought being saved meant a big ceremony in front of a church minister.' But she was to discover it would be one of the easiest things she would ever have to do. It happened as she routinely went about her work as a home help with elderly people. One of her colleagues had been saved many years before and Betty Harris quizzed her about what she had to do in order to give her life to the Lord.

Her friend simply asked: 'What would you do if I offered you twenty pence?' Betty Harris replied: 'I would take it.'

'That then,' said her friend, 'is all you have to do with the Lord.'

Far from being a religious ceremony in the presence of a minister all Betty Harris had to do was simply to accept the Lord into her life there and then. 'I had visions of her trailing me up to a church but she explained that being saved was just being offered a gift and that all you had to do was accept it.'

Betty Harris accepted the Lord that very day as her Saviour and now admits that she has never been happier. 'My whole life has changed. It took away the bitterness and even though I can still feel angry over all of the killings and troubles around me I don't feel bitter any more. I just pray now that all people can be saved. Hundreds of people, including paramilitaries, are being saved and baptized and maybe, just as the Devil once used people during the troubles, then the Lord is now leading them away.'

While exploring her faith Betty Harris is learning from Geordie Aitken. 'During the times I have spent with him I have seen how he brings things down to earth and to a level that people can understand. He goes out amongst people and I have learned a lot from that.' She also knows the value of his work in general. 'He has been called a miracle by some people as he has worked and prayed with people from all walks of life and has brought people together from both sides of the divide.'

It is people like Betty Harris and Margaret Holland who Geordie Aitken genuinely admires for taking a basic message into the streets and to the people who need to hear it. 'Such people are very close to my heart as they themselves have seen a lot and can go out and relate the Lord's message right from their very hearts. Every one of these people is a miracle of God's grace.'

Both Betty Harris and Margaret Holland made the trip to Scotland with Geordie Aitken and the party of children from deprived areas of Belfast.

Margaret Holland, herself a saved Christian, was once as troublesome as her male counterparts. She has firsthand experience of the sectarian violence and admits to having a 'troubled background'. She was actually visiting a relative in the Maghaberry Prison, in Lisburn, Northern Ireland, when she first met Geordie Aitken. Now he regularly stays at her home and the two of them witness and preach along the rough Shankill Road.

Geordie's wife, Marion, with visiting Irish mothers Margaret Holland and Betty Harris.

Margaret Holland also speaks to hardened prisoners from both sides of the divide, both in the notorious prisons and on their release. Following her conversion she started taking the word of the Lord around the pubs she once sat and drank in. Once the booze fuelled her hatred and she left the pubs in very mean moods. She can relate to Geordie Aitken's background and also knows how important he is to the people of Northern Ireland.

'Everyone loves Geordie Aitken. He is one in a million. The Lord has worked miracles with Geordie Aitken, and he has worked miracles with the people over here.'

Margaret Holland was saved after realizing she was wasting her life fighting and drinking. She was so bad even her own daughter told her she would go to Hell when she died. She knew there was something happening but tried to block it out with drink. Then one night, seventeen years ago, her drinking days finished and she found salvation. 'I just thought to myself, if I'm going to Hell then I'm going to Hell because of this lifestyle.' The Lord accepted Margaret Holland on the night she was due to throw a party for her wild friends and neighbours. She had stockpiled £50 worth of drink, which she had ordered from a catalogue, but the only invitation she issued was one to the Lord. 'I asked God that if he could take me the way I was then I would give my life to him. I was saved that night and even went around telling everyone that the long-awaited party was off. I was cleansed by the Lord that night and it was as if a massive burden had been lifted from me.'

Margaret Holland now witnesses in pubs, streets, church halls and prisons spreading the message that Jesus saves and Jesus loves. She knows how difficult it can be in her native country and knows the extra hardships endured by Geordie Aitken. She also knows that he has helped lead members of her family to the Lord. 'We can relate to Geordie Aitken because people like us from the troubled areas of Belfast are also just rough and ready Christians.'

Despite the similarity in their troubled backgrounds Margaret Holland knows that Geordie Aitken has taken a Christian message further, and to more people, than she will ever be able to. 'The people in Northern Ireland, from both sides of the divide, love Geordie Aitken. He has done things in the name of the Lord that nobody else could ever do. God is using Geordie Aitken in just the same way as he once used his disciples. If the world had more people like him it would be a much better place.'

Firmly believing that Geordie Aitken has a uniqueness about him, Margaret Holland is happy to learn from him and help spread the same evangelical message that he does. She now travels around Belfast ministering and visiting people from differing religious walks of life and has herself led many of them to the Lord. 'Christ is the only answer to the problems in Northern Ireland.'

It is Geordie Aitken's closeness to the people on the streets and the down-to-earth message he preaches which endear him to them. One place in which Geordie Aitken felt at home was a gospel hall in the middle of a housing estate which drew people of differing but hurtful backgrounds.

'The Zion Gospel Hall sure made me feel welcome as the folks were just ordinary folks with some having backgrounds of booze and violence similar to my own past but now their lives have changed so much since coming to believe in Christ. I have spoken in this wee hall twice and I certainly felt humble doing so.'

Speaking and relating to people is what Geordie Aitken enjoys most and that has been appreciated as much as anywhere at the Meeting House in Randalstown. When he first spoke there his message was a simple one to the people who turned up to listen. 'Be yourself and don't try to be someone you're not'.

George Bates, himself a fiery, but respected evangelist, and subject of the book *This Is For Real*, knows from firsthand experience the true worth of Geordie Aitken. 'He is a powerful man.'

It is that power which has taken the fiery Scotsman into the high security wings of notorious Irish prisons where he witnesses to hardened terrorists from both sides of the divide. It is not uncommon for former paramilitaries who have now been saved to sit side by side in a room to listen to his words. In the past such men would have gladly put a bullet through each other's heads without a second thought.

Geordie Aitken challenges them that they now have a different weapon with which to get their message across, the Bible. The Lord seems to open doors to Geordie Aitken which he doesn't quickly open to others. The prisoners accept him because they know exactly where he is coming from and what he is interested in. Saving souls.

'Geordie Aitken is crossing the divide because he is only interested in bringing Jesus into their lives. He is interested in them as people not what religious denomination they happen to belong to. They can see that he is not being divisive but is genuinely interested in their needs. He is prepared to go and live amongst these people and that is what makes him really special.'

George Bates also knows that a hapless drunk or dire depressive will get the same treatment as any deadly terrorist. To Geordie Aitken it is souls, not just bodies that matter. The Lord came to preach the Gospel to the poor and common people heard him gladly and Geordie Aitken can equate to that more than anyone George Bates knows.

'He has a depth in regard to preaching that in itself is remarkable. They broke the mould when they made him. He is reaching people that might not otherwise be reached.'

George Bates himself was saved after a chequered past and knows what it is like to live at grass roots level and why people can appreciate Geordie Aitken for what he is. 'He is unspoilt as far as his witnessing for Christ is concerned. People need to see today that there is a manliness about serving the Saviour. Geordie Aitken portrays the character of a man's man and not the image of a cissy with a Bible. This lets people see that God has his people everywhere.'

Getting straight to the point and letting people know about God in a down-to-earth way is the strength of the man. He has proved on countless occasions that he can lead people to the Lord in his own inimitable way. So many can testify that they have been pointed to Christ through the words and teachings of the remarkable Scottish evangelist.

George Bates proclaims simply that in the relatively short time of eleven years that Geordie Aitken has been saved: 'He is a short-circuiter for God. He gets right to the very heart of things.' It is his background, according to the Irish evangelist, that makes him extra special and his notorious background makes him all the more a trophy of grace. 'You can see he is a rough diamond and with him everything is pared right down to the bare bones. His firing from the hip-type preachings are natural to him and are appreciated by countless people.'

Many people across Northern Ireland could add their testimony to the life of Geordie Aitken and the work that he does in the troubled country. 'Scotland's son of thunder certainly is some man, he has lived a remarkable life and is a unique servant of the Lord.'

Geordie Aitken has visited the Meeting House in Randalstown, on a number of occasions and always receives the same high level of hospitality. Congregations, familiar with the powerful preachings of George Bates know that he has a soulmate in the shape of the rough and ready Scotsman. The two men can complement each other and give people their own perspective of Christianity. Both had chequered pasts and while Geordie Aitken is at his happiest preaching at street level he knows that God dragged his Irish friend out of the mire to use him in the pulpit of a church.

Geordie Aitken admits that he does not have the same technique as George Bates, while the Irishman knows he could never do the work of the Scotsman. Neither man would want it any other way. In unison they proclaim that it proves that the Lord has His servants at every end of the scale. Their mutual respect knows no limits. 'George Bates is the finest preacher I and many others have heard and a blessing of the Lord is that his preaching is more refined than my own. I am so used to working with the people of the streets and the prisons that I speak their language.'

But both men know that there is a long way to go before people can live in peace. On his last trip to Northern Ireland Geordie Aitken took a friend with him on the visit but it was to sadly illustrate just how bad the situation still is.

Simply because of a Catholic tattoo, on his arm, depicting his innocent allegiance to nothing more than a particular Scottish football team followed by Catholics, his friend was stopped and grilled by police on arriving in Belfast after making the ferry trip from the Scottish port of Stranraer.

It was the man's first trip to Northern Ireland but it was to leave an impression on him that he would never forget in a hurry. He had made the trip in faith, having himself been saved after leaving the Catholic church, but he was to return home enlightened about the troubled country.

Far from being a potential terrorist or troublemaker the poor Christian was actually terrified of visiting the troubled country and had only accompanied Geordie Aitken as a gesture of faith. As with many other people he did not fully appreciate just how bad the situation really was but knew of the strife from the news bulletins that regularly announced more murders and mayhem. He knew the general picture but was not prepared for the tension and fear that affects everyone when just going about their daily business. It was bad enough for him actually going to the country but by the time he returned to Scotland he was all but a nervous wreck.

The final straw came when he unwisely, but in good faith, got his camera out and took a picture from a taxi window in the notorious Protestant area of Belfast called Glencairn Estate. No sooner had the flash gone off than two armed policemen, toting sub-maching guns, stopped the taxi and ordered the two men out and demanded the film from the camera. As Geordie Aitken tried to calm down the petrified man the officers took the roll of film from the camera and destroyed it before questioning the man in the back of an armoured vehicle about his motives. They knew only too well that many of their colleagues had been murdered after terrorists had photographed them at work and later passed the pictures around hardline groups. Geordie Aitken's appearance admittedly did nothing to help their cause. 'While he was shaking like a jelly I tried to explain that I was a preacher visiting men in Maghaberry Prison but their answer was that I looked more like an escaped prisoner coming out of Maghaberry Prison as my head was almost clean shaven. At the end of the day I wished, both for his sake and for mine, I had never taken him to Northern Ireland because he ended up with his nerves almost completely shattered.'

Even today RUC officers live a very tense existence to the point where some of them in certain areas of Northern Ireland cannot even wash and hang out their uniform shirts on a washing line for fear of reprisals. They live on a knife edge and the last thing they need is a stranger poking a camera out of a taxi window photographing them at work.

But despite the validity of the policemen's actions the sight of their machine-guns and being quizzed in the back of an armoured patrol vehicle on a busy street in the middle of the afternoon was all too much for Geordie Aitken's friend. That and the trouble at Belfast docks over his football tattoo left him paranoid believing that the Protestant factions were watching him and his every move. In his shaken state, every time he heard a bang he thought someone had taken a shot at him. With shattered nerves he was taken back to Scotland by Geordie Aitken. On his recovery he was to testify to exactly what Geordie Aitken was up against in his fight to spread a Christian message on the streets of Northern Ireland.

He himself had barely been able to cope on the streets let alone in such places as the Maze Prison and Maghaberry Prison. But Geordie Aitken is determined to continue his evangelical work in the troubled country. Scores of people have already put their faith in the Lord but, sadly, countless others have yet to be reached. Those are the ones Geordie Aitken is determined to get to as he believes that faith could be the only answer to the bloodshed.

'The only solution I believe possible for Northern Ireland is the blood of Christ shed all over that dear land so that brother can live with brother in the love of Jesus.'

There is a man called Benny Lee
who came to Jesus on his bended knee
He drank the booze and womanized
his cardinal sins the Lord despised

Benny took an inventory
he decided to tell the Lord his story
The sins of the flesh were killing his soul
so he asked the Lord to make him whole

Save me Jesus he cried with tears
My sinful life is full of fears
The hurts cut deep into my heart
Satan is tearing my soul apart

Come unto me for your rest
and put my power to the test
The sins you committed belong to me
that's why I hung upon the tree

To save the souls of men like you
for you to live a life so true
I hear your cry directed to me
your soul is mine, Benny Lee

So walk in faith each new born day
my skies are blue never grey
Benny Lee you are my son
go out and make the Devil run

Lead the souls of men to me
and remember the Cross on Calvary
Tears and blood ran down my face
to heal broken souls with my saving grace.

Benny Lee

# CHAPTER 10

# Taking America by Storm

Throughout his years prison visiting, and running the soup kitchens, Geordie Aitken had been relying on social security benefit money to keep himself and his family. He had even played host to American evangelist Pastor Benny Lee who had been told about him by Jeff Sindelar, the man who witnessed the argument outside East Mains Baptist Church, when Geordie Aitken had severed his ties with the established churches. Benny Lee had never forgotten what Jeff Sindelar had said of the lonely Scottish evangelist and arranged to visit him at his Glasgow home.

On his return to St Charles, Missouri, Benny Lee spoke highly of Geordie Aitken whenever he addressed his Celebration Fellowship services. After hearing how their pastor had visited Geordie Aitken, and spoke in prisons and churches the American congregation donated enough money to pay for his air fare to take him across the Atlantic to speak to them in his rough and ready way.

A rejuvenated Geordie Aitken now needed things he never once dreamed of owning, an up to date passport and a half decent suitcase. Having obtained those he then had to kit himself out, with the second-hand clothes he still collected for the needy. All he had to supplement his search for clothing was a £5 note which he had saved up. 'My search through the donated bags of clothing was a laugh because the down and outs would fight with me to see who could get the best gear.' But Geordie Aitken managed to get himself a pair of training shoes, a lightweight jacket and two pairs of underpants.

Then it was off to the Barras Market in a bid to add to his wardrobe. Clutching his £5 and mouthing a prayer he set off winding his way along the canvas stalls. The prayers must have worked. He came away with a pair of denim jeans, two pullovers and three short-sleeved shirts. 'What a bargain and what a Jesus.' Now he was beginning to feel like a holiday-maker. Clutching his two carrier bags he set off home but decided to call into the council chambers to ask the Lord Provost if he would give him an official letter to take to the American city of St Charles. He finally got his letter of greetings but not without a struggle.

Striding through the massive entrance lobby with its marble pillars and brass rails, he was soon stopped by the building's security staff. Standing looking up at the distinguished looking commissionaire, a tattooed and scruffy Geordie Aitken, complete with carrier bags, informed him he wanted to see the Lord Provost. After explaining he was on a mission of mercy the guard looked at him in disbelief. 'He looked at me with such suspicion that he must have been wondering what this tattooed criminal was doing in his building. When I told him I wanted a letter of greeting to take to America, he must have thought he was looking at a candidate for the nearest funny farm.' Not exactly sure how to handle him the burly guard passed the buck and told him to report to the security guard on the second floor.

As Geordie started walking up the winding marble staircase his mind wandered back to his old days. 'First the chandelier caught my eye, and then all of the valuable paintings of former Lord Provosts and historical figures. What a nice bit of pocket money they would have got me. Given half a chance I would have tried to steal the lot in my thieving days.' At the top of the stairs stood the towering security guard he had been told to report to. Instead of being dispatched back down he was greeted with the words: 'Are you the man that Jesus told to visit the Lord Provost?' A minor miracle, thought Geordie Aitken unaware of the walkie-talkie system used by the security staff. He repeated the story of how he had been walking home from the market when the Lord had laid it in his heart to approach the Lord Provost for the goodwill greeting letter. Unimpressed the guard told him to sit on the leather settee which already seated a queue of people waiting to see the civic leader. But seconds later a giant of a man, with a voice to match, walked into the corridor and boomed: 'Is Geordie Aitken here?'

Once inside the office he was offered a cup of tea and told that the Lord Provost was on official business and would not be back until tomorrow. Undeterred he started telling the secretary of his life story, conversion and planned trip to America. It was an hour and a half before he left the council chamber. 'We finished up on first name terms with me calling the Lord Provost's secretary Willie and him calling his uncouth visitor Geordie.' He left the office with an invitation to return the next day. On arrival he reported straight to Willie, ignoring the queues of people and was duly shown into the Lord Provost's suite. But before meeting him he was given a cup of tea by secretary Willie. 'He thanked me for having him in stitches the day before and that he had laughed all afternoon at the drunken escapades I had told him about. I think he wanted a wee laugh with me before dealing with all the stone-faced zombies waiting on the leather settee in the corridor.'

Once in the main office Geordie Aitken came straight to the point with the Lord Provost of Glasgow, and told him that he was an evangelist dealing with drunks, prostitutes and homeless, and that he was going to America to preach to the people of Missouri. Before he left the oak-panelled office he not only had his letter but two bags of gifts to pass on to the civic leaders of the city of St Charles. He walked out clutching everything from gold cufflinks, to tie pins, to pewter tankards to tea towels. All bearing the city's coat of arms.

Weeks later he was to return to the Lord Provost's office with gifts from the other side of the Atlantic and a plaque proclaiming that the mayor of St Charles had bestowed the freedom of his city on the Scottish Lord Provost. In accepting the gifts Geordie Aitken managed to spend the whole afternoon in the mayor's civic suite. In conversation he told the Lord Provost how his American counterpart had, during his visit, explained that he could not see him out of the office himself, as he suffered varicose veins and was having a particularly bad day with them.

'I decided to tell him abut my old grandmother's cure and told him to roll up his trouser legs, and send a man out for some olive oil, and I knelt down and rubbed it into his legs. He later put his arms around me and gave me a big hug for my help. I left the office with the American smelling like a box of oiled sardines.'

The plaque, complete with gold key and the inscription: 'This is the key to our hearts and our city' still adorns the Lord Provost's office wall in Glasgow.

With his presents, passport and holiday clothes sorted out, his next task was to inform the local social security office of his plans, and tell the benefits maanger that he would not be around to sign for his giro cheques. That nearly landed him in prison. 'Little did I know that after my visit he would be blowing a gasket and threatening to call the police.'

In his typical forthright manner Geordie Aitken informed the manager that he was going to America for nine weeks to work. He left it until the end of the interview to explain that he would be working for the Lord. In between which the amazed benefits manager called in two clerks to witness the conversation in which Geordie Aitken admitted he wanted to claim his benefit while 'working in America'. He also added that he had been working twenty-four hours a day, seven days a week in Scotland and Northern Ireland. The manager didn't know what was going on and called his witnesses. 'As I answered his questions two little Hitlers were making out their statements with an obvious joy as they must have thought they had captured someone for working while claiming benefit money.' By the time he had finished answering the questions the three office staff were standing open-mouth in amazement.

In reaching for the telephone to call in the police, the manager asked: 'Oh, by the way, who is your employer?' The Lord Jesus Christ, came the answer. Down went the telephone and up jumped the benefits manager. Scarlet in the face and shouting and cursing he demanded the statements from his two members of staff and ripped them into pieces. In the background queues of unemployed people laughed and cheered as the crimson faced office worker struggled to get his words out. When he did he spitefully informed Geordie Aitken that he would not be eligible for benefit money as he was not effectively eligible for work, and that his family would have to live on a destitute payment while he was out of the country. The joyful evangelist left the building promising to send the social security office manager a postcard from America.

'I skipped down the stairs knowing in my heart that the manager had not been able to upset me even by saying we would only get a destitute allowance. Despite his antics I had left the office smiling and happy where in my old days I would have left him unconscious with a lump on his head so big he would not have been able to pull his jumper on for a fortnight.' Changed times indeed for Geordie Aitken.

On the day he was due to fly out his benefit money was due to arrive and he had economized over the past weeks so that he could use some of it for his trip. Mysteriously, it never arrived. 'I still wonder if the unemployment office manager had anything to do with the money not arriving.'

What he did know was that he was flying out to America for nine weeks with fifteen pence in the pocket of his second-hand denim jeans.

Settled in his seat for the eight hour flight on the North West Orient aeroplane his trip got off to a good start when a James Bond film was screened. Seconds later that turned sour, having just placed his earphones on his head to hear what 007 was saying, he was tapped on the shoulder by an air hostess who wanted £1 for the use of the earphones. He duly handed them back. 'I often wonder what James Bond was saying in that film. I told her that I only had fifteen pence, but that the Lord would provide for my needs. She smiled, but still took the earphones from me.' Very soon the other air hostesses were quizzing this 'madman' about his fifteen pence trip to America and by the end of the flight he had made six more friends.

As he stepped out into the American sunshine every one of them kissed him on the cheek and wished him good luck. He was to travel to America on another six occasions to preach in the Mid-West and amazingly met many of the girls again. 'The service I received was great. One man, sitting behind me with a cheesy grin and designer clothes asked all the way to Missouri how I managed to attract the women. He never found out.'

As his feet touched American soil he muttered a quiet prayer to himself which was only interrupted by the booming voice of Pastor Benny Lee welcoming him to America. In front of hundreds of airport passengers the two men hugged each other and loudly proclaimed their faith in Jesus. During the trip from the airport Geordie Aitken was like a kid with a new toy. 'I was that excited that I couldn't take it all in. In my old drinking days I could not even afford to go to the other side of Glasgow, yet here I was in the sunshine of America. I might have only had my fifteen pence but what a change from sleeping rough in a Glasgow field.' When they arrived at Pastor Benny Lee's home Geordie Aitken was greeted by crowds of people eager to meet this Scottish evangelist. 'My hands were soaking because of the heat,

With Pastor Benny Lee.

excitement and countless hand shakes, but what a change. These hands were being used to greet people instead of punching them in the mouth.'

During his first stay in America Geordie Aitken used up every minute of his time counselling people in the St Charles area of Missouri. 'Nine weeks of bliss just lying in the Missouri sun, I had thought. Little did I know what Christ had in store for me.' What he did know was that people the world over, in Scotland, or America or wherever have the same problems and suffer from the same things.

At one of his first meetings in the Celebration Fellowship, which normally attracted 100 people, over 300 packed the church. After the first session the congregation thought he was an Irishman and asked him to speak slower because they could not understand him. 'The pastor told me that I would have to speak politely and slowly which were two things I had never done except for when I had been practising in front of the mirror and learning enough words to help me con my way into jewellery stores before pinching rings and necklaces.'

Before the start of the second session Geordie Aitken sat in the hall's toilet and prayed for help. 'Dear Jesus could you help me to speak slowly as I have your message to deliver and if the punters haven't got a clue what I'm saying I won't be able to get your message across.' With the Lord behind him he knew he would manage, and he did. He delivered his message that night in a polite, slow way which everyone understood. 'I can only praise the Lord because everyone in that hall understood the foreigner with the funny accent that night.' When not speaking to the local parishioners Geordie Aitken took his message into the state penitentiaries and spoke the language of the criminals.

One inmate who met Geordie Aitken was the imposing Kenneth Eugene Seidler, a convicted armed robber and rapist who is currently serving a forty-year sentence in Menard, Illinois. Despite a history of violence and drug-related crimes the 42-year-old American, of an explosive Irish, German and Cherokee Indian ancestry now lives his life for the Lord. He was saved while in a prison cell serving time for his latest crime.

Already Kenneth Seidler has spent twenty years of his 24-year adult life in prison and has another ten years to serve before he can be released. He was first jailed at the age of 18 and when he sees his fifty-second birthday on the outside he will have spent thirty of his thirty-two year adult life behind bars.

His troubles effectively started when he was introduced to drink and drugs as a teenager. At 16 he quit school and a year later joined the US Navy where he was introduced to Marijuana. Twice he went AWOL and less than a year later he was discharged from the Navy. He moved back in with his parents in Jerseyville, Illinois, but soon began his dark descent into the world of LSD and Speed. Very shortly he was serving a twelve month sentence for burglary, theft and criminal damage. Following his release Kenneth Seidler tried various jobs but relied on his criminal skills to feed his drug habits having now started shooting drugs and taking Rock Crystal Speed. His life was on a downward spiral and he remembers 'aged 20 I acquired a nickname that fitted my lifestyle perfectly and one that has followed me for twenty-two years—"Caveman".'

Another two to three year jail sentence was imposed and following his release from that he moved into serious crime to feed his drug habits. At the age of only 24 he was given an eight to twenty-four year prison sentence for armed robbery and attempted murder. After serving almost seven years of the sentence he was released and settled down into some semblance of normality following marriage to an old flame. But trouble was to dog him and despite never going back on hard drugs he continued taking marijuana and drinking heavily. After less than two years of freedom Kenneth Seidler was arrested for rape and sentenced to forty years in prison. When he first met Geordie Aitken he still had twelve years to serve. Yet remarkably it was only two weeks into the forty year sentence that the hardened criminal was saved.

'What has made this time so bearable is that on 24 February 1984, only two weeks after my arrest, I met a man named Jesus Christ and he completely changed my whole outlook on life and has been re-modelling me ever since.'

With his own hardened background Kenneth Seidler is not easily impressed and does not lavish praise on anyone lightly. But one man he does respect, for his work in the name of the Lord, is Geordie Aitken. 'He has a beautiful way of expressing his stories about his life and makes them become real in your mind. He is not afraid to go out into the streets and spend time with the undesirable and there is a lack of this in the church today. In I Corinthians 9:22 Paul said: "I am made all things to all men, that I might by all means save some". That is what Geordie Aitken does. He comes down to the level of the people he is ministering to and his is a life story that needs to be told for I believe it will touch many lives.'

Geordie Aitken knows that Kenneth Seidler is another example of the Lord taking people the way they are and that despite being behind bars has a deep love of Christ.

'I spoke with a different accent to the convicts but I spoke the same language. I had walked the walk the same as them and it is a true saying that if you can walk the walk you can talk the talk. Street talk and prison talk are the same the world over no matter what country you are in. I thank God for letting me have a stinking, sinful past, as people today can recognize themselves in my past and realize it is not a life worth living.'

One thing from his past that did come back to haunt him was the dreaded shakes and sweats. Not from any wine bottle but from tins of Coca Cola. Because of the American sunshine Geordie Aitken gulped down gallons of the fizzy drink, and had to be rushed to the doctors where he was given tablets to combat the amount of caffeine his body had taken in. From once being on a liquid diet of alcohol he was now on a liquid diet of water. Such memories only served to strengthen his faith and he took that strong belief in Christ to the Americans.

Wherever he spoke he was appreciated and loved by the Americans he met. He was introduced to Pastor Bob Tindall, head of the Victory Church in St Charles, Missouri. But having learned to tone down his Scottish accent he was immediately told to resurrect it. He was asked to speak at church services in front of hundreds of people but told to speak in his own way. 'Bob Tindall was a cracking guy who used to try to impersonate my accent when addressing the congregation. Here was me trying to get rid of it and there he was trying to learn it.'

Away from the public arenas Geordie Aitken carried out his work

With Pastor Bob Tindall at the Victory Church Missouri.

on his beloved personal level. One churchgoer took him to meet an elderly blind woman, who was having horrendous problems with her heroin-addicted son. After speaking to the woman he arranged to meet her son and confront him about his problems. It emerged that the youngster had once been his blind mother's eyes and worshipped the ground she walked on. But following his parents' divorce she had remarried and the boy had felt shunned. He started to rebel against his new father and out of a misguided sense of revenge had turned his back on his mother and started dabbling with drugs. He soon became addicted and his filthy heroin habit soon led him away from the mother whom, deep down, he truly loved. But meeting Geordie Aitken was to be the turning point in his wasted existence and he was to find his way back to normality and indeed his mother.

He poured his heart out to Geordie Aitken, in relating the story and after hearing how his Scottish friend had overcome his own alcohol addiction he vowed to battle against his. Geordie Aitken later discovered, on a subsequent trip to America, that the young man had overcome his heroin addiction and had been reunited with his mother. 'It was a terrible state of affairs. To see his blind mother crying, almost killed me. I had never known that a blind person could actually shed real tears, because I always thought that with them having no sight they would not be able to cry. I'm pleased I was able to get through to Ricky as he is now off the heroin and his mother is once again proud of him.' He took on a new ministry of visiting elderly people after he was taken to a sumptuous nursing home.

Outside it looked fantastic but, inside, the suffering of the elderly residents brought back memories of his friends who lived in squalid dosshouses. The furnishings and fittings were worlds apart but the problems of the people were the same. 'The smell was terrible because many of the old men and woman were paralysed and wore nappies because they were incontinent. The strong smell of faeces and urine was nothing new to me because I had spent years in dosshouses, and the smell of urine is the same in America, as it is in Scotland. As is the pain and suffering of the elderly.' Walking through the home he instinctively threw his arms around many of the residents telling them that both he and the Lord loved them. 'The first old woman in a wheelchair burst out crying because I don't think anyone had ever told her they loved her. I was just as tearful, as hugging elderly people who had messed themselves was all new to me. But love can overcome any type of smell or hardship.'

Geordie Aitken will never forget his first ministry with the elderly. 'I thank God for allowing me to go amongst those old American people. It is heartbreaking to think that at one time they were young and full of life, and now they are old and ready for death in sheer loneliness. The visit to the home opened my eyes, because despite the outside of the building looking so luxurious there was so much loneliness and suffering behind those walls. Just like human beings who behind their smiles are suffering.'

Each time Geordie Aitken returned to America he was given stark, but heartfelt reminders of his previous visits. A year after his first visit, during which he met and befriended an elderly cancer sufferer, he learned the man had died. The man's dying wish was that: 'My Scottish friend should help carry my coffin'. Geordie Aitken made the trip to Missouri, and carried out the old man's wish. 'I had watched as he died in severe pain from cancer and I felt honoured to carry out his wish.' Geordie Aitken made a big impact on the American communities he visited and has been praised for his work across the Atlantic. His no-nonsense approach to the gospel has been, and still is, appreciated by thousands of Americans. Since first being introduced to the country by Pastor Benny Lee, he has spoken in countless church halls, prisons, homes and meetings across the Mid-West of America.

Pastor Benny Lee, the former head of the Celebration Fellowship church in Missouri, and who now leads Bible study classes and has written about Christianity once commented: 'God, why in the world would you give me a friend so close, that's so close to me, yet so far away in miles.' Pastor Benny Lee and Geordie Aitken built up a tremendous friendship through their shared love of Christ and belief in Christianity. He has witnessed him leading countless American people to the Lord and puts a lot of it down to his 'simplistic faith' which he relates to people.

'He is a person who can bring people to the Lord and it is so natural to him. I have seen him lead a lot of people to the Lord in America. He has touched people I felt were untouchable just through his life's experiences, his personality and through the simple faith that he portrays.

The Lord wants us to have a simple faith, and he wants us to come to him as a little child. A little child simply believes. Children do not pray for their fathers to provide them with a home, food and clothes, they just simply believe that daddy will provide. And that's how it is with our heavenly Father. That is the simple faith that I have seen in Geordie Aitken over and over again. I have seen him grow in the Lord and that is something we all have to do. I thank the Lord for people with the conviction of Geordie Aitken. He has been a real strength in my life and there have been times when I have wanted to talk to him so badly. Sometimes I would talk to him about a problem, and the answer would be just so simple. In the old days there was a saying of, "just praying through with a person just praying until they knew in their hearts and spirits that they had touched God with the problem and it was in his hands whatever the outcome would be". Nowadays in America it seems that every man and his brother are receiving counselling. It is something a person has to approach very carefully as a lot of it is just plain common sense. I have seen Geordie Aitken give counselling and most of the time it is plain common sense and getting priorities right. I have seen more things happen in faith with Geordie Aitken than probably anyone I have ever been around.'

Both of the men have preached and worked in each other's country, with Pastor Benny Lee having worked in the red light areas of Glasgow and its soup kitchens. He has also accompanied Geordie Aitken during his prison visiting in notorious Irish prisons.

On his first visit to Scotland he saw first hand the power of Geordie Aitken's prayers and his simple belief that the Lord provided people's needs not their wants. After twelve months of writing to each other, the American pastor made the trip to Glasgow, to be met at the airport by his host.

One man Colin Mulgrew, was to give his life to the Lord simply by witnessing the welcome. 'We just embraced and hugged each other at the airport. Colin received the Lord simply by witnessing our reactions to one another. We embraced and just loved each other in the Lord and we had never even met before.' Shortly before the trip a concerned Geordie Aitken had been wondering whether his tight budget would suffice when it came to feeding his guest.

He had prayed for food and the next day received a telephone call from a Glasgow friend asking if he wanted any shop-soiled food. The packets were damaged but the contents were intact. A grateful Geordie Aitken took the lot. It was only weeks later, with Benny Lee feeling at home and looking through a kitchen cupboard that the truth came out. Inside the cupboard were dozens of packets of mixed nuts. 'I thought it kind of strange that someone should have so many packets of expensive mixed nuts in his kitchen. We all love them but I couldn't understand why in the world he would buy that many nuts. I later discovered that it had been the food that had been brought over following his prayers. God certainly supplied his needs not his wants on this occasion, and I have seen that happen over and over again in his life.'

Another time when Geordie Aitken's prayers were answered the American was on home soil. Desperate to pay his way and earn some money while in Missouri, Geordie Aitken suggested making wooden bird boxes to sell locally. The only stumbling block was a lack of timber. Together the men prayed for wood. Amazingly, the next morning Jeff Sindelar telephoned the pastor to ask if he could use any lumber. He had a pick-up truck full of wood which he had taken from a nearby mill and now had no use for it. He said it was too good to throw out and even suggested that it would be perfect for making little bird boxes. 'Geordie duly made his bird boxes, and he sold those crazy things all over St Charles, Missouri. This really showed me something in the area of faith. He took his problem before the Lord and it was taken care of.' That was one of the examples pastor Benny Lee witnessed to lead him to believe in the depth of Geordie Aitken's simplistic faith. 'If there's anything a person can learn from Geordie Aitken it is simple faith. It is not a "Name it and Claim it" faith, just a "I believe, let's pray and the Lord will take of it! The Lord always does." I have seen things like this happen with Geordie Aitken over and over again.'

In public his faith was illustrated countless times as Geordie Aitken took his street level evangelism to the people of Missouri. 'Geordie Aitken has been a tremendous blessing to the people in America that he has spoken to and administered to, and I have found him to be very effective with young people. Everywhere Geordie went people were blessed and God blessed what he did. We need more Geordie Aitken's in this world today.'

Bird boxes made by Geordie for US charity.

When Pastor Benny Lee first invited Geordie Aitken to minister in America he was head of the Celebration Fellowship Church in Missouri. He later left that to move into other areas and knows from his own experiences how difficult it would have been for Geordie Aitken to move from the Loaves and Fishes soup kitchen, to open up other ministries in the Irish prisons.

Benny Lee now 54, with three grown up children, was himself saved in 1968 and started attending the Assembly of God Pentecostal-type church. Four years later he was part of a massive charismatic movement in the St Louis area of Missouri. They used to hold their meetings in a building known locally as the sheep shed.

It was a great movement and up to 2,000 people would attend. I witnessed many miracles of the Lord and people literally saved by the multitude.' He later spent eight years as pastor of the Celebration Fellowship and since hearing of Geordie Aitken and developing a deep friendship has visited Scotland six times. 'After I first wrote to him I got this ten page letter back and I just thought, wow. He had just been saved, loved the Lord and was trying to fit in but basically none of the established churches would accept him. When I arrived in Scotland it was like brotherly love at first sight. We just loved one another in the Lord.'

On subsequent trips he saw first hand the work Geordie Aitken was doing in soup kitchens across Glasgow and compared it to his own church nearly 7,000 miles away across the Atlantic. Geordie Aitken's soup kitchens were battered Transit vans with soup urn, bread and a few helpers.

The Celebration Fellowship Church also ran a soup pantry but it was house in a ninety foot long building, now worth over $500,000, and incorporating thirteen classrooms, a nursery, offices, a sanctuary and furnished basements. Pastor Benny Lee had helped build it up from nothing from the days when he and his fellow Christians took over the payments on the once-ramshackle building that was worth only $49,000. Despite the physical differences in their ministries both found it heartbreaking to move on from them.

Pastor Benny Lee moved on to teaching and secular work and Geordie Aitken into prison visiting amongst hardened criminals. 'When I walked away from that, I walked away with nothing. When the Lord told me to leave I just left. I waited until we could find a suitable replacement to do my work and I just laid it down and left. Geordie Aitken had to do the same with the soup kitchen, and it was a very difficult thing to do. It is almost like walking away and leaving your own baby.'

But Pastor Benny Lee knows the fruits of his Scottish friend's labours will blossom and continue to serve the needy people of Glasgow. 'Geordie Aitken set up the ministry in the name of the Lord, and if God is in something then he will make it work.'

Over the years the two men have had their differences and shared many emotional experiences which have tested their friendship. Pastor Benny lee likens it to the parable of the mountain tops and valleys.

'Nothing grows on the mountain tops everything grows in the valleys. The mountain top experiences are wonderful but you can't live by them and have them for ever. They do not produce fruit but are just blessings. The Lord knows that fruit grows in the valleys. If you show me a Christian who has never been in the valleys then I will show you a very immature Christian. One whose faith has not been tested. Geordie Aitken's faith has been repeatedly tested but he has a tremendous belief in the Lord.'

As with the mountain tops and valleys the two men had their ups and downs, but came through them in faith, and are deeply bonded together in the Lord. 'Even gold is tested by fire and friendships are tested the same way. If you have got a friend that will stick with you through thick and thin, no matter what it is, then you have got a tremendous friend. Most people in their lives are fortunate if they have got one friend like that. Some people don't ever have a one. I have such a friend in Geordie Aitken and he is the closest friend in the world to me. I have had many blessings in my life but one of the biggest blessings ever was when I met Geordie Aitken.'

Together the two men shared numerous spiritual experiences in America that ranged from the incredible to the insane. They travelled thousands of miles speaking in church halls and ministering to countless people across the Mid-West of America. One of their venues was a predominantly black congregational church in downtown St Louis, in Missouri. En route to the church the two men stopped in an all-black area and pulled over at the local Sheriff's office to seek directions. Benny Lee went into the office leaving his white friend sitting in the car and under strict instructions not to open the doors or windows to anyone. Geordie wondered why but didn't want to argue with his host, though it rankled with him, especially when the large gang of black youths, which had appeared from nowhere, seemed to be waving at him.

Moments later he was to discover why Benny Lee had told him to keep the car secure and he would also discover that the black youths were not exactly waving at him out of friendship.

The gang of vicious looking youths, wielding sticks and baseball bats menacingly patrolled the street opposite the car staring at the little Scotsman sitting alone. In waving their sticks and bats the amiable talk-to-anyone evangelist thought they were being friendly and actually waving him out for a chat. Unknown to him, the proceedings were being watched from the window of the Sheriff's office and seconds before Geordie Aitken would have left the car to join his black 'friends' Benny Lee rushed out of the police building and dived into the car. With him he had brought directions to the church but also a message from the Sheriff: 'The church is two miles up the highway on your left—now get that bloody white friend of yours and yourself out of this town.'

With tyres screeching the two white men sped off just as the black youths approached the car. 'We shot away from them because I later found out that they would have half-killed us both just for being white. At least I found out why Benny had told me to keep the car locked but at the time it seemed like nonsense because the thoughts going through my head were that surely if I could mix it with terrorists in Northern Ireland then surely I could handle a gang of friendly-looking black guys. But thankfully Benny showed a lot more wisdom than me and we beat a hasty retreat out of that black ghetto.'

A few miles up the road they duly found the church they were looking for and were welcomed with open arms as that part of the town housed both blacks and whites in harmony. But the area itself had the same physical problems of the ghetto from which they had just been forced to flee in fear of their lives. 'This area made the slums of Glasgow look like hotels in comparison to the houses in this broken-down dump of an area.'

But what the buildings lacked the people more than made up for. Once inside the church hall the two men sampled first hand the renowned Gospel singing of black Christians. 'There were about 200 of them all singing their happy hearts out and you could almost taste the joy and happiness that filled the room. These folks were black but they were so much different from our friends with the baseball bats.'

Once the singing stopped inside the San Francisco Temple, the leader, Elder Williams invited Geordie Aitken to share the platform with him and minister to the congregation. Because of their own deprived and harsh backgrounds the people readily accepted his testimony and clapped and cheered loudly throughout his address. 'Many of them were crying when I told them about the time in my past when I had wished I was dead but did not have the nerve to take my own life. They could see themselves in my past because they had obviously also endured hardship in theirs.'

Elated and emotional the two men left the church and headed back for St Charles, in Missouri, and another round of testimony meetings. But the elation was short lived for only days after Elder Williams had greeted the two men as his brothers and welcomed them into his church he met an untimely end. Geordie Aitken later heard that Elder Williams had been travelling to Colorado to address a meeting on how blacks and whites could live together when he was hijacked and shot dead by a notorious American racist group.

'It just shows how deep-rooted hatred can be because Elder Williams paid with his life for trying to get his message across. This and many other incidents really opened my eyes about life in America.'

But not all of his eye-opening experiences were so tragic. Having watched, and helped Geordie Aitken at work in his native Scotland's soup kitchens Pastor Benny Lee invited him to see how the soup pantry at the Celebration Fellowship in Missouri had developed. On his return from Scotland Benny Lee had opened up the kitchen in the plush American church and watched it grow into a thriving venture. It served the same purpose as the Scottish one but could not have been further removed in terms of size and management.

While Geordie Aitken doled out soup and bread to the street people of Glasgow the needy people of Missouri were treated to the finest food and drink thanks to a government initiative to supply the hungry and needy through a network of churches and charities.

'At home all I could provide was bread, hot soup and large helpings of love, but here I was witnessing something so much different from my own soup kitchen work. The food that the American government supplied was the best of gear. Tinned peanuts, fresh bread, butter, candy and even shaving foam, razor blades and toothpaste. Everything you could mention you could get from the government warehouses.'

Organizers of American soup kitchens only had to contact the agency and arrange to collect the required goods from a central warehouse. On one occasion Geordie Aitken joined in one of the runs but was heart-broken by the end of it. The foodstuffs and merchandise were sent along conveyor belts to a point where people would lift off their orders and load them into their vans before taking them back to their own churches and charities to be distributed to local needy cases. But such was the scale of things, and because of strict hygiene regulations, any damaged tins or ripped packets had to be discarded and thrown into special wastebins before being destroyed. That stuff alone would have kept Glasgow's earthy soup kitchens stocked up for months.

'My heart was breaking seeing all of this terrible wastage and tears were coming to my eyes thinking about how we could have fed scores of people at the Glasgow soup kitchens with what was being thrown out.'

He knew the Government legislation had to be obeyed but could not stop himself making the comparison between this food factory and his way of obtaining supplies in Scotland.

'Back home I would search through bins behind fruit shops for old vegetables so that I could cut off the good parts and make soup in my own home to take to the soup kitchen to feed the hungry, homeless people of my city. I could not handle this terrible wasting of food just because tins had a dent in them or because labels had fallen off but the strict Government rules had to be obeyed.'

After returning to the Celebration Fellowship Church where the food was to be distributed he endured even further conflicting emotions. He could not understand how the poor, hungry people, deemed in need of a handout invariably arrived to collect their goods by car. 'Many hungry families would come to the church and leave laden down with food but one of the things I could not comprehend was how most of them owned cars. Most of the folks we fed in Glasgow didn't even have shoes let alone cars. It truly showed me that different countries have different levels of poverty.'

Whatever the cultural differences the two men are on the same level when it comes to Christianity. They regularly cross the Atlantic and cement their extraordinary friendship in the Lord through their dealings with the needly people of both countries. Both men know that there are millions of people across the world who could yet experience such friendship and love, by giving their lives to the Lord and finding that something special which the true Christians share.

Having been introduced to America by the then Pastor Benny Lee, Geordie Aitken was to find himself speaking in meetings and churches across the massive country. Missouri, Ohio, and even the sunshine state of California were beckoning the street-level evangelist from Glasgow. Despite the cultural differences he was welcomed in all walks of American life.

Such was his influence at the church of Pastor Bob Tindall, in Missouri that he was to be adopted as the church's Scottish missionary. Worshippers at the Victory Church are greeted by his picture and name and address when they arrive for services at the Christian Center in St Charles. Both Bob Tindall and Geordie Aitken share a common respect and admiration for each other's work. Despite their differing backgrounds both men work hard in their respective communities to spread the Christian message.

Bob Tindall, a former salesman was himself saved at the age of 34 and after dedicating his life to the Lord actually witnessed to people as he continued working for a pharmaceutical company. But his real calling was in a church and after joining Hope Church in St Louis, Missouri, as an associate pastor, he spread his wings and opened the Victory Christian Center, in nearby St Charles. In its early days the church was founded with only three families but now draws larger congregations and plans are in the pipeline to extend the work of the center. From the earliest days when the church held services in a rented waterfront store with only thirty people in the congregation Pastor Bob Tindall has turned the center, at its new premises in Parkway, into a booming and joyful church center. His wife Gale helps at the church, his son Ty plays at services and his eldest daughter Tamra, gave up her lucrative job with American Airlines to oversee a Christian Day Care Center for local children.

Bob Tindall knows there is a lot of hard work to be done in bringing people to the Lord but states that with people like Geordie Aitken and himself preaching the message countless numbers will eventually see the light and give their lives to the Lord.

'The most important thing to us is that people come to know Jesus Christ. Geordie Aitken is loved by us because of the mutual feelings we share. I believe that the Lord brought Geordie Aitken into our lives and it was because of the love that we have for him that we adopted him as our Scottish missionary. There are two things that I look for in a person, honesty and integrity and I see both of those in Geordie Aitken. We are friends and brothers in the Lord and I have seen his ministry grow and grow. Some people can serve the Lord for a short time and if nothing seems to be happening, or they are not getting anything back then they just stop. But Geordie Aitken works tirelessly to spread his message and never looks for any personal credit as he knows the source of his inspiration. He does not do it for glory but through a deep love for the Lord and a deep love for people.'

Such were the mutual feelings of love and respect between Geordie Aitken and the Victory Christian Center that on one visit he was given a cheque for 1,000 dollars. When Geordie Aitken approached the man who had given him it to see if he had made a mistake the man promptly replied: 'Why, do you want me to put another nought on the end?'. Bob Tindall knows that the offer was a genuine one and that the cheque would have been upgraded had Geordie Aitken wanted it to be.

'He was shocked by the offer but it was made out of sincerity and a love for Geordie Aitken. Whenever he came to us there was a mutual feeling of love and friendship and we want him to come here every year. The reason that people take to Geordie Aitken is that he can stand up and be real. When he first came over he had no money and his clothes hardly fit him but the people at our church took to him not because of pity but because of love. He has a heart for people, especially those that are hurting and he has such a commitment that is not found in very many people. Everything he does he does through his genuine love of the Lord and not for any personal glory.'

Bob Tindall knows there is a great revival underway and that 'people are coming back to their first love' but he fears that America is soon to witness some hard and terrible times as the Lord leads people back from their financial and worldly desires. 'There is a great gap at present between the world and the Church and my whole purpose for living is to help people to met the Lord, get to know him and become like him. There's a reason for people being on earth and it is not what most people think it is.'

Geordie Aitken has seen firsthand the sincerity and faith of Pastor Bob Tindall and knows that he is the right man to help many lost souls find Jesus Christ. 'Bob Tindall has a tremendously powerful message to get across to people and he delivers it in a genuine and caring way that can let people see that the only way to true happiness is through salvation and living in harmony with the Lord and by dedicating their lives to Him. Bob Tindall knows that there are changes coming and through his deep faith and beliefs he is a man who can help people change their own lives.'

As the Victory Christian Center continues to grow Geordie Aitken visits the center whenever he can. Usually his visits are multi-purpose. Because of the obvious distance between his native Scotland and America he tries to schedule his trips to take in other churches and organizations across the Atlantic.

But whatever church it is, and in whatever part of the sprawling United States of America it happens to be he is welcomed as a friend and brother. Since his first visit in 1986 he has returned seven times, on an almost annual basis and after each trip comes away with even more friends and evangelical exploits to use in his witnessing for the Lord.

A close friend of former singer and now churchman Ed Fasnacht, Geordie Aitken has witnessed to people caught up in the devastating flooding that destroyed scores of homes in the Chesterfield Valley area of St Louis, Missouri, when the Missouri River broke its banks and left acres of land submerged in up to ten feet of water. Hundreds of people had to be evacuated when the waters descended upon them without warning in the summer of 1993. Ed Fasnacht and wife Patti were among the congregation of the St Louis Family Church which went to the aid of the stricken homeless families under the guidance of church Pastor the Reverend Jeff Perry. Together the church helped flood victims rebuild their lives, their homes and, just as importantly, their spirits.

Ed, now a devoted Christian, first met Geordie Aitken years before the flooding and recognized in him a deep belief in the Lord. He also knew what sacrifices Geordie Aitken had made in order to drag himself out of the gutter and dedicate his life to the Lord. Ed Fasnacht himself knew life at its lowest.

Now dedicated to helping others, and helping to establish the church and the Christian message across Missouri Ed Fasnacht was once, admittedly, a drunken and lost soul who would have died at an early age from drink and drug abuse had he not been saved. Like Geordie Aitken his saviour was the Lord Jesus Christ.

'Ed Fasnacht is living proof that the Lord does save lives if people are prepared to give their lives to Him. He has seen the dark side of life and was into everything in a big way but he is now a caring Christian with a beautiful testimony to tell. His own life story is an inspiration to everyone and through our shared faith we have become firm friends who have a great deal of time, and deep respect for each other. People will probably never know just how caring and dedicated to the community he really is.'

The way Ed Fasnacht was going in his early days it is nothing short of miraculous that he is even alive today let alone preaching the Lord's message in the St Louis area. By the time he was 6 he was already sampling alcohol and by the time he was 12 he was 'a real user'. Throughout his teenage years his habit developed and at one time he even stole from the local church youth group to help feed his addiction. The youngest of nine children he was brought up in traditional family virtues where by the time children were 18 they either joined the armed forces, moved out of the house or married. Fate decreed that he would take the third option and even today he still thanks God for sending his wife Patti into his life. But in the early years of their marriage Ed was a burden to his wife through his wild drinking and partying. Money was never a problem as he held down a regular decorating job and also played in an acclaimed rock band. In the 1970s the income from the band alone was over $10,000 a year but that was spent on drink and drugs. For five years he was on a monthly diet of thirty hits of speed and 120 Valium tablets along with a daily diet of a litre bottle of bourbon, three six-packs of beer and a steady intake of marijuana and LSD. 'I was on a collision course with death and heading for hell. Inside I was crying out for God but knew that I would have to give all of this up and to be honest I didn't want to.'

Instead he continued to drink and do drugs up until the point where he began lying to Patti about his habits. Even when taking Patti to work or picking her up he would stop off at convenience stores and buy two six-packs of beer but tell his wife he had only drank two bottles of it. On the eve of St Patricks Day in 1976, Ed Fasnacht was to change for ever and embark on a life with the Lord after eventually fighting off his alcoholic addiction.

It was while painting his boss's house that he finally cracked. Being a competent decorator he would usually work flat out every morning to get through his workload and then hit the nearest bar to feed his addiction. In a one-hour lunch break alone he would get through twelve beers and four glasses of whiskey. But on this occasion when

he returned to the house to finish the job he could not hold the
paintbrush steady. 'My whole life flashed in front of me and I could
see myself lying to Patti and ignoring her. Everything just caved in on
me and I ran through the house screaming "no more, no more, God
help me".' With the help of his sister-in-law he booked into a treatment
clinic for three weeks in a bid to curb his drinking. Such was the scale
of his problem that he got drunk even on the way to the clinic. When
he came out he stayed off the drink but knew there was something
missing in his life. 'When I got out I was sober but I was empty.'

At work his foreman urged him to go to church with him and seek
out the Lord in a bid to save his life. It was then that Ed Fasnacht
realized that the Lord had saved him for a purpose. To be a Gospel
singer. To this day he is an acclaimed singer in churches and performs
at concerts in front of thousands. 'When I walked into this chuch the
people were so real and alive. When I learned that God will meet you
where you are at it felt like a great weight had been lifted from my
shoulders and I began to see things differently. I knew that I had been
called by the Lord to sing the Gospel.'

A week after Ed Fasnacht gave his life to the Lord in Grace Church,
St Louis his wife Patti did the same. It was his Gospel singing that was
to lead him into contact with Geordie Aitken at Pastor Benny Lee's
former church.

'There was this little guy there dressed in plaid trousers and wearing
a tam on his head. I gave him a tape of me singing "All the losers
win" and for some reason knew deep down that this would not be
the last time we would meet.' A year later the paths crossed again and
the foundations of a deep friendship were being lain. 'That was when
we really connected. I saw a man who was so full of the love of Jesus
and so loud for the Lord. He is a man who is so full of humility and
is not just a sayer of the word but a doer of the word. All of the things
I noticed about Geordie Aitken proved to be a real inspiration to me.'

Despite his own harrowing background and the obstacles he had
overcome in giving his life to the Lord, Ed Fasnacht learned a lot from
Geordie Aitken. 'After hearing him speak about his own life it made
me realize that I was a very fortunate man and should not complain
about anything. I had met Christians who thought they were something
else but I saw a genuineness in him and he impacted into my life in

With Ed and Patti Fasnacht.

a major way. He has a way of getting across to people that this is not a game but real life.'

Like Benny Lee the only complaint that Ed Fasnacht has about Geordie Aitken is that he lives so far away. Many times when he has been down Ed Fasnacht has wished he had his Scottish friend close at hand. 'At all-time lows in my life there has been a man called Geordie Aitken who has loved me for who I am. He has encouraged me not to look to men but to look to Jesus as he is the one who will never let us down. I have been honoured to have been in his presence and it is an honour to call this man my friend as this little man is a giant in the kingdom of God.'

On one of his last trips to America Geordie Aitken accompanied

Ed Fasnacht around the devastated Chesterfield Valley area where church workers and relief teams are still trying to pick up the pieces of the massive flooding. With the Reverend Jeff Perry from the St Louis Family Church, Ed Fasnacht, wife Patti and scores of helpers are busy rebuilding homes and lives. Two days after the July 1993 flooding Jeff Perry preached to a flock of about 200 people from the middle of the closed-off Highway 40 just yards from where his church stood in ten feet of water. To date the church has restored its own building and helped refurbish 45 houses and 70 businesses over an area of eighteen square miles. Ed Fasnacht, who runs a contracting business in St Louis put his own life on hold to help out with the mission of mercy. But he knows that faith is just as important as bricks and mortar and he saw firsthand just how encouraging Geordie Aitken can be when it comes to bringing hope to people. He was not surprised when Geordie Aitken finished addressing a group of relief workers and was duly invited by many of them to visit their hometown churches the length and breadth of America and speak to the people of their communities. Ed Fasnacht had known for years what the assembled workers were just finding out. 'Geordie Aitken is sold out for the Lord. His testimony is an inspiration to everyone who meets him.'

Patti Fasnacht herself knows just how much of an inspiration he really is. After first meeting Geordie Aitken she felt compelled to get up and take a Christian message into the lives of people. She admits that she was never a bold person but after meeting the Scottish evangelist felt an inner strength and an urge to do more practical work for the Lord. 'He has been a great example to me. I was never a bold person but seeing his boldness for the Lord has helped me and made me want to get up and go outside of my comfortable zone and help. He has got an endearing quality to reach people and is willing to take as much time as is needed to get to know a person as he is genuinely interested in their welfare. He lives the Gospel and lives Christ on a daily basis.'

She also knows that only the Lord could have changed Geordie Aitken from what he once was into what he now is. 'Who he used to be and who is he now is remarkable. To see how someone who was once so torn up with hatred and committed to a violent cause, can make a full U-turn and be even more committed to Christ is amazing and it is fantastic to hear of the countless lives that have been changed as a result of his ministry. That is why we know God created Geordie Aitken with a specific purpose in mind. He is a real-life Christian straight out of the Bible out there amongst people doing what Jesus himself did.'

Throughout Geordie Aitken's travels across America, Christian couple Bobby and Terry Grapenthin have provided him with the homely support needed by the travelling evangelist. Whenever he visits the Ohio and Missouri areas of the United States their home becomes his home. Their moral support and native knowledge of America has proved invaluable to Geordie Aitken on his evangelical travels. Not only because they literally know the lay of the land but because they and their two children share a deep Christian faith and are fully committed to the Lord. As much as Geordie Aitken can help others they too can offer him a place of rest and times of comforting fellowship. As well as a deep friendship they also share a deep and genuine belief in the Lord.

Bobby and Terry, like many other Americans, were impressed by Geordie Aitken after meeting him for only the first time, despite most of the congregation initially thinking he was Hungarian! Despite the language barriers the couple soon came to love Geordie Aitken and offered him accommodation whenever he visited their part of America. As the friendship blossomed so did Bobby and Terry begin visiting Scotland to share their faith with the Scottish people. It was during one of the trips that they realized how special Geordie Aitken was. While there Geordie Aitken encouraged the couple to take an active part in his ministry which is something Bobby Grapenthin will never forget.

'Because Geordie loved us the people of Scotland loved us and, similarly, because we loved Geordie we also wanted to love his people. Simply because of Geordie Aitken a lot of love passed between complete strangers. Out of all the ministers we have ever known Geordie Aitken is the only one who has urged us to become involved in his ministry. He is the only one who has shown that he trusts people enough to let them get involved with people and that is a very important thing. When we do this we are not only representing the Lord but also Geordie Aitken and it is his good name and reputation that is on the line and we will always respect the fact that he trusts us enough, and

With Bobby and Terry Grapenthin.

believes in us enough, to keep that intact. We respect that and would put our reputations on the line for him.'

Bobby and Terry Grapenthin now spend their lives helping others, and although they realize that they could never do the street work of Geordie Aitken they know they are vital cogs in the Lord's work by backing him and supporting him during his American trips. 'We all serve the same God but while Geordie Aitken's ministry is in evangelizing ours is in helping people. We can help the people like Geordie Aitken who are actually out doing the work and it is an act of God that our paths came to cross. If I'm helping Geordie Aitken I'm helping the Lord.'

Bobby herself is more than happy to help Geordie Aitken spread his evangelical message after years of heartache when she was diagnosed as having a rare form of life-threatening cancer. At one stage doctors told her she might only have days to live. But she and husband Terry pulled through by the power of prayer. Trouble flared after Bobby noticed a hard lump in the side of her neck and despite years of tests, hospital visits and trips to cancer specialists the lumps grew until she had them under her arms and on her legs and stomach. 'Here they were giving me only days to live and yet they didn't even know what was wrong with me.' Finally, specialists called Bobby in to tell her they had discovered what was wrong with her but could not offer her much hope in the way of treatment. They gave her three options, do nothing, risk taking medication that could be highly dangerous or even fatal because of the advanced state of cancer or simply pray. Bobby and Terry decided prayer was the only answer.

Amazingly, five long and tiring days after they began praying the lumps began to disappear. After all of the worry and hospital visits the problem was over and the cancerous lumps simply vanished. During their darkest days the couple studied a great deal on what the Bible says about healing and Bobby Grapenthin has regularly demonstrated spiritual healing powers both in America and while visiting Geordie Aitken in Scotland.

At one meeting she actually healed a crippled woman and watched as her deformed leg actually grew half an inch to come back into line with her other leg. 'As long as God can trust me to say that he did it then it will continue to work. This girl came up to me and said that the Lord had told her that the deformity was going to be cured and as I held her the shorter leg just grew out by half an inch.' Amazed by what was happening other people took to the stage to be cured of various ailments leaving Bobby to remember how: 'We were hardly touching people and they were being touched by the power of the Lord and dropping to the floor all around us. People were coming up to us because they recognized God was doing this and not me.'

Over the years the Grapenthin family have witnessed enough 'miracles' to leave them convinced the only explanation is the power of the Lord. Now the mother of two beautiful daughters, Bobby suffered eight miscarriages as she strived to have a family. Despite treatment at the Boston Fertility Clinic she was destined to endure more heartache as the pioneering treatment saw her go into cardiac arrest and rushed her into the intensive care unit of the hospital. After going into labour both she and a Christian nurse prayed throughout the night that Bobby might for once have a successful and healthy pregnancy. She did and that was to herald the arrival of a baby daughter.

Bobby and Terry Grapenthin say they have a lot to thank the Lord for and are now content to spend their lives repaying him. Even during their working days they minister to people they come into contact with when the opportunity arises. The fact that Geordie Aitken shares such a deep faith with them is what makes him special to both them and the Lord.

'When we first met Geordie Aitken we were not touched so much by his life story but by the heart of the man. He has been such a blessing in our life and it is refreshing to see someone who is so bold and active for Jesus. He has a freight train approach and he is bold enough to say to people "if you don't like me then I'm not bothered but I'm coming through anyway". He has been a tremendous help to us, and countless others as people need people like Geordie Aitken to drag themselves out of where they are.'

Bobby and Terry Grapenthin's honesty and caring nature is not lost on Geordie Aitken who classes the couple as being amongst his closest friends. 'I have never seen so much kindness put my way by other people than that shown to me by Bobby and Terry. The best things anyone can give me is their love and kindness and they have been given to me in abundance by Bobby and Terry Grapenthin. They are the kind of caring and compassionate people who would put most so-called Christians to shame.'

In Lorain County, Ohio, Geordie Aitken has been welcomed at the Church on the North Coast Christian Center where Pastors Louis and Tina Kayatin are building up a Christian empire where the actual church is only one building among dozens that include schools and other educational establishments where fundamental Christian beliefs are taught. Housed on the sprawling complex is the Family Life Center and the North Coast Christian Academy.

Despite the size of the complex the church is also looking to acquire over sixty acres of adjoining land where a new sanctuary could be built together with buildings where visiting missionaries and people from across the world can rest and study. The innovative plans could also include a landing pad where people could be flown into the Christian Center.

At the helm of the Center, and behind the proposed developments is Pastor Louis Kayatin whose faith in the Lord knows no bounds. The powerful preacher, who reaches into the very hearts of his congregation has travelled a long road in his walk with Christ since his early days

With Pastor Louis Kayatin at North Coast Christian Center.

when he was drinking whiskey at the age of 12. He would pinch the whiskey from his father's drinks cabinet and top the bottle up with water to hide his crime. Before he was 18 he was running around the streets fighting, stealing, drinking up to twenty-four beers a day and taking LSD and speed. Even after joining the US Navy he was heading for disaster. Often he would be left lying on a back street of a foreign country drunk out of his mind when the rest of the crew returned to their ship. It took a former alcoholic to lead him to the Lord at the age of 23.

'I knew what a mess this former drug addict and alcoholic used to be and when I saw the change in him I knew there had to be something and wanted to know what it was that had happened to him.' Louis Kayatin, at the time was working at the US Steel Mill and had everything a man could want. A beautiful wife, three young children and a fantastic job which brought all of the trimmings from his house to his flash car. But he also had severe drink problems and was empty inside. 'Before my conversion I was selfish, egotistical and materialistic and had everything I needed but my life was going downhill fast with firstly my marriage and then my drinking.'

Having given his life to the Lord, Louis Kayatin started serving the Lord at the Church on the North Coast before studying at Florida Bible College and returning to the church as Youth Pastor in 1979 where he worked with troubled teenagers. In 1981 he became Pastor and took over the reins of the church which at that time had less than 200 members. Now it is a sprawling Christian Center with over 1,000 members. As the numbers continue to grow and the Center expands, Louis Kayatin and wife Tina use their life's experiences to prove the power of the Lord.

'I was released from a prison without bars when Christ gave me a new life. I was a zombie, a living dead person, and I was dying every day a death that brought much pain with it but now I'm living a life that is free from those pains. I'm a person now that never existed before. It is like a marriage because until you come to the Lord there's a part of your life that you will never know about. When you become one with the Lord you become a new creation. We are trying to reach out into the world and tell people the story of what God has done for us. We want others to feel special because in the eyes of the Lord they are special.'

Just as Geordie Aitken travels to America and Northern Ireland to bring people to the Lord so, too, does Louis Kayatin leave his native country to spread an evangelical message in other countries. Missions from his church regularly leave Ohio to spread the word in all corners of the globe from Russia to Israel, and Mexico to the Bahamas. Louis Kayatin has himself travelled to the eastern-bloc country of Russia where he has ministered to thousands of people. He will never forget one night when 6,000 Russians attended a stadium meeting on the outskirts of Moscow and over 5,000 of them gave their lives to the Lord.

'I could not speak their language and they could not understand mine so I would just hold up the Bible where I went.' With twenty members of the Church on the North Coast, Louis Kayatin was given the opportunity to speak in schools and colleges in the town of Orel, near Moscow, which had a population of over 400,000. With the help of interpreters and bi-lingual Christians the message was accepted by many of them. 'We gave our testimonies and shared Christ and were each doing at least four meetings a day. We all became missionaries for two weeks to take the Lord's message out to the world.'

Closer to home, the church helps the needy and deprived people of its own area. An area which has fifty-two different nationalities living in it and which has some terrible ghetto areas. Children are brought into the Center by bus to learn the Bible which is made easier for them by Tina Kayatin teaching it in a music and drama form. Over the border in Mexico, the church runs a bus through the squalid shanty towns equipped with a shower and medical supplies. 'In these areas people actually live on rubbish dumps and we take old school buses around fitted with showers as some of these people have never had a bath in their lives. We also feed them, clothe them and tell them about Jesus and the church.'

It is the ambition of Louis and Tina Kayatin to take the Lord's message worldwide and already they have linked up with a radio station to take that message further afield. The Far East and China is the next destination for the Christian church. 'We believe we have to reach out into the world and deliver God's message to people. In China alone there are two billion people who have never heard the message and it is our obligation to tell them about it.' That plan is working at the church where twenty-six flags from different nations across the world proudly fly above the sprawling Center depicting the different countries from where numerous visiting missionaries have come. Louis Kayatin respects Geordie Aitken for taking his simplistic faith across the oceans and into different cultures. Within one day of meeting Geordie Aitken he asked him to speak at the weekly Bible meeting in front of hundreds of people.

'Geordie Aitken has got a fantastic testimony to tell and speaks straight from the heart. He has a deep love for the Lord and it is the powerful, yet simplistic manner in which he relates his testimony that draws people to him. It is wonderful for people in churches and centers like ours to hear his testimony. We are all brothers in the Lord and it is refreshing to see someone like Geordie Aitken, who has given his life completely to the Lord, preaching in the forthright way that he does.'

Since his earliest trips to America in 1986 Geordie Aitken has returned to the country on numerous occasions and with every visit adds to his tally of people he has led to the Lord. But he can also be found in Alcoholics Anonymous meetings in heady sun-drenched areas of Los Angeles or in nursing homes and hospitals across the Mid-West of America. Whether in America, Scotland or Northern Ireland he is not averse to just stopping in the street and ministering to a person.

That was fully demonstrated over 2,000 miles away from Ohio when Geordie Aitken visited Santa Monica, in Los Angeles, California. Far

from the back streets of his native Glasgow Geordie Aitken knows that
the problems suffered by those walking the sun-drenched boulevards
are fundamentally the same as those experienced by his fellow Scotsmen
dodging the rain showers in Glasgow. Alcohol, sadness and depression
are not reserved for Scotland. Whatever new ministries he opens up,
be it in a street, a church or a prison, people are people to Geordie
Aitken. Their problems are his problems. He has ministered to people
from all walks of life but in the sunnier climes of Los Angeles he has
recently opened up a new ministry with the help of fellow Glaswegian
John Keaveney.

Far from the Scottish suburbs he has worked with American servicemen traumatised by the active service they have seen in numerous
wars. Many of the men, and women, still relive the horrors of Vietnam.
Many of them resorted to drink and drugs to forget the horrors of the
war and now rely on heavy counselling and support to pull them back
from the brink.

With John Keaveney of New Directions.

John Keaveney, a little Scotsman, is a scriptural mountain of a man when it comes to helping veterans of various wars. He himself is a Vietnam veteran who saw first hand the horrors of the controversial conflict which even today many servicemen still 'don't know what the hell it was all about'. But John Keaveney is now fighting an even bigger battle than the days when he carried a rifle and wore the American uniform as he strives to get his fellow veterans the help and support many of them need. It is a battle with bureaucracy and red tape that he is determined to win for the sake of all servicemen. To date he has won many battles but knows those individual victories alone have not won him the war. While there are still suffering veterans to be helped he will continue fighting. John Keaveney and a band of dedicated helpers now run a rehabilitation programme under the banner of New Directions Incorporated. The volunteers kept the innovative programme going after the American government pulled out of it and stopped

With US Army veterans in California.

funding it. The news, was a devastating blow to hundreds of veterans who knew it was their only hope of getting back into a normal life.

They were saved by John Keaveney who took over the disbanded programme and set it up as a private concern although he and his fellow directors work on a voluntary basis. To date he has a home for veteran men and a separate home for veteran women and has just negotiated the lease on a sprawling building which he hopes to convert into a rehabilitation centre for scores of homeless and suffering veterans. He estimates that in Los Angeles alone there are up to 30,000 veterans walking the streets and living a squalid life. He wants to help every single one of them.

He knows exactly what they are going through. Born and raised in Scotland, where he even once attended the same Bernard Street School, in Glasgow, as his close friend Geordie Aitken, he was destined to lead a life of heartache before finding his true calling in life. He is a respected and loved man in veteran circles but gives the credit for everything he has achieved to God.

In his early days God was the last thing on his mind. Having seen the squalor of both Glasgow and Belfast during his early years John Keaveney set off for America, age 18, and a year later joined the US Army. During his years in Vietnam, between 1969 and 1972, he changed from being a willing recruit into a heroin-addicted savage soldier. Back in America he embarked on a drug-taking and criminal spree that saw him in and out of prison and sleeping rough for years. Even a return trip to his native Scotland could not pull him out of the mire and he returned to Los Angeles in 1982. Months later he was back before the courts and facing a prison sentence of up to life for his violent drug-related crimes. But in placing him with the Veterans Association programme the American judge had saved his life and heralded the start of John Keaveney's mission to help other veterans.

Shad Meshad, President of the National Veterans Foundation, knows only too well how far John Keaveney has come. When he was accepted into the programme in 1983 John Keaveney actually took Shad Meshad hostage at knifepoint as his crazed mind again took over from reality. But today Shad recounts how: 'He was one of the most dangerous and angry veterans I have ever seen and he almost killed me in 1983 so the change in him has been miraculous. He is on a mission like nobody

I have seen in a long time.' Two years after completing the programme John Keaveney immediately took to the streets to bring homeless veterans into the government programme. He was given a job with the Veterans Administration but continued to evangelize for the New Directions programme for many years. When the Government pulled the plug on it he and two volunteers opened it as a private non-profit making concern.

With his Christian beliefs John Keaveney has also worked with Mother Teresa in Calcutta and indeed with veterans of the Afghanistan war hooked on hard drugs. Because of his pioneering work in the United States with his fellow servicemen he was invited into Russia to consult on programmes for Soviet veterans of the Afghanistan War. Back in Los Angeles his dedicated team of volunteers are working the clock round to help as many veterans as possible. Today there are various schemes and programmes available to veterans and most of them have been based on the work of John Keaveney. It is no surprise he has picked up such honours as the Congressional Award which was presented to him in Washington DC by Congressman Matthew Martinez for his pioneering work. Shad Meshad knows John Keaveney will never give up until every veteran is given a fighting chance of making a new start and offered help. He remembers how he once took him to speak at a university:

'In twenty minutes he owned 1,200 people. John's single-mindedness and charisma will make him a potent social and political influence on the way society treats its veterans and homeless and if something is to get done it will be done by someone like John. He's just a miracle. He is on a mission, just the same way as he used to hunt people down on the streets, to get the respect that veterans need and the basic health care and shelter.'

At the rehabilitation center where John Keaveney runs New Directions the residents also know his full worth. Veteran George Vanderford, who used to load the body bags in Vietnam has been to hell and back both in the combat zone and on the streets of America. Since his discharge he has been in sixty-four detoxification programmes, eight halfway houses and two mental institutions. When he talks about something he chooses his words carefully. Of his mentor John Keaveney he simply states: 'This man saved my life. I don't consider this a programme but a new start in life and the family and home that I never had.'

As the programme blossoms and expands so, too, do John Keaveney's own horizons and personal plans. He has also extended the New Directions concept into the streets where he hopes troubled teenagers and the young gang members from notorious areas of Los Angeles can be given a new start and a direction in life. Under the guidance of fellow volunteer Larry Williams the gang members are being offered the chance to make something of their lives before it is too late. John and Larry are hoping to get to them before they meet a premature end by a bullet or a knife in areas of the sprawling city where drive-by shootings, gang warfare and murders are everyday occurences.

They had their work cut out at the height of the infamous Los Angeles riots in 1992 when hundreds of people went on the rampage after the controversial court case in which white policemen were cleared of battering a black motorist. For days shops burned and vicious fighting and looting was the order of the day as disgusted black people and street gangs wreaked their warped revenge.

The importance of the work Larry Williams does in the South Central area of Los Angeles was demonstrated in a direct telephone call from Congresswoman Maxine Waters at the height of the troubles. The message was a clear call for help with Maxine Waters telling Larry: 'The police and the military can't do anything so could you please try.' They immediately swung into action and now many of the young gang members are finding a new reason for living. A centre has been opened where they can work and give themselves a sense of purpose. It stands in the middle of an area where drive-by shootings are commonplace and near to a motel where an estimated six murders are committed every week. But for the youngsters working at the Center the violence is now only a part of their history as they strive to drag themselves away from it.

Larry Williams, who knows he is giving the gang members a new lease of life through the New Directions programme, will never forget how much John Keaveney and the people involved with the programme have given him. 'I have been brought back from the dead and I have now got a purpose in life and it is all because of people caring for me.'

Working the troubled streets with the programme is a blessing in

With Larry Williams of New Directions.

disguise for Geordie Aitken. 'There is so much that can be done with youngsters if people have the faith to go out and do it.' It is such sentiment that John Keaveney knows can make Geordie Aitken an important part of his mission to bring stability, peace and comfort into the lives of many people in Los Angeles, if not America itself.

He knows the future of the country depends on its youth. A pending project is to arrange exchange visits between youngsters from Glasgow and Belfast and the youths from the troubled streets of South Central Los Angeles. He hopes Geordie Aitken can help him get it off the ground through his own involvement on the streets of Scotland and Northern Ireland.

'I hope to set up some exchange visits between the kids from Scotland and Northern Ireland and the youngsters from Los Angeles to widen their horizons and that is where Geordie Aitken can really come into things. The Lord uses impossible men to perform his impossible miracles and that is why he picked out Geordie Aitken. He is not only open to the Lord but really believes in him. He was a guy who once believed

Spreading Christianity on the streets of Los Angeles.

in nothing but hate but now believes in the good of God and that in itself is a powerful testimony to Geordie Aitken. If you really believe in something you show it in the way you try to give something back and that is what Geordie Aitken is doing and the places he is trying to take his message into really are the bellys of the beasts.'

Geordie Aitken knows how horrific and soul-destroying it can be working with desolate street people.

'One of the most heartbreaking experiences I ever went through happened while I was in Los Angeles and had the privilege of being invited to "Skid Row" to share some fellowship with my less fortunate brothers and sisters who sleep rough on the streets and in hostels. To my amazement I witnessed with my own eyes hundreds of zombie-like people and what made the situation even sicker was that many of the sidewalk people were ex-Vietnam veterans who had fought bravely for the country they loved and were proud to call America.

'The trouble with this situation, in my opinion, is that these men fought battles in Vietnam that would have been nothing more than

Away from his street-level ministry Geordie Aitken has even witnessed to Governor
John Ashcroft during a visit to Jefferson City, Missouri.

manoeuvres compared to the suffering and pain they are now enduring today on the streets of their own country.

'Some of the folks I witnessed to were not different from the homeless folks I feed and clothe back home in Scotland but the multitudes of homeless people all together in one area really blew my mind. Why can America with all of its wealth and biblical belts allow this situation to continue. The immense wealth in America should be able to finance such organizations as New Directions and the Vietnam Veterans Foundation to help obliterate this sick situation among the homeless and unloved Vietnam veterans who have lost all purpose for living. There is a road back for all of these people through such organizations but first the problem has to be acknowledged as it is too horrendous to just sweep under the carpet of a very, very respectable Los Angeles society.

'John Keaveney, an ex-Vietnam veteran has, like myself, found the road back to normality through some folks who loved and cared for

To get his message to a wider audience Geordie Aitken was invited to speak on an
Illinois radio station by Christian presenter Joanne Bateman.

him despite the way he once was. Like myself in Scotland, John is
now working with limited finances to help alleviate the problems of
the twilight world and the desperate people who live in it.

'With the backing and support of Shad Meshad of the Vietnam
Veterans Foundation they are working in the areas of the unloved and
unwanted. These two men sure have a great love and concern for the
homeless and especially the Vietnam veterans who are fighting the
biggest battle of their lives against enemies called heroin and alcohol
brought on by the lousy, worthless Vietnam War.

'Every country has its own Skid Row but it is not every country
that has had a negative Vietnam War like America. If only I could help
in some small way then I would feel better because anyone with a
heart would not be able to look upon Skid Row and not want to do
something about the lonely streets of desolate people.'

It is a challenge that Geordie Aitken is relishing as he continues to expand his ministries. 'Just to help John Keaveney in some small way would be a blessing to me as he has done so much good for the people it is unbelievable. The beauty of it all is that the credit for everything he has done, and he has done a tremendous amount, goes to the Lord. If anyone doubts that God exists they only have to look as far as this man. He is an inspiration to everyone.'

Since his first trip to America avenues have opened up in all walks of life for the Scottish evangelist who knows no boundaries. Working with Vietnam veterans and other war veterans, street gangs or addressing collar-and-tie church groups is all in a days work for the man who repeatedly takes his simplistic message and powerful testimony across the Atlantic.

It is not just paying lip service to him when the American people he has met and influenced call him a 'blessing to the people of America'.

If trees could speak of days gone by
the tales they would tell would make you sigh
Of battles fought with lance and spear
dating back for many a year

Where knights were bold and castles strong
this era of time with harp and song
What a joy if the trees could see
and to view past times with ecstasy

Then again if trees could hear
the sound of the river and the drinking deer
On the knuckled branch the feathered friend
can perch with joy that has no end

This poem I write is written by thought
from a heavenly gift that cannot be bought
That gift is Jesus my Saviour and friend
who created the tree that His wind can bend

These heavenly words come from above
by a Holy Ghost power full of heavenly love
This poem for you I pray will bring joy
that is the purpose of a heavenly ploy

So go on with Jesus the Saviour of man
and stay close to him as close as you can
Your past life is forgiven by his saving grace
just look upon Jesus with the heavenly face

Trees

# CHAPTER 11

# From a Lord to a Layabout

Whatever country or continent Geordie Aitken has visited during his evangelical travels it is the ordinary man on the street whom he tries to reach.

But whatever is put in his way he will cope with. His targets are the unfortunates of the world but anyone with a problem will find that Geordie Aitken has a spare moment to listen to their worries. People have always been the most important thing in his life since his conversion to Christianity. In his early days he did not have a decent thought for anyone. Not even his own family. But in a dramatic turn-around the physical well-being and the spiritual welfare of his fellow man became all important to him.

In the last twelve years, since the night that the Lord took over his life and saved him from an early grave, he has encountered thousands and thousands of people. Many of them he has led to the Lord while for many others he has been a much-needed shoulder to cry on even if they were not interested in giving their lives to Christ.

The people he has met and influenced have come from numerous countries, various walks of life and highly different backgrounds. From Lords to lice-infected down-and-outs he has left his amazing mark on countless people. Many of those meetings have been serious but also humorous while many others have been serious but also, sadly, heart-breaking. Before, during and now after his conversion Geordie Aitken's life has always been full of incident.

But in a far cry from his earlier dark days when he was always looking to take from people he now has something to give. And all he ever gets back, and it is all he wants to get back, is the knowledge that in some cases he has led another person to the Lord, while on other occasions he has simply earned the respect of his fellow man.

That in itself bears testament to the man who once slept in field, fought with anyone in sight and was once branded 'an excuse for a man' by an old school friend who saw him begging outside pubs.

Now people will testify that far from being an excuse for a man Geordie Aitken is a man amongst men. And these tributes come from people who deal with everyday life and know what they are talking about. They are Geordie Aitken's kind of people. The people who live and work the mean streets of Glasgow and know from their own bitter experiences what life in some areas of the tough city can be like. To walk them after dark is classed by many as an achievement. Actually to have an impact on them is classed by many others as a miracle. The streets are where Geordie Aitken wants to preach but because of the very nature of his powerful message he knows he can never settle for just helping the lepers of society. Because of what he is he has ministries in just about every walk of life. Prisons, schools, churches and hospitals. But wherever he goes he preaches the same forthright way whether it be to aristocrats or alcoholics.

Social standings have never been a barrier against the evangelical preachings of Geordie Aitken. People's problems are the same whether you are on the top rung or the bottom step of the social ladder.

Prostitutes, drunks and dossers have all been led to Christ by the tough talking Scotsman. Media personalities, people with mental problems, tramps and terrorists have all been addressed by him. Not only does he bring Christ into people's lives he also brings comfort.

One who knows such comfort, and is far removed from the everyday street people in Geordie Aitken's life is the nobleman Lord Hugh Douglas Hamilton. The Scottish aristocrat said he feels 'honoured' to be a friend of Geordie Aitken. The friend who helped him through a difficult spell when he had problems with alcohol. As with all public figures Lord Hamilton finds himself a source of unwanted media attention whenever things go wrong. They did just that when he was convicted for his latest drink driving charge and hauled before a Scottish court of law. His name was daubed across the front of most newspapers eager to tell of his downfall. But one reader was more interested in his future welfare than his present predicament. The reader was Geordie Aitken.

Knowing the pressures and pain that an alcoholic problem can bring he wrote a letter in the hope that it would reach Lord Hamilton. It did but more remarkably it was answered. But that nearly turned into a farce when the well-spoken Scottish lord rang Geordie Aitken at his East Kilbride home three weeks after receiving his letter of comfort.

Because of the delay Geordie Aitken was not expecting a reply and when he heard the educated tones of Lord Hamilton he instinctively thought it was his old friends up to their tricks. Often they would ring him up, feign accents and pretend to be someone else. Lord Hamilton's telephone enquiry of: 'could I speak to Mr Geordie Aitken please, this is Lord Hamilton here' was met with response: 'Get a grip of yourself, you daft sod, and stop taking the Mickey.' But it really was Lord Hamilton. Dozens of apologies later the two men finally entered into a lengthy conversation about the letter. The aristocrat said he would like to meet Geordie Aitken but because of a busy social diary and the fact that he had just been banned from driving for seven years he was unable to make the trip to East Kilbride but invited his new pen-pal to visit him at his farmhouse in the Scottish countryside.

The letter that sparked the invitation, and the beginning of a close friendship, was one of the scores that the public figure receives weekly. 'I get a lot of letters from people and I have learned to distinguish between what are genuine ones and what are not. I don't reply to very many but there was something so real and genuine about Geordie Aitken's letter that I knew he had something to offer me. When he came to see me this proved to be the case as I thought we had a lot in common and a lot to talk about. That letter was the means by which I became very friendly with Geordie Aitken.'

The two men kept in close contact but their first meeting was straight out of Geordie Aitken's handbook of street-level evangelism.

Without transport, and knowing that his trusted mountain bike would hardly get him to the farmhouse, he commandeered the Loaves and Fishes soup kitchen Transit van, along with a driver and a group of his friends. 'If you had seen the state of us you would have thought we had gone to burgle the place. What a motley crew we were.' Included in the group was John 'Shotgun' Elliott, a man who had served twenty-four years of his life in prison for various heavy crimes. His last sentence was imposed for the shooting of two men. John, himself reformed and a Christian would later witness the true value of Geordie Aitken and his work in the prisons and on the streets.

When they arrived at the nobleman's farmhouse Geordie Aitken toyed with the idea of leaving his friends in the van and out of sight. 'I was afraid that he might not open the door if he saw them.' Geordie Aitken strode up to the door and began knocking. After a while he started peering through the window for signs of life, His host popped his head out of an upstairs window and bellowed: 'Is that you Geordie?' An affirmative answer of: 'Aye, is that Hughie,' and Lord Hamilton was on his way down the stairs to open his door to the Scottish evangelist for the first of many times.

Geordie with Lord Hugh Douglas Hamilton.

After Geordie explained that his friends would wait in the van Lord Hamilton exclaimed: 'Tell them to come in, any friend of yours is a friend of mine.' So in walked the unkempt quartet for what was to end up as a three hour visit. Despite their social differences the group got on famously with their host, repeatedly disappearing into the kitchen to refill their coffee cups. Geordie Aitken declined the offer and settled for a glass of Coca Cola. He was to discover that Lord Hamilton had recently invested in a homemaking kit and had yet to master the art. Following the request for a soft drink the nobleman duly brought his guest a pint of homemade Coca Cola minus the bubbles for him to quench his thirst. Their host returned to the kitchen to bring out the coffee and a dismayed Geordie Aitken wondered what to do with the 'flat as a pancake' drink. Knowing his face would give the game away if he tried to drink the uncarbonated pop in front of his host he quickly gulped down what he could and watered a couple of nearby plants with the remainder, and prayed that his eyes would have stopped watering before his Lordship re-emerged from the kitchen.

When Lord Hamilton returned and noticed his empty glass he promptly took it back and filled it to the brim. Geordie Aitken tried to disguise his grimace with a smile. But he was not the only one to be sitting suffering in silence.

Wherever the motley crew of former thieves, villains and conmen looked there were obvious signs of wealth. In their earlier days the lot would have been rolled up in a tablecloth and taken off the lord's hands. Now they were Christians but human none the less. As they sat talking, in the absence of the coffee-making lord, they expressed a preference.

'The first thing I would have taken in my old days would have been the Highland claymore hanging on the wall.

'One of the lads said he would have blagged the collection of valuable clay pipes. As we heard Lord Hugh returning I told everyone to shut up.' After the lengthy conversation the last thing on any mind of the born-again group was thieving. Instead, they left his house with a deep liking of their new friend. And for Geordie Aitken, the right to fish on an exclusive stretch of river. Geordie having explained that he was a fisher of men, Lord Hamilton asked if he did any fishing and said that he could use his land whenever he wanted. He declined the offer but the immensity of it was not lost on one of the shoddy visitors. 'I fish my Lord, I fish,' piped up one of them before receiving a quelling glance from Geordie Aitken.

With that, the social misfits trooped out of the farmhouse and into the battered soup kitchen van for the second leg of their trip.

Before returning to Glasgow they were going to visit nearby Nunraw Abbey and the friendly monks who had become a part of the evangelist's life—with 700 cans of EEC stew. They had been donated for the soup kitchen but Geordie Aitken knew they would be appreciated by the self-sufficient monks who lived in the 600-year-old abbey.

On a subsequent visit Geordie Aitken later asked if they had been of any use. He was told, 'Oh yes, we really enjoyed the stew. We had it for breakfast, dinner, tea and supper for the last three weeks.' With their trip proving a double success the four men clambered back into the battered van and headed for Glasgow and its waiting streets.

Since that first trip Geordie Aitken has returned to visit Lord Hamilton on numerous occasions. Arriving unannounced, he discovered his aristocratic friend was away on business. Undeterred, he decided to make the most of his trip and popped in to see his friend's mother—the Duchess of Hamilton. He was welcomed as warmly at her farmhouse, as he had been at her son's, and he is now a family friend of the highest order.

As Geordie Aitken goes about his daily business on the streets of Glasgow so, too, did Lord Hugh Douglas Hamilton work to help the unfortunate and homeless people. Three years ago he started voluntary work at the charitable Jericho House, one of many homes across Britain administered by the Jericho Benedictine Order. As appeal secretary he helped fundraisers collect over £67,000 towards the target. Brought up as a Presbyterian, with his parents both members of the Church of Scotland, he changed his faith to Roman Catholic when aged 23. That was his religious turning point and unlike Geordie Aitken is not in the ranks of the born-again Christians. But he admitted that since meeting his down-to-earth friend his view of evangelicals had changed considerably. 'Until I met him I did not have an awful lot of time for evangelicals. But I admire enormously what he does and his street-level evangelism is of enormous value.'

He knew that both of them, in their own way, were doing a tremendous amount to help alleviate the suffering of Scotland's street people. 'Christianity means a great deal to Geordie Aitken and that is exactly how it comes through. He is reaching people who are not being otherwise reached and he takes a terrifically positive message to them. He takes light where there is darkness.' While Lord Hamilton arranged the fundraising campaign for the Edinburgh homeless Geordie Aitken and his band of helpers had been taking their unorthodox evangelism to the people of Glasgow. Having been involved with homeless people, albeit on a different level, he knew the value of Geordie Aitken's work.

'Geordie Aitken is infectious. He has a burning zeal to communicate the Gospel and a lot of people are just waiting to hear him. People who are perhaps contemplating suicide can meet Geordie Aitken and suddenly there would be something worth living for. There are all kinds of people in all kinds of places who need him.'

Since Geordie Aitken first wrote that hopeful letter to the unknown aristocrat the two men shared many experiences, and Lord Hamilton admitted to being 'honoured' to be part of his life. 'He has got a unique, positive way of doing things and I am very proud to be part of his life. I have the highest regard for Geordie Aitken and the invaluable work that he does.'

Lord Hugh Douglas Hamilton knew that Geordie Aitken had more to offer than just spiritual guidance. He comforts people and gives them hope simply by relating his own past experiences. It was not rare for Lord Hamilton to pass on the name of a person he knew was having a hard time to Geordie Aitken with the hint that a comforting chat might not be out of place.

In a far cry from his wild drunken days Geordie Aitken is now a respected speaker at Christian Police Association meetings in his native Glasgow and has earned the respect of veteran police officer Inspector Roy Logie of Strathclyde Police. The pair became firm friends over twelve years ago and the respected community policeman acted as a trustee when Geordie Aitken opened the charitable Loaves and Fishes soup kitchen on the streets of Glasgow. Inspector Logie first met Geordie Aitken when he spoke at an association meeting and witnessed firsthand the down-to-earth nature of the street evangelist. 'What thrilled wee Geordie was the fact that there were such things as Christian policemen. He thought that had to be a contradiction in terms.'

Inspector Logie, a police officer for thirty years and a member of the Christian Police Association for twenty-nine years, knows that Geordie Aitken's love of the Lord is genuine and deep rooted through the work he does in the Glasgow area. For such work Geordie Aitken was given a top award by Strathclyde Police for his work in the community. Whether it be at Christian Police Association meetings or on street corners Geordie Aitken takes every opportunity to witness to people and Inspector Logie has seen the results of his testimony.

'When feeding the down-and-outs at his soup kitchen in Glasgow he would also witness to the people who came along and quite a number of them committed their lives to the Lord Jesus. He was always involved in telling others the "good news" from the Bible and would travel anywhere to help people and assist them both physically and spiritually. I know that in some of the campaigns he has been on people have been converted by his life story and his witnessing.'

The respect and admiration between the two men is a mutual thing.

Geordie Aitken knows how important to the Christian policemen the work of the association is. Members of the Christian Police Association, of which Roy Logie was branch chairman for twelve years and is still a member of the Council of the Christian Police Association, its governing body, share fellowship and encourage each other in their faith. 'Roy Logie is both a dedicated policeman and devoted Christian who does a tremendous amount of work both in the community and in the association.'

Geordie Aitken with Inspector Roy Logie of Strathclyde Police, in Scotland. Mr Logie is a leading member of the Christian Police Association which has a worldwide outreach.

The Christian Police Association was founded over 100 years ago and now reaches out across the world with foreign policemen regularly contacting each other. The association established a police orphanage and school and also convalescent homes for police officers. Over the years the need for the orphanage and school has disappeared but the convalescent facilities have continued to grow and are now largely overseen by the Police Federation.

The main aim of the association is to offer fellowship between Christian police officers and support each other. The non-denominational association is open to every Christian involved with a police force and Geordie Aitken knows how reassuring it can be for many Christians to have a like-minded believer to talk to.

'I know from my own experiences that the Christian walk can be a very lonely one at times and probably even more so for policemen. People, including myself at one time, just cannot comprehend the idea of Christian police officers. The work they do can leave them cynical and bitter but because they have the power of the Lord in them they can handle the pressures. Through people like Roy Logie and other Christians you can see that the Lord does indeed have his people everywhere.'

Such is the strong bond between the two men that Roy Logie still regularly visits Geordie Aitken's mother whenever he is in the Cumbernauld area of Scotland where she lives. Geordie Aitken will be eternally grateful to the busy seasoned police officer who always finds the time to 'look in on my wee mother'. He knows that it is no small sacrifice because as well as Inspector Logie holding down a demanding job, his involvement with the Christian Police Association, he is also a member of Gideons International and helps distribute scriptural literature to schools, hospitals, hotels, aged peoples homes, nurses, firemen and policemen in the local area. But whatever the workload he knows that he has the power of the Lord to sustain him. The same power that keeps his friend Geordie Aitken going.

'Geordie Aitken is a great soul-winner who loves the Lord and loves to serve him to the best of his ability. He has travelled extensively to give his testimony and tell others of the Lord. I feel sure that Geordie Aitken still has a lot of work to do for the Lord Jesus and that many more folk will come under the influence of the Gospel because of his testimony.'

As is typical of Geordie Aitken he is prepared to cross any divide to take the Lord's message to people and, as if in stark contrast to his work with the Christian Police Fellowship, he is just as much at home working with criminals and convicts. His work in the prisons has earned him the respect of the Prison Fellowship in Scotland whose members regularly visit hardened criminals inside the nation's jails.

Prison Fellowship director Colin Cuthbert admires the way he will roll up his sleeves and get stuck in at grass roots level. 'Geordie the evangelist and, therefore, the one-man band, was introduced to me many years ago and has been a blessing ever since. He came along to a meeting in Renfield Street, Glasgow, for ex-offenders and immediately got his sleeves rolled up providing food and clothing for men and women coming out of prison. His 'hands-on' approach to the Gospel and his Glasgow patter endeared him to all.'

Following his work with the soup kitchens, for which he once had some signs painted for him in Perth Prison with the immortal words 'Jesus loves prostitutes and destitutes' he strengthened his ties with the Prison Fellowship over the years.

'Geordie continued as a prison visitor, letter writer and Prison

Fellowship Volunteer in many localities, having established strong links today with the prisons in Northern Ireland, such as the Maze and Crumlin Road, and in the USA where he makes regular trips. What amazes me is his wonderful ability to write letters to men in various institutions, in encouraging men to come to faith in Christ and in going on through thick and thin.'

Colin Cuthbert also knows that there is a lot more to come from the man he has labelled the double of a certain Duncan Donaldson the close friend and source of inspiration for Geordie in his early Christian days.

'Geordie's gifting as an evangelist and encourager to others will, I'm sure, continue to grow as he grows in the Lord. I know how many people, both in and out of the Prison Fellowship appreciate him. We all say thanks and keep up the good work.'

One of the men Geordie Aitken has witnessed to while prison visiting was John 'Shotgun' Elliott, a former hardened convict who now takes a Christian message to inmates himself following his last release from prison. Of his forty-two years John Elliott has spent twenty-four of them in prison for various offences, usually violent. His last sentence was for shooting two men, which he denied, and he met Geordie Aitken when he was ministering in Dungavel Prison in 1991. He had heard of the 'wee man' through the prison grapevine but was still amazed at the power and sincerity of him when he first heard him speak.

John Elliott had earlier given his life to Christ while waiting to be sentenced after being convicted of the double shooting. Following the trial he was on remand awaiting sentence when the Lord came into his life.

'I had just served six years in Barlinnie Special Unit and by rights I should have been given life for this but the judge only gave me nine years. I realized then that something unreal was happening and I believed it was the Lord through the power of prayer. I had been thinking about it while on remand and all of my earlier memories came flooding back and I dedicated my life to the Lord.'

In his early Christian days he discovered the loneliness of the Christian walk but was helped and encouraged by the power of Geordie Aitken's own deep love of the Lord and strong beliefs.

RE teacher Anne McKay with pupils of John Ogilvie High School.

'His preaching is on a different dimension. God uses him in a special way as people are transfixed by the way he preaches the Gospel. People think that when you become a Christian everything is rosy but Geordie Aitken tells it as it is and in a very forthright way. He experienced the loneliness and hurts that dedicating your life to Christ can bring and it is a blessing to others to hear him talk of how he overcame it. The Lord uses Geordie Aitken in a down-to-earth way and people can relate to him.

'We all have our ups and downs but Geordie Aitken perseveres and is a tremendous inspiration to people. He has got a genuine heart for people and he is unique in his personality.'

Geordie Aitken listens to such tributes and immediately gives the glory for them to his Saviour the Lord Jesus Christ. 'It is me who should be thanking the Prison Fellowship for allowing me to work with them and for allowing my story to be told in the prisons. It has been a blessing of God for me to participate in a small way in the recovery of prisoners.'

Since his conversion Geordie Aitken has always looked at helping

George and Denise Craig who help Geordie Aitken with his English outreach since welcoming him into their Sunderland home. A former criminal, George Craig now spends a lot of his time helping deprived children and those in need of care. Despite not being born-again Christians both he and Denise are staunch supporters of Geordie Aitken's community work.

people as a two-way thing and says that helping them come to the Lord only serves to strengthen his own conviction.

Whether it be to policemen, prisoners or indeed pupils it is his forthright and sincere manner which gets him noticed and which helps him get his evangelical message across. He is respected for that, as much as anywhere else, by the staff and pupils of John Ogilvie High School in Hamilton, Scotland. He was invited to speak at the school because staff were looking for someone 'different' and religious education teacher Anne McKay was soon to realize she had found just that. Yet had she not been close at hand when he made his first appearance the pupils might never have got to hear him speak.

Now he is welcomed at the school and regularly witnesses to both staff and pupils but on his first visit was very nearly thrown out. Anne McKay remembers how: 'When Geordie first came to the school in jeans and T-shirt sporting an armful of dubious tattoos he was almost thrown out by an assistant head teacher who mistook him for an "undesirable" who had come in off the street. Thankfully I managed to rescue him and perform the introductions because Geordie is now on the best of terms with all of the staff at the school who now pop along to hear him whenever he is speaking.'

Geordie Aitken loves his work with those with special needs. Geordie and his friends have organised appeals to help such people as the residents of a children's village which caters for Downs Syndrome sufferers, pictured below.

From that day he has gone from strength to strength and has lived up to all expectations and indeed surpassed many of them since the day he spoke to fourth year pupils during a one-day conference on marriage and family life.

'I wanted someone who was down-to-earth and I was attracted by Geordie's reputation, his casual approach, his entertainment value and style of delivery which is so unusual for religious education. Geordie works very hard while in school and is happy to fit in or take workshops and also makes himself available for pupils to chat to on an informal basis.'

The power of his conviction and Christian beliefs is not lost on the teacher, who like many others, is attracted by his simplistic faith.

'Geordie gives witness to

the transforming power of Christ in our lives and does so with utter conviction. This appeals to young people who readily spot insincerity. He has had an interesting past, which endears him no end, and has an abundance of stories which he uses to lend realism to his talks. His language is never offensive but he uses a street-level vernacular and represents the macho side of Christianity which is very rare.

'His spirituality appeals to many young people because he is a rebel with a cause and an anti-establishment character with a freelance ministry not affiliated to any particular church. He lives at the interface between faith and life and practises what he preaches in a haphazard way.

'His message is simple—put your trust in Jesus.'

It is that simplicity in his beliefs which has endeared Geordie Aitken to people across the world from Scotland to Northern Ireland and England to America. Whether he is speaking to young children, hardened criminals or hopeless dossers he always delivers the simplistic message which people can relate to. They not only take in his words but also take a close look at the man delivering them and realize from his testimony that there has been a miraculous change in his life and that perhaps a power greater than man's has been responsible for it.

I looked for an answer and could not find
the way to leave my past behind
Satan he has pulled me down
hence the reason I always frown

What is the secret of a smiling face
The way I cry is out of place
Why do people smile today?
they must know an answer to a better way

Yes my friend we know the way
the smile on our face is here to stay
To our Lord Jesus is the way we go
that is why our faces glow

Our faces show our hearts condition
To work for Jesus is our mission
Join our workers for the cause
and praise the Lord with loud applause

I now have an answer for my strife
I will direct my feet to the tree of life
He died for me and rose again
to save the souls of sinful men

What a joy to know I am saved
I have left the road that Satan paved
Now I walk on the King's highway
on this road I am here to stay.

The Way

# CHAPTER 12

# My Future with Christ

To date Geordie Aitken is still taking the word of the Lord out into the streets and continually opening up even more ministries. He still lives by what he once told the social security benefit office manager before his first evangelical visit to America many years ago.

'My employer is the Lord Jesus Christ and I work for him twenty-four hours a day, seven days a week, fifty-two weeks a year.'

Geordie Aitken's home telephone is a hotline for help to scores of desperate people and recognized organizations who know they can rely on the street-level evangelist to get a no-nonsense but often life-saving message across to those who need it most.

One such telephone call recently led him away from his native Glasgow to a Christian revival centre in the remote countryside that forms the border region between Scotland and England. In opening up yet another new ministry for the Lord he was to find himself counselling people with life-threatening problems who had been thrown a physical and spiritual lifeline at the Peniel Revival Centre in the Scottish Borders.

The Revival Centre is owned and administered by Englishman Brian Wilkinson who urged Geordie Aitken to visit the centre and counsel many of the men who reside there. Brian Wilkinson himself, was saved in 1959, aged 25, as he served a prison sentence for theft. He gave his life to the Lord and made his commitment in Portland Prison, England. He remembers how he prayed for a convicted killer, John Vickers, on the morning he was due to hang for killing an elderly woman. 'On the morning that he was hanged I remember the soft music being played in his cell and I offered up prayers for him. I was not a Christian in my earlier days but I made a commitment to the Lord as I was serving a sentence for theft.'

Like Geordie Aitken, Brian Wilkinson, has led a colourful life, albeit

Peniel Revival Centre.

in a different manner to the Scottish evangelist, and without the involvement of alcohol. But he knows the value of having someone at the centre who can relate to the men, through past experiences, and the value of Geordie Aitken's counselling. As a teenager Brian Wilkinson joined the Royal Navy but five years into his twelve year stint he went AWOL. For good measure he also stole a 50ft patrol boat and had to be chased by a Royal Navy destroyer and a naval helicopter. The chase only ended when he ran aground in the Mull of Kintyre in Scotland. While on the run he started stealing and when he was finally arrested he was jailed for theft. That was to herald a life with Christ.

Following his release from prison he attended a Bible college and graduated from the Assembley of God Bible School with a diploma in theology. He then gained his teaching diploma after studying at Bede College, Durham University and for many years in the middle part of his life was a respected church leader in his native Sunderland. After teaching he opened up an antique dealership near his home and blossomed as a businessman. But throughout his varied working life, he always had a heart for the needy and the homeless.

Often his own home would be an open house to the destitute and his involvement with the Peniel Revival Centre was a natural progresion of his love for the needy. He bought the centre in 1989 from the Christian organization Youth With A Mission (YWAM). Before their involvement with the building it had formerly been a plush riding lodge and used by the likes of former English Prime Minister Sir Harold Macmillan. After further years in use for various leisure activies it was bought by YWAM and used as a hostel. Now, under the guidance of Brian Wilkinson, it is an accredited rehabilitation centre drawing people from all walks of life who want to turn their backs on their former lifestyles. Usually those lifestyles included heavy involvement in drink, drugs or crime. Most of the men at the centre are referred to Brian Wilkinson through a network of churches, social services departments and the Prison Fellowship organization. The only criteria are that the men genuinely want to make a new start and want the guidance and help on offer at the Peniel Revival Centre.

In both Brian Wilkinson and Geordie Aitken that help is available from two men who have seen life at its harshest but from different angles. The theological approach by Brian Wilkinson complements the rough and ready streetwise approach adopted by Geordie Aitken. Together they have been responsible for reshaping many lives. Brian Wilkinson knows exactly the challenge faced by the two men. 'People come here who have life-controlling problems, either because of drink, drugs, crime or because they have suffered abuse. The greatest joy of all is seeing some of these men who have come through the centre, not only regaining their place in society, but going on to help others who have had similar problems.'

One such man who now spends his life helping people with their problems is Geordie Aitken and Brian Wilkinson has seen at first hand how important he is to the men at the centre.

'All of the lads have the greatest respect for Geordie Aitken because they know he has been where they are coming from. He is a man they can relate to because he has been through it and he has a great empathy with them and he will often sit and talk with them and counsel them into the small hours of the morning. When you have been through something yourself then you can help others overcome it and the great strength of Geordie Aitken is that he has walked the walk.'

The problems of the people at the centre are nothing new to Geordie Aitken and he relished the challenge of helping the unfortunate residents get a grip on their lives. 'It is at the foot of the Pennine Range away from the hustle and bustle of everyday life but inside the walls of the Centre the problems of the outside world are housed in the bodies and spirits of the people living there.' Geordie Aitken worked at the Centre on a voluntary basis because he knew the importance of the work Brian Wilkinson had undertaken. Although the residents were housed in a former riding lodge in a picturesque valley the problems they had were the problems of street people. Amazingly, one of the young men Geordie Aitken counselled was the son of a Glasgow woman who knew Geordie Aitken from his own wild drunken days.

'John is a miracle. He was only 24 but hooked on drugs and thinking that there was no road back for him. But he gave his life to Christ and has never looked back. The strange thing about meeting him at Peniel was that John's mother knew me from my own wild days and here I was actually counselling her son. The miracle of this is that John is going to work among drug addicts in a vicious area of Glasgow. John, like myself, will have his own personal experiences to share with the drug addicts, where I have been able to share my personal experiences with the alcoholics and depressives. He is another example of the Lord at work in various walks of life. I am certain that anyone attending the Peniel Revival Centre and embarking on its recovery programme will made the grade back to normality because their physical needs are catered for but also, more importantly, the troubled person can find God there.'

Over the years many troubled people have found God at the Centre and gone back into society with a positive approach to life. Residents range from former prisoners to former policemen. Their backgrounds may differ dramatically but their problems are usually the same—drink, drugs or violence.

John Findlay and Martin Lalley shared the everyday chores at the Centre as they set out on the road to recovery from their own problems. As they passed their time at the lodge there was no difference between them. Years ago they were from both ends of the social scale. John, the son of a Scottish steel magnate, was admittedly one of the 'Original Yuppies' spending up to £1,000 a week in plush London restaurants while working in the cosmopolitan capital city of England. Martin, at the other end of the scale, was continuously in and out of Scottish jails for his violent behaviour in his troubled teenage years.

After years in London, John Findlay had developed a drink problem, even though not an alcoholic as such, drink governed his life. Family life had always been strained for the upper-class man with him blaming his parents and in later years his parents blaming his drinking. In a bid to get away from his Edinburgh roots he tried his hand at almost everything. Still only 35 he has been a commodity broker in London, once losing over £100,000 on the city markets, and at the age of 22 found himself 'wiped out' and owing £30,000. After dragging himself out of that he had a stint as a professional hunter in Africa, a security guard/policeman in troubled South Africa and then in later years patrolled the streets of Edinburgh as a policeman.

That job went the same way as many of his previous jobs and he continued trying various avenues of employment—while hitting the drink. It soon caught up with him and left him miserable and depressed. But throughout the years he had never realized he was drinking heavily until it began to spoil his life. 'It was the classic progression really, it was a gradual process with me drinking large Scotches in my earlier days and continuing from there.' But it dawned on him one day while at college that he had a problem. 'I can remember that day eight years ago when I was sitting in the college classroom feeling miserable, depressed and downhearted. I just walked out of the college at the first break, bought a bottle of vodka and took it home to drink.' The signs took years to come out as, unlike the alcoholic, John Findlay could go long spells without a drink but when he did drink he drank heavily in bursts.

Various jobs later he eventually found himself living in rented accommodation in the heart of Edinburgh and seeing his family only on the very rare occasions he was invited to the family home. Unfortunately, on one visit to the family home at Christmas he tried to escape the hostile atmosphere by sleeping in his car in the lavish grounds of the family mansion. That deed was reported to the Press and he found himself in the *Daily Record*, a national newspaper in Scotland, under banner headlines proclaiming that a Scottish tycoon's son had been sleeping in the garden of his father's house. He learned of the

Two men from the Peniel Revival Centre who owe a lot to Geordie Aitken are Martin Lalley, above, and John Findlay, below.

story only when he went into a pub on Boxing Day and saw a copy of the article.

It made terrible reading for him but in the neighbouring city of Glasgow it made interesting reading for a certain Geordie Aitken. Having read of John Findlay's plight the little evangelist, with a heart for everyone and never one to miss a chance to take God's message to those who needed it, contacted his family offering to help John. His father took the message, Geordie Aitken's telephone number, and that of the Peniel Revival Centre, and promised to pass them on to his son if and when he next saw him.

The message was relayed and John Findlay was to make the telephone call that he now admits has put a purpose back into his life.

Following the call Geordie Aitken immediately arranged to meet John at a bus station in Edinburgh and with the help of Brian Wilkinson took him back to the Peniel Revival Centre. Now he has a reason to live a decent life.

'I went on the basis that I had nothing to lose and everything to gain and after only a couple of days thought it was great. Brian Wilkinson and Geordie Aitken were the most amazing guys I had ever met.' Soon he looked at life in a different way and was soon taking it one day at a time until he felt ready to head back into the world in a positive way. 'I had been unfit, without energy and had lost my zest for life. It was not so much the drink alone but not knowing what I wanted to do with my life and feeling so insecure at home.' But, under the guidance of Brian and Geordie Aitken, he took not only what they had to offer but also what God had to offer.

'Though I would have described myself as a Christian, although non-denominational I have never read the Bible. Having been here I now feel that I have learned so much about Christ and feel that this is something which is very much for me. I am still learning and taking it very very easily as at times it is still very hard for me with regards to other things but it is proving very beneficial as I have learned a great deal about myself, God and other people. When I have the strength to go back into the world I will hopefully be a much better person.'

Martin Lalley is also looking to put something back into society.

Brian Wilkinson, at the head of the table, with guest and residents at the Peniel Centre.

Ten years ago as John Findlay was dabbling with the money markets and travelling the world a teenage Martin Lalley was heading for the approved schools and prisons of his native Scotland. Still only 23, he has spent most of his life behind bars for one reason or another. His last prison sentence was for the attempted murder of a partygoer whom he stabbed at a house party. He was only released in September 1993, age 22, and referred to the Christian Centre. Apart from rebellion there was no reason for his violent behaviour and criminal activities throughout his teenage years.

'I was brought up by respectable parents but became the black sheep of the family and to this day I still don't know why I used to act the way I did.' But regardless of why, he did act that way and paid a heavy penalty. Even while inside the juvenile prison and serving his sentence his rebellious violent streak surfaced and he would often be in trouble with the warders. Towards the end of his sentence, although shorter than normal because of prison overcrowding, he was transferred to a low security wing as part of the prison's Training for Freedom project.

To prepare inmates for their pending release they were given outside visits and six hours freedom every Saturday afternoon in Falkirk. Once he and a friend overstayed their welcome and did not return as planned. But the following day Martin Lalley telephoned the prison to offer himself up. 'That's when I started thinking about Christ. There was a presence within me but it was like being in a dream.' But he was still the same person on the outside even if inwardly something was happening.

Following his parole from prison he went to live with his sister but invariably got into a fight and after battering three men he was back inside. While inside he continued reading the Bible and struggled to take in the confusing emotions he was experiencing. 'I asked God to come into my life but I never felt any change and thought it was a farce but deep down I was praying for it and even though I thought nothing was happening things were changing.' With the help of Colin Cuthbert, the Director of the Prison Fellowship Association, he struggled to come to terms with what was going on in his life. Following his last release from prison he returned to his mother's home in Hamilton to try to settle down. But he still fought and was soon back into his old ways. 'I was still fighting but deep down I did not want to hurt anyone.'

Confused at what was happening to him he finally got the sign that was to see him fully commit his life to the Lord. Sitting in his bedroom one day he got the feeling that he had to leave the house. He did not know why but he had an overwhelming urge to leave the house. He did and he later discovered that only minutes after he had left three men arrived at his home to settle an old score by beating him senseless. He was desperate to know more about what was happening to him and contacted Colin Cuthbert. Knowing of the invaluable work carried out at the Peniel Revival Centre, Colin Cuthbert referred him there. It was a move that was to change his life and compound his Christian beliefs.

But his first meeting with Geordie Aitken was to leave him wary. 'To be honest I did not like him at first because he tried·that hard to help you that it is frightening. But one night I was sitting talking to him properly and I actually shed tears. Weeks later I felt right about everything and wanted to give my life to Christ. I went to see Geordie Aitken and actually made the commitment in his bedroom. That night I slept the best night's sleep I have ever had in my life.'

Despite his initial misgivings Martin knows that Geordie Aitken has proved to be a saviour. Over the ensuing months Geordie Aitken nursed and assisted Martin through his early days of Christianity. 'Geordie Aitken has so much to offer people like myself because he has been through it all before and can explain things in a way you can understand and appreciate. He always had time to talk with people and is a tremendous help to everyone struggling to come to terms with what has happened. He has been through a lot himself and can use his own experiences to get his message across.'

In time, Martin hopes to be of benefit to others in the way that Geordie Aitken has helped thousands. 'The reason I know that Christ is in my life is because I once thought I could never change. My biggest worry after finding Christ was what people would think, but now I honestly don't care. I'm still weak in my faith and having to persevere but at least I have the strength to stand up and say that I am a Christian. My future lies in evangelism but in an active way and hopefully I can help other young guys with the problems I once had.'

Seeing the likes of John Findlay, Martin Lalley and dozens of others rebuild their lives is what makes his work at the Peniel Revival Centre so worthwhile to Geordie Aitken. 'The greatest gift of all is seeing a changed life. My reward is seeing the recovery of these men, seeing them making it one day at a time and walking the road back to normality.'

Despite the efforts he puts into the Centre Geordie Aitken never distances himself from the countless other ministries that he continues to work in and indeed open up. Back at his East Kilbride home his battered typewriter continues to churn out countless letters. He can write up to seventeen a week to scores of desperate people. Such is the amazing life of Geordie Aitken that there is even a heart-warming tale behind how he got his typewriter.

Knowing of the countless letters he typed every week to scores of people his good friends Bobby and Terry Grapenthin presented him with a brand new expensive word processor to enable him to continue his work from home. But to Geordie Aitken it was no good. 'I couldn't even understand the instructions let alone the keyboard.' Knowing that a local nun wanted such a machine for the convent Geordie Aitken got in touch with her and offered her his on condition she found him something more manageable. She gladly swapped her little battered manual typewriter for the American word processor. She went away beaming, and he now had something he could use. The fact that it is probably worth about a twentieth of the brand new word processor never bothered him. What did bother him was having to tell Bobby and Terry that he had effectively given away their gift. But the Christian couple only remarked that it was for the best of reasons and that the main thing was that he himself had something with which to type his invaluable letters of comfort.

On that battered typewriter, which he still uses today, in the makeshift office in the kitchen of his home, thousands of letters have been typed. Most of his state benefit money goes on buying stamps. Once he lost his wallet and in reporting it to the police found himself receiving funny looks when asked if it contained anything valuable. Driving licence, credit cards and the like. 'The most important thing in it is a book of stamps,' he told the desk sergeant, 'because to many people the letters I write are a lifesaver and without the stamps I won't be able to send them as I will have to wait until my next benefit payment.'

Many of the letters he types are sent off to prisons across the world. Only recently he has started corresponding with a woman in a British jail who is serving a life sentence for murder. He was asked to contact her through a church movement and after the first set of letters had been exchanged between them the woman asked if he could send her one of his testament tapes so that she could watch it in the prison. She added that she was going to ask the prison governor and the prison chaplain if she could show it to other inmates but did not know if she would get permission.

After sending the video tape to the jail Geordie got word back from the woman that permission had been granted and that scores of prisoners were looking forward to seeing him talk about his former lifestyle and how he had been saved from this dark past. Like other prisoners, from Northern Ireland to America, the woman asked if she could share his letters with other inmates in a bid to bring some comfort into their incarcerated existence, too. As always, he readily agreed. The prison ministry is an important part of his life as he knows that a massive revival is taking place behind the bars of countless prisons across the world.

'Many, many people who have done wrong in their lives are now realizing that there is only one real Saviour and that it is the Lord Jesus Christ. Even amongst terrorists in the Maze Prison there is a major revival going on.'

With his work at the Peniel Revival Centre and his constant round of mission visiting Geordie gave up prison visiting recently. In the near future he hopes to go back into the prisons physically and take a personal message to the people he is currently writing to. Already he and Prison Fellowship Director Colin Cuthbert are looking forward to the day when he gets a little more time to go back into the jails and help spread the evangelical message. But before that happens he has another pressing matter to attend to.

Away from evangelical circles, to a certain degree, he is currently challenging council chiefs about the standard of housing in his native Glasgow and is taking them to the High Court in Edinburgh. He is doing it for himself and ten other families from the East Kilbride area as a test case. If successful it could open the doors to scores of other claims from families who are living in what Geordie Aitken claims is sub-standard housing. He has the backing of top civil lawyers but says that outside legal circles he has the best lawyer available—his Lord Jesus Christ. 'This is a fight for the underdog against bureaucracy and the fact that councils and corporations can let people live in such conditions. It is right versus wrong and we cannot fail with the Lord on our side. He is the best lawyer you could have in your corner when fighting an injustice.'

For legal reasons, the matter being *sub judice*, the exact details of the court case cannot be published but the bottom line is that the development corporation designed the houses badly and then held back in carrying out vital renovation work. The development corporation has always denied that the prefab-style houses were sub-standard despite agreeing to carry out insulation work. Residents, who set up an action group to protest at the state of their homes, claim the corporation's decision to carry out the work, which they have fought for years, is proof that the houses have always been below standard. To prove the point Geordie Aitken is challenging them in Edinburgh High Court at a date to be announced. Indeed, Geordie Aitken could have been called to present his case at the plush legal chambers while living in a caravan. While the re-roofing and wall-cladding was being carried out the affected families were temporarily housed in caravans.

Geordie Aitken moved into the house of Dornoch Place, East Kilbride, sixteen years ago from their marital home in Barlanark because it had an extra bedroom and their son Adam had just been born. But from day one they were going to be beset by problems with damp and condensation.

'Little did we know we were going to be living in a metal hell-hole called a house. Despite years of arguing the corporation refused to carry out any improvement work saying that the houses were up to standard. In a bid to challenge that I applied for Legal Aid to get the services of a solicitor and also to get an independent survey done. The surveyor actually condemned the roofing of the houses and found numerous faults within this excuse for a house. The corporation later reneged on its claims and said it would be carrying out repair work but I am still going to court for the principle of the matter and because there are another ten families relying on me to win my case against landlords who definitely couldn't care less.

'I am a test case and if I win, which I know I will, then the rest of the families will also win their cases. My whole adult life has been spent fighting for the underdog whether as a counsellor in numerous organizations or when running the soup kitchens. The message to any other people in the same position as myself and those other unfortunate families who feel they are banging their heads against brick walls in trying to combat bureaucratic injustice, or indeed injustice of any sort, is to keep looking forward as the system can be beaten.'

Geordie Aitken's whole life, since the age of 30, when he overcame his alcoholic addiction, has been spent helping others come to terms with their problems. He is known by thousands of people for his no-nonsense and down-to-earth approach to Christianity. What keeps him going is his simplistic, yet passionate faith which he can take into areas where other people can not or, indeed, would not even try. He is prepared to go into places that many people don't even want to know exist, let alone venture into. But Geordie Aitken knows that it is the people who have to live in such areas and lead decadent, deprived and spiritually-void lives that need him most.

Indeed, it is any ordinary man or woman with a problem of any kind, whether self-inflicted or tragically incurred that he wants to help and comfort. And, whether on a street in Glasgow or a boulevard in America, heartache and horror walk hand in hand on an almost daily basis. Tragedy has always dogged the little evangelist but as dire as a situation may appear he will never shirk an opportunity to help a distraught or suffering person. That was graphically illustrated on the tragic occasion that a young Scottish couple lost their little child in a bizarre but heart-breaking and tragic accident. If anyone ever needed help then the distraught and near-suicidal father of the dead youngster was that person. And he got it from Geordie Aitken.

He read of the tragedy in the Scottish newspaper the *Daily Record*. A 4-year-old boy had died after choking on a toy snooker ball, the snooker set a gift from his parents. One morning, after the table had been left out, the youngster crept downstairs to play with his new toy but sadly put one of the balls in his mouth and it lodged in his throat. Frantic fireman and paramedic crews tried to resuscitate the toddler but he died on the floor of his Glasgow home. After reading the heart-breaking tale, Geordie Aitken tried to contact the young couple by letter. Weeks passed without any reply and he thought either they were not interested in his offer of help and comfort or, had not received the letter. Either way, he carried on his daily routine of helping the scores of other people who needed his help.

One day, while at the notorious Paddy's Market in Glasgow, a Christian couple whom he knew from his earlier days called out to him as he passed their market stall in the pouring rain. Huddled up and crouching to protect himself from the downpour, he hadn't noticed them until they called out his name as he passed. Recognizing the couple he hurried over and greeted them. He was amazed when the woman thanked him for the comforting letter he had written to her son. He discovered that this couple were the parents of the young man whose son had choked to death on the snooker ball.

The reason the son had not replied to the letter was because he had been living with them since the tragedy and had only just returned to his own home and found the letter. He had told his parents about it but had not bothered replying as all he was now interested in was alcohol. Since his son's death he had turned to drink and was now walking the streets in a drunken stupor ranting that he was a murderer and that he had killed his son. His drinking was worsening by the day and he had turned suicidal. Whenever possible his parents tried to get him to live with them, as his wife had suffered a nervous breakdown, left him and gone back to her own family. More often than not he would be sleeping rough and drinking himself senseless.

In relating the story to Geordie Aitken, the couple broke down in tears and the three of them stood there crying in the pouring rain in the bustling market as startled shoppers hurried by giving just passing glances to the tearful trio. After praying together, Geordie Aitken left to go on his way reminding them that when they did see their son he was still willing to help and to try to take some spiritual comfort into his life. He was less than a hundred yards away when the still-tearful woman called out his name and on turning back he saw her son standing at the market stall. 'Except for the power of the Lord I will never be able to explain how that young man came to be standing there in the middle of Paddy's Market or why he chose that very day to seek his parents out.'

Hurrying back to the stall, Geordie Aitken could see that the young man was already drunk out of his mind and looking like death warmed up. 'He asked me if I was Geordie Aitken and when I said yes he threw his arms around me and thanked me for the letter I had written weeks before.' The four of them now stood crying in the rain-soaked market as the man poured out his heart. 'He was breaking his heart crying and telling me "I have killed my kid, I have killed my kid." It was heart-breaking because he really thought he was the cause of the child's death simply because he had left the snooker table and the balls out during the night.' Instinctively, Geordie Aitken helped the man in the only way he knew and got right to the heart of the problem.

'Listen, your wee son is in heaven with the Lord and some day you will meet him. But there is one clause in the matter, as it says in the Bible that if you want to enter the Kingdom of Heaven you must be born again. Therefore, son, if you ever want to see your boy again then you need to give your life to the Lord, ask him to come into your life as your personal Saviour and he will be your key to heaven.' Geordie Aitken then tried to explain to the distraught young father that he was not to blame for his son's death.

'Maybe the Lord had seen a lot of trouble and suffering ahead for your wee son and decided to call him home but I cannot answer why it happened in the way that it did. But if you give your life to Jesus it is a guarantee that you will meet up with him again. Don't think that I am spiritually blackmailing you into becoming a Christian but, if you don't believe in Jesus, or you rebuke him, then there is a place called hell: and if you don't accept Jesus into your life and your soul goes to hell while your son is in heaven then you will never ever see him again. If you do want to see him again then the only way you can get into heaven is by asking Jesus into your life and then it will be a certainty that one day you will see your wee son again.' I was only relating what is in the Bible and not making a story up just to comfort the man and after I had spoken to him the big man broke his heart.

So engrossed in the man was Geordie Aitken that he and the parents stood in tears unaware of where they were. In fact they were not bothered about their public display of faith. 'While this was going on every social leper you can imagine, drunks, dossers, prostitutes and hawkers were scouring the market stalls looking for bargains in the notorious area of Glasgow.' Not just because of the rain Geordie Aitken believes that the heavens literally opened that day when the man threw his arms around him and asked how he could find the Lord.

'He asked me what he had to do to become a Christian and I told him that he just simply had to ask the Lord into his heart and that he would forgive every one of his sins past and present. The Lord says in the Bible: "I will never leave you or forsake you and will be with you until the end of the age" and those words were a marvellous blessing to this young man. He just stood there in this market, in the pouring rain, and simply uttered "Lord Jesus will you come into my life and be my Saviour". As he said it the young man just broke down and accepted Christ into his life.' For what seemed like an eternity, but what in reality was only minutes, the four of them stood and hugged each other as the rain mingled with the salty tears running down their faces.

'I still pray today that the young man is doing well and I know for a fact that in giving his life to God then he and his young son will be reunited in heaven. That is a stone wall certainty.'

Such heart-breaking incidents are a part of Geordie Aitken's evangelical life as he fights to take a Christian message out into the streets. Wherever he is needed he is willing to go if people call upon him for help. In some bizarre and harrowing instances he has helped people he has never even met and who live hundreds of miles away but who have begged him for help in finding the Lord and to help them overcome serious addictions and life-controlling problems.

Once he was called upon to help a heroin addict who had started mainlining heroin since moving to London from his native Glasgow. To this day Geordie Aitken does not know whether the man, his girlfriend and their young child survived on the rough streets after their brief meeting but for one day at least the family knew happiness of a sort.

The day that Geordie Aitken met them at Buchanan Street bus station in Glasgow he led them to the Lord in the presence of the man's parents. He met the man after a remarkable set of incidents while the addict was living a squalid life in London. Geordie Aitken had spoken at a meeting in Scotland where a doctor had taped his testimony for future reference and to help him deal with many of the sad cases he treated every day. That tape was to find its way down to London and subsequently if not save the life of the heroin addict at least prolong it.

The addict was lying on the floor of his aunt's home ready to inject himself yet again when the woman urged him to listen to the testimony tape of a Scottish man who had once been addicted, not to drugs, but to alcohol. One sentence on the tape saw the addict throw down the needle, remove the tightened strap from his upper arm and vow to meet the man who might be able to save him.

On the tape Geordie Aitken could be heard saying: 'I always wanted

to be a good guy but never knew how to go about it until Christ
came into my life.' The words struck a chord with the heroin addict
because, amazingly, he had always said to his family that he wanted to
be a good guy but didn't know how. After listening to the rest of the
tape the man set out to find this speaker. With the help of Alcoholics
Anonymous they managed to track down a certain Beardie Geordie.
The organization contacted their former member and asked permission
to pass on his telephone number to the distraught addict in London.
Two days later and Geordie Aitken was standing at the Glasgow bus
station waiting for the London bus to pull in.

He had never met the man before but when a dishevelled couple
holding a scruffy baby got off the bus he knew the man who needed
his help had arrived. The man, dressed in tatty overalls walked towards
the little Scottish evangelist, asked him if he was Geordie Aitken, then
threw his arms around him. The two men were soon joined by the
woman and the young child and formed a tearful group in the busy
bus station.

'The woman was in a worse state than him and the child looked
like death warmed up. The man asked me to go to his mother's house
with him and talk about Jesus. When we got there I discovered that
his mother was a chronic alcoholic and his father was a drug addict.'

Despite the filthy surroundings of the council house Geordie Aitken
spent three hours talking to the hapless family in a bid to win them
over for the Lord and possibly save their lives. By the end of the day
the heroin-addicted man, his girlfriend, his mother and his father had
all given their lives to the Lord.

'The house was filthy and when we got there his father was freaked
out on drugs and drink but by the end of the visit I had the joy of
leading them all to the Lord.' To date Geordie Aitken still does not
know what happened to the man, his girlfriend and the baby. The man's
mother is still doing well after coming off the drink and taking up a
voluntary job, but her husband relapsed and died after swallowing his
own vomit during a heavy session. The worry of Geordie Aitken is
that the heroin addict might also have passed away. 'The man and his
girlfriend looked as if they were HIV positive and had the deadly AIDS
virus. I can only pray that they recovered, and indeed survived, but
they were that thin and unkempt that I believe they did have the virus.'

Anyone who needs help is assured of it, but it is the heart-broken, the homeless, the drunks, the drug addicts, the prostitutes and the prisoners who have a special place in the massive heart of Geordie Aitken.

Those are the people whom he still meets while working at the Oasis Soup Kitchen. The soup kitchen, in the heart of Glasgow, is overseen by John Brown, co-ordinator of the Therismos Christian Outreach, and devoted friend of Geordie Aitken. The two men met while working as volunteers at a Lanarkshire Christian Centre.

'It was here that I learned that Geordie Aitken had once been involved with soup kitchens feeding the homeless for over twenty years, and that he had a street-level Christian ministry reaching out to the groups in our society which are normally ignored—drunks, drug abusers, prostitutes and down-and-outs. This was an area that appealed to me as I wanted to become involved in a ministry that reached out to these particular people. These were people in our society who had hit upon hard times yet society was too busy to help them.'

The two men went their separate ways but John Brown could not get away from wanting to help the kind of people Geordie Aitken had spent decades caring for and comforting. It was to happen after a typical piece of Geordie Aitken advice.

John remembers how: 'I was telephoning him from time to time for advice and on one occasion told him that I felt a burden to help people in Glasgow who were on the streets. He suggested that I should just go into the city with a big pot of soup and wad of gospel sheets. It was down-to-earth advice given in typical Geordie Aitken style.'

Soon John and a band of dedicated helpers were looking for premises in the heart of Glasgow and quickly stumbled upon an office that was available at a cheap rent. From those early days the Centre now feeds over 200 people every Tuesday and Saturday night.

'During this time I kept in constant contact with Geordie Aitken, sharing with him concerns about the work, seeking his advice and inviting him to join our ministry. Before too long he was coming to the soup kitchen and even he was amazed at the number of people we were feeding and with the best of food, too. Geordie suggested the name Oasis for the soup kitchen and that is what we called it. In a very short time we have helped hundreds of people and never at any

John Brown organized Oasis Soup Kitchen.

time have we needed to worry about money. In the early months we raised over £10,000 and it just keeps on growing. It is very early days for us but we have a very sincere and committed bunch of helpers and a great big God. So we have everything in our favour to help the needy and hungry people in our society. Just like the Lord Jesus, we take people just as they are, taking time to speak to them and build up relationships with them sharing the love of Christ.'

Since his conversion to Christianity, Geordie Aitken has ministered to people worldwide from high society to hapless drunks but he knows that whatever people's social standings might be they are all the same in the eyes of the Lord. He knows that just as he was taken as he was so, too, can anyone be.

Many people have labelled him unique and not without good reason but whatever accolades he receives he dismisses with a shrug of the broad shoulders that have carried many burdens throughout his fascinating life. He knows that the glory belongs to God.

Everything he does he does in the name of his Saviour and offers up daily prayers for the strength and conviction to continue his spiritual work. He will not rest until he has reached as many people as is humanly possible. The man that has been called the 'Unique Servant of God' is determined to preach until his very last breath is taken from him. Then he knows he will meet up again in heaven with the people he has lost over recent years and who helped him through the difficult early years of his conversion.

He knows he wasted the first thirty years of his life in a violent, drunken and criminal stupor before realizing his real calling in life. He

Helping the destitute in Glasgow.

is determined that nobody else should waste as many years as he did before recognizing there is only one real Saviour, the Lord Jesus Christ. 'Too many people worship various gods in the shape of money and possessions but there honestly is only one God worth having and it is so easy to get him.'

Every day new ministries are opening up for the little tattooed evangelist and what the future holds for him God only knows. But whatever it is it will centre around helping the people who need him.

'The power of Christ is unbelievable as he can literally raise the dead. He raised me and I was spiritually dead. To date I have led over 1,000 people to the Lord and the majority of them were those society rejected. They are now putting something back into society and leading decent lives. The sooner people take Christianity back into reality and street-level then the sooner we will see a revival throughout the whole world.

'And believe me—that day will come.'